The Achieving
of *The Great Gatsby*

The Achieving of
The Great Gatsby

F. Scott Fitzgerald, 1920–1925

Robert Emmet Long

Lewisburg
BUCKNELL UNIVERSITY PRESS
London: Associated University Presses

For my mother and my sister Carolyn

© 1979 by Associated University Presses, Inc.

Associated University Presses, Inc.
4 Cornwall Drive
East Brunswick, N.J. 08816

Associated University Presses Ltd
69 Fleet Street
London EC4Y 1EU, England

Associated University Presses
Toronto M5E 1A7, Canada

First printing 1979
Second printing 1981

First paperback edition 1981

Library of Congress Cataloging in Publication Data

Long, Robert Emmet.
    The achieving of The great Gatsby, F. Scott Fitz-
gerald, 1920-1925.

        Bibliography: p.
        Includes index.
        1. Fitzgerald, Francis Scott Key, 1896-1940. The
great Gatsby. I. Title.
PS3511.19G864   813'.5'2   77-92572
ISBN 0-8387-2192-3 (cloth)
ISBN 0-8387-5026-5 (paperback)

PRINTED IN THE UNITED STATES OF AMERICA

Contents

Preface

In his boyhood F. Scott Fitzgerald sometimes told the story that as an infant he had been left on his parents' doorstep, wrapped in a blanket bearing the royal name *Stuart*. He had, in fact, been born to his own parents, Edward and Mollie Fitzgerald, on September 24, 1896, in the city of St. Paul, Minnesota. But the story is in a certain sense true, insofar as it reveals his imaginative origins as a fairy-tale prince who has somehow, wrongly, been given the social garments of a middle-class youth. This foundling fantasy persisted throughout Fitzgerald's career. It can be seen in "Absolution," in the young boy's disbelief that he is the son of his middle-class parents, and even at the very end, in the unfinished novel *The Last Tycoon*, in Monroe Stahr's assumption of an earthly princehood, as he descends from the heavens to the "warm darkness" of the Hollywood dream capital. In boyhood dreams began a commitment to romantic largness that was to lead Fitzgerald to his exploration of the American dream in *The Great Gatsby*.

In considering *The Great Gatsby*, I am concerned primarily with its evolution and art, the peculiar "shape" the novel comes to have. I am interested in the large and complicated development of Fitzgerald's art in the early twenties, his movement from uncertainty to achieved vision; and I give particular attention to Fitzgerald's literary-cultural milieu, the way it acted on his imagination, the writers from whom Fitzgerald learned in coming to maturity. In the chapter on the early fiction that prepares for *The Great Gatsby*, I examine Fitzgerald's two apprenticeship novels, along with the most relevant short stories, to illustrate the direction of his imagination, the formation of his attitudes toward his young protagonists and their discovery of themselves in relation to America. *This Side of Paradise* announces Fitzgerald's theme of romantic disillusionment but does not focus it clearly; in *The Beautiful and Damned*, influenced by Mencken, Fitzgerald's social perspective is sharpened. His view of contemporary society is wholly depreciatory, and his protagonist, who is committed to a higher aspiration than his culture's, is doomed to failure. The novel is an attempted study in the ironic mode endorsed by Mencken, and although it fails, it does lead Fitzgerald toward *The Great Gatsby*, in which the irony of aspiration has been maturely grasped. *This Side of Paradise* and *The Beautiful and Damned* both reflect Fitzgerald's preoccupation with illusion, and in a number of the apprenticeship stories, such as "The Diamond as Big as the Ritz" and "Winter Dreams," I indicate how he schooled himself further in the subject of illusion—that of both the individual and the nation—before the vision of *The Great Gatsby* was achieved.

In the chapter following, I show how Mencken introduced Fitzgerald to the writing of Conrad and how Conrad's early fiction was influential on Fitzgerald's conception of *The Great Gatsby*. In Conrad's early novels, romantic illusion is treated authoritatively and given sharp outline; and in *The Great Gatsby* there are many indications that Fitzgerald made adaptations from Conrad in giving outline to his own, distinctly American vision. In the next chapter, I examine the art of *The Great Gatsby* and the aesthetic strategies it involves. Dramatic in the presentation of character and scene, poetic in the deployment of imagery, Fitzgerald's aesthetics reveal an exceptional delicacy together with an extraordinary compression, a tension that is the mark of a powerful vision. In particular, I emphasize the duality of Fitzgerald's imagination, which accommodates both social satire and tragic myth and reconciles a strong sense of alienation with a deep sense of involvement, through the firmness of Fitzgerald's social criticism. The final chapter places *The Great Gatsby* in the context of the American literary milieu of the early twenties, out of which it evolves and which it also expresses; and the Appendix treats the growth of Fitzgerald's conception as it is revealed in the manuscript versions of the novel. The book is thus an in-depth study of *The Great Gatsby*, an anatomy of an imaginative conception.

In the relatively brief time between the beginning of the twenties and the completion of *The Great Gatsby*, Fitzgerald absorbed an enormous amount of his immediate milieu, and to be fully appreciated Fitzgerald's achieving of the novel must be understood as a very large and complicated act of cultural assimilation. When Fitzgerald wrote *The Great Gatsby*, he was only twenty-seven years old, but he had already reached artistic maturity and touched his age deeply, achieving a contemporary vision that remains a permanent part of American awareness of itself. Fitzgerald's swift and early arrival as an artist has about it, indeed, an aspect of fairy-tale princehood.

Acknowledgments

I would like to express my appreciation to the Byrd Library, Syracuse University, and the Penfield Library, State University of New York, Oswego, which have been indispensible for my research on this and another book. I am particularly indebted to Mr. George Scheck, Interlibrary Loans, Penfield Library. My gratitude is acknowledged, also, to Walter Sutton, Syracuse University English Department, and to Matthew J. Bruccoli, University of South Carolina English Department, for reading the first draft of the manuscript. My largest thanks, for innumerable services and great loyalty, go to my sister Carolyn.

An earlier version of the chapter on Conrad and *The Great Gatsby* appeared in *Texas Studies in Literature and Language* (Summer and Fall 1966), published by the University of Texas Press, as "*The Great Gatsby* and the Tradition of Joseph Conrad," and is reprinted with permission of the publisher. In the chapter on "The Intricate Art," I have drawn on some observations made in my essay "The Opening Three Chapters of *The Great Gatsby*," published in *The English Record* 26 (Fall 1975), reprinted with permission. Material in several notes is taken from short articles of mine that appeared in *The Fitzgerald Newsletter* and *The Fitzgerald/Hemingway Annual*, both edited by Matthew J. Bruccoli, and is reprinted with permission. Quotations from the works of F. Scott Fitzgerald are reprinted by permission of The Bodley Head from The Bodley Head Scott

The Achieving
of *The Great Gatsby*

I was rereading The Geat Gatsby *last night, after I had been going through my page proofs, and thinking with depression how much better Scott Fitzgerald's prose and dramatic sense were than mine. If I'd only been able to give* [I Thought of Daisy] *the vividness and excitement, and the technical accuracy of his! Have you ever read* Gatsby? *I think it's one of the best novels that any American of his age has done.*

Edmund Wilson, *Letters on Literature and Politics 1912–1972*

All they think of is money.

Myrtle Wilson, referring to menials,
in *The Great Gatsby*

1

Toward *The Great Gatsby:* The Apprenticeship Period

This Side of Paradise is a dream-haunted first novel that questions what dreams and reality are. It begins with adolescent dreams, fantasies that before long evaporate, of Amory Blaine's supposed boyhood background of riches and privilege. The riches mysteriously vanish, and Amory becomes a middle-class youth who enters Princeton, where he is more impressed by its casually aristocratic tone than he would have been had his wealthy and sophisticated background been real. Amory is, apparently enough, a fictionalized version of Fitzgerald himself. The reader follows him through his college days and later experiences after World War I; his romance with Rosalind Connage who, although in love with Amory, finally breaks off their engagement because he hasn't the money to make her future secure; and his subsequent discouraging experiences in New York that lead to the cul-de-sac of his belonging nowhere. Finally, in a cemetery beyond Princeton after midnight, with Amory alone in his anger and confusion and pain, the novel ends. *This Side of Paradise* is like a kaleidoscope of glimpsed, glittering dreams that come apart before it ends in isolation and

17

darkness, a forecast of Fitzgerald's concern with the dream nature of American reality in his next two novels.

Fitzgerald used much of his own personal experience in writing the novel, but its form was dictated largely by contemporary models. Fitzgerald's assimilative approach to the work can be noticed in its atmosphere, an American translation of *fin-de-siècle* writing, as Sergio Perosa has pointed out:

> The atmosphere in which Amory's portrait becomes credible is the typical atmosphere of the English *fin-de-siècle,* with its enthusiasm for Verlaine and Rimbaud, for impressionistic writing and symbolistic poetry, for an ideal Renaissance and a decadent form of Hellenism. English decadence idealized the figure of man in tired attitudes and blasé forms, or reproduced it in their paintings as a pale medieval phantom. . . . Together with a predilection for Tennyson's drowsy poetry and for Swinburne's languid sensuality, these aspects of the decadent movement exercised a notable influence on practically all writers who flourished at the beginning of the new century—on Tarkington and Cabell—on young Faulkner and even on Dos Passos, and they are clearly discernible in T. S. Eliot's and Ezra Pound's early poetry as well. They permeated the whole cultural atmosphere which Fitzgerald had to absorb while at college, and it is small wonder if in his first book he repeated these forms, these attitudes, and these formulas to the point of satiety.[1]

Fitzgerald's collegiate exposure to *fin-de siècle* poetry is apparent particularly in his friendship with his classmate John Peale Bishop. Fitzgerald spent part of the summer of 1917 with him at his home in Charleston, West Virginia, where Bishop prepared the final proofs of his first volume of published verse, *Green Fruit.* The book reveals a great deal about the poetry Bishop admired, a taste for which he inspired in Fitzgerald, for he was writing at the time under the spell of romantic poets—Keats, Swinburne, Verlaine, and Rupert Brooke. Bishop's poems are etched with an exquisiteness of feeling and convey the delicate impression of "violet dusks" and the "sobbing" of rain and wet leaves. They contain the imagery of lutes and peacocks, the incense of "ambergris and cinnamon," and are concerned with the pain of early love and beauty that is ephemeral. The romantic poetry, with its *fin-de-siècle* styling and themes, that Bishop introduced him to that summer was to leave a deep and lasting impression on Fitzgerald. Its immediate effect may be seen in the poems he wrote at that time, scattered through *This Side of Paradise*, and, more importantly, in his conception in that novel of a young man whose personal identity is shaded by the romantic verse of Keats and Brooke.

In the period when *This Side of Paradise* was written, Rupert Brooke was practically a personification of romantic youth and tragic circumstance. Still in his twenties at the time of his death in the Aegean in 1915, while serving in World War I, Brooke came almost at once to symbolize the tragedy of the war and the waste of the best of young English manhood. *The Collected Poems of Rupert Brooke* (1918) was widely read, and with its appearance Brooke seemed to pass into legend. Part of the great appeal of Brooke perhaps was that he was personally the image of the young romantic; strikingly handsome, looking the part of the idealistic dreamer, his physical appearance in photographs seemed to complement the youthfully romantic verse he wrote. In Brooke, what is important is the moment of youthful intensity—a quick apprehension of beauty and love together with a consciousness of their transience. Brooke gave Fitzgerald's novel its name, the line "this side of Paradise" coming from "Tiare Tahiti," one of a group of poems written in the South Seas a year before Brooke's untimely death. Its closing lines are also used by Fitzgerald as his epigraph, and their sense can be understood by noting their context in the poem:

Hasten, hand in human hand,

. . . .

And in the water's soft caress,
Wash the mind of foolishness,
Mamua, until the day,
Spend the glittering moonlight there
Persuing down the soundless deep
Limbs that gleam and shadowy hair,

. . . .

Snare in flowers, and kiss, and call
With lips that fade, and human laughter
And faces individual,
Well this side of Paradise! . . .
There's little comfort in the wise.[2]

Brooke's poem celebrates youth's sentience, its ability to *feel*.
The living moment of physical sensation is preferred to "wis-
dom," since reason cannot compensate for the brevity of happi-
ness or the tragic nature of life. Fitzgerald's choice of this poem
as the source of the title of his novel and its epigraph clearly
implies a sympathetic identification with Brooke's romantic
attitude toward youth's experience.

But Brooke is present in *This Side of Paradise* in more than
its title, since his poetry is said to be one of Amory's earliest
discoveries in college. By the outbreak of the war, "everyone
bantered in public and told themselves privately that their
deaths would at least be heroic. The literary students read
Rupert Brooke passionately."[3] In the Eleanor Savage episode,
Amory is even told that he resembles Brooke, and he begins to
act out the part consciously:

"You ought to be a materialist," she continued irrelevantly.
"Why?"
"Because you look a good deal like the picture of Rupert
Brooke."
    To some extent Amory tried to play Rupert Brooke as long

as he knew Eleanor. What he said, his attitude toward life, toward her, toward himself, were all reflexes of the dead Englishman's literary moods. Often she sat in the grass, a lazy wind playing with her short hair, her voice husky as she ran up and down the scale from Grantchester to Waikiki. (P. 248)

In the novel, Fitzgerald attempts to portray Amory Blaine as a gilded being, responding sensitively to poetry and life; and his association with Brooke reinforces this characterization.

But in addition to Amory's association with Brooke, the influence of many other literary figures is apparent in the work, particularly that of Compton Mackenzie. It was his friend Father Fay who first encouraged Fitzgerald to read Mackenzie's *Sinister Street*, which ends with the conversion of its hero, Michael Fane, to the Roman Catholic church. A sequel to *Youth's Encounter, Sinister Street* was published in 1914, and was thus quite timely—the very latest depiction of modern youth. A popular work, *Sinister Street* was also widely praised, and was praised on the Princeton campus. Reviewing *Youth's Encounter* in the *Nassau Lit* in 1913, Fitzgerald's friend T. K. Whipple wrote that Michael Fane possessed "passion of the intellect, of feeling, and above all, charm." He concluded by remarking that *Youth's Encounter* was one of the few novels he wanted to "reread . . . again and again."[4] Fitzgerald's own interest in the novel's hero, Michael Fane, was extreme, as Arthur Mizener has noted:

He was enchanted by *Youth's Encounter* and *Sinister Street* and began a period of seeing himself as Michael Fane and all his friends as appropriate subsidiary figures. Wilson and all his other friends fitted in admirably, as did Fay, who took him to dine in suave splendor at the Lafayette and got confused in Fitzgerald's exuberant imagination with Mr. Viner. Thus with his imagination full of the romance of *Sinister Street*—so that, seeing a man disappear silently into a doorway in Greenwich Village one night he had an almost physical sense of the pressure of evil— . . . he plunged into being a writer.[5]

Mackenzie's depiction of Michael Fane appealed to Fitzgerald particularly because he was the same age as young Fane and because he was then attempting what *Sinister Street* was—a "college novel." Delicately evocative, *Sinister Street* creates the atmosphere of Edwardian Oxford. Cyril Connolly, himself displeased by the novel, has explained the nature of its appeal:

> It is a work of inflation, important because it is the first of a long line of . . . novels of adolescence, autobiographical, romantic, which squandered the vocabulary of love and literary appreciation. . . . It popularized schoolboy friendship, Oxford and the English countryside, literature as the pool of Narcissus into which one gazes, the romance of prostitution, of priests, of murderers, and the ugliness of London and first love. It is a pastiche . . . of Pater . . . and Wilde. . . . It is prose Rupert Brooke.[6]

There is an aesthetic aura about Michael Fane. From an upper-middle-class family, he is physically attractive and impressionable to poetry and love. In the first volume, *Youth's Encounter*, Michael Fane falls in love with Kathleen McDonnell while he is seventeen, she being slightly older and already engaged. It is not out of character that in his disappointment of first love he should be reminded of love in verse, of a line from Swinburne: "Oh love, my love, and no love for me." His most intense love affair, which also ends in disillusion, occurs near the end of *Youth's Encounter*. Michael meets Lily Haden in Kensington Gardens while he is reading Verlaine, and the entire meeting is stylized and has an aesthetic cast:

> Games were a great impediment after all, when October's thin blue skies and sheen of pearl-soft airs led him on to dream along the autumnal streets. Sometimes he would sit

reading Verlaine, while continually about him the slow leaves of the great planes swooped and fluttered down ambiguously like silent birds.

One Saturday afternoon he was sitting thus when through the silver fog that on every side wrought the ultimate dissolution of the view Michael saw the slim figure of a girl walking among the trees. His mind was light with Verlaine's delicate and fantastic songs, and this slim girl as she moved wraithlike over the ground marbled with fallen leaves, seemed to express the cadence of the page. There was no one else in sight . . . then a breath of air among the treetops more remote sent floating, swaying, fluttering about her a flight of leaves.[7]

Later Michael thinks of Lily in connection not only with Verlaine but also with Poe. "It was almost as uncanny as the poem of 'Ulalume' and Michael found himself murmuring, 'of my most immemorial year,' half expectant of Lily's slim form swaying toward him."

The meeting between Amory Blaine and Eleanor in Maryland in *This Side of Paradise* is distinctly reminiscent of Michael Fane's meeting with Lily Haden. The scene in Fitzgerald in which the young couple meet is also delicately stylized; and with recognizable echoes of Mackenzie, Amory recites "Ulalume" and Eleanor speaks lines from Verlaine during a rainstorm. But more important than the similarity between these scenes is the larger pattern or design that Fitzgerald derives from *Youth's Encounter* and *Sinister Street*. The epigraph of *Youth's Encounter* comes from Keats and suggests the peculiar nature of youthful experience that Mackenzie treats: "The imagination of a boy is healthy, and the mature imagination of a man is healthy; but there is a space of life between, in which the soul is in ferment, the character undecided, the way uncertain." Mackenzie's subject is youth's turmoil, the difficulty of knowing one's mind and of achieving a stable relation to life. Michael Fane's sense of life shifts with each new set of experiences.

From his earliest years, Michael is an idealist. In childhood his favorite book is *Don Quixote*; in his teens he reads Keats and Swinburne, and romances like *Manon Lescaut*. But life is baffling, and he is uncertain of an identity (significantly perhaps, he does not know the identity of his father). Catholicism has an early appeal for him that is, again, related to his idealism: "Michael was a Catholic because Catholicism assured him of continuity and shrouded him with a sensuous austerity." But his faith fades, and for a time he takes up with a worldly sinner and sometime monk named Henry Meats, who brings him to sexual awareness, and then with Arthur Wilmot, an aesthete who, in an atmosphere of incense and preciosity, awakens Michael's interest in the Symbolist poets. The Boer War makes him begin to question the English government's morality, and disturbing also are the series of love affairs he has later in the work. *Youth's Encounter* concludes with Michael Fane's departure for Oxford, as an entirely new world opens before him. *Sinister Street* begins where *Youth's Encounter* leaves off, and Michael's life at Oxford is described in detail, including his college friendships, the clubs to which he belongs, and the literary magazine (the *Oxford Looking-Glass*) to which he contributes and of which he is an editor. Beyond Oxford is London, which he comes to know in its ugliness and poverty; at one point he attempts to "save" Lily Haden from her surrender to a life of prostitution. The man Meats is met again, as the perpetrator of a sordid murder involving one of his mistresses. The novel concludes in Rome, with Michael's conversion to Catholicism and to a life, presumably, as a priest. "Rome! Rome!" he cries at the end, "How parochial you make my youth!"

Sinister Street no doubt suggested to Fitzgerald the possibility of a college novel with an American setting that would be as evocative as Mackenzie's. His novel would be impressionistic, like Mackenzie's, and his hero would be similar to Michael Fane since he too would be both self-centered and impressionable. Mackenzie's description of Michael's interests at Oxford—his clubs and the circle of friends who are published in the

Oxford literary magazine—set an example for Fitzgerald, who describes Amory's clubs at Princeton, along with the group of undergraduates who write for the *Nassau Lit*. And when Fitzgerald "squanders the vocabulary of love and literary appreciation," he does so with the knowledge that Mackenzie had done the same in a novel that was widely admired. Amory is by no means a carbon copy of Michael Fane, but there is a kinship between them.

Fitzgerald was not served entirely well, however, by Mackenzie's model. *Youth's Encounter* and *Sinister Street* possess charm and are very gracefully written; they establish a pattern of youthful uncertainty, an atmosphere, an ambience. But they have a weak thematic outline, as Edmund Wilson has observed in his comment that Mackenzie "lacks both the intellectual force and the emotional imagination to give body and outline to [his] material." From the beginning, Mackenzie's model worked against a sense of unity, and eventually led Fitzgerald to an impasse. In the first draft of the novel, entitled "The Romantic Egotist" and twice rejected by Scribner's, Fitzgerald followed his hero from his early years through his college experiences, but was then unable to find an adequate ending for the work, which concluded with Amory's leaving college to die in the war. It is not surprising that this version was rejected, since it lacks the weight of sufficient experience, and its killing off of Amory in the war is too arbitrary an ending. The real problem, underlying the others, was that Fitzgerald had failed to locate the *meaning* of Amory's experience. In his revision, written after his own disappointing experiences in New York, Fitzgerald incorporated a version of his own embitterment; and as he attempted to give this new section shape, he turned to another contemporary model, H. G. Wells. As Fitzgerald groped for a social theme in Amory's alienation, he was guided by Wells's conception of outcast heroes, or idealistic outsiders. In the earlier part of the work, Amory is drawn as an individual functioning *within* the framework of a social group; by the end, he is an outsider and critic of the society in which he earlier aspired to succeed.

Tono-Bungay was Fitzgerald's favorite of Wells's novels, and it has the closest affinity of any of his novels with *This Side of Paradise.* The experience of his hero, young George Ponderevo, brings him into contact with many different levels of society until at the end, when the bubble of his uncle's prosperity bursts, he becomes a disinherited figure, attempting to find meaning and value in society, a pattern that Amory's experience resembles. Ponderevo and Amory, moreover, have one great love affair, which is thwarted by their belonging to the wrong social class. Ponderevo's love affair is with Beatrice, who, because she is a member of an aristocratic English family, cannot marry him even though she loves him. It becomes part of Ponderevo's indictment of English society that wealth should have the power to destroy love. His situation is reproduced in different form in *This Side of Paradise*, when Rosalind Connage finds that she cannot live without money; even though she still loves Amory, she breaks their engagement and marries a man of secure wealth and social position. Amory then becomes an angry critic of the society in which "the richest man gets the most beautiful girl, if he wants her, where the artist without an income has to sell his talents to a button manufacturer" (p. 299).

At the end of *This Side of Paradise*, Fitzgerald consciously adopts the stance of Wells, as Amory argues for socialism with Mr. Ferrenby. At different points in this section, he speaks of the "critical consciousness of the race" and "the active knowledge of the race's experience"—phrases that come directly from Wells's novels. Fitzgerald also repeats Wells in Amory's espousal of an open and experimental view of life and in his rejection of the "spiritually married man." "Opposed is the man who, being spiritually unmarried, continually seeks for new systems that will control or counteract human nature. . . . It is not life that's complicated, it's the struggle to guide and control life. That is his struggle. He is part of progress" (p. 293). Amory speaks here as a surrogate of the Wellsian hero.

But as a Wellsian hero, Amory is less than convincing. Even as he finishes his defense of socialism, he admits to Mr. Ferrenby: "Until I talked to you I hadn't thought seriously about [socialism]. I wasn't sure of half of what I said" (p. 299). A few pages later, Amory contemplates turning to the Catholic church for guidance in his confusion. "Yet," he remarks, "my acceptance was, for the present, impossible" (p. 303). There is a curious lack of logic in Amory's indecision as to whether he will embrace the authority and conservatism of the Roman Catholic church or commit himself to a radical revision of society and its institutions. He makes tentative announcements of a new self emerging from the disillusionment he has experienced (as he stands, symbolically, in a cemetery with the aspiring spires of Princeton in the background), but his affirmation is vague. When he cries, "I know myself but that is all" (p. 305) one is inclined to think that it is precisely himself that he does not yet know.

Fitzgerald's fuzzy ending, however, is not absolutely ineffective. If Amory's recognitions do not seem as valid as those of Wells's heroes, Fitzgerald has managed to project a convincing sense of Amory's disillusionment. In particular, in the situation with Rosalind Connage, who breaks their engagement because Amory does not have money, he touches upon a somber reality of wealth, which is quite different from his romanticization of wealth in the opening pages of the novel. Money is heartless, as Amory learns, and life without money, as he discovers when he works for an advertising agency in New York, can be harrowing. Amory's earlier dreams have been shattered, but there is nothing in New York City, as Fitzgerald has described it realistically, that can compensate for their loss. He has come out on the "other side," and it is a very barren world he has found. Fitzgerald has registered the pain of Amory's dilemma, and in doing so has given his experience a larger relevance, has suggested that his recognitions may not be his alone but also those of his generation. In this respect, at least, the novel achieves an *emotional* climax.

A number of critics have described Amory as an authentic Wellsian hero, who undergoes a profound change and reaches mature understanding, an interpretation that seems to me to miss the ambivalence of Amory's state of mind at the end. Robert Sklar finds Amory at the end committed to constructive social values, so that his life has been an "education," with a distinct contour, rather than "shapeless autobiographical writing"; and Milton Stern believes that Amory has developed from the mere "personality" he was at the beginning to the "personage" he is at the end, when he repudiates the values he once admired. There is, of course, a movement in this direction, a sense of dreams centering upon wealth being exploded as a form of illusion, but Fitzgerald does not focus Amory's final attitudes distinctly. At the end of *Tono-Bungay*, Wells himself comes forward as the spokesman of the novel, which is in fact a vehicle for his ideas, and there is no question of the hero-author's commitment to social change. Amory's Wellsian stance, on the other hand, seems dubious and tricky. It is impossible to imagine Amory as a Socialist. It is very difficult to believe, despite his disillusioning experiences, that he has outgrown his romantic attitude toward the world, which is the deepest fact of his psychology.

One may say reasonably only that Amory has been chastened by his experiences, that he is moving toward *becoming* a more mature person, even if he is still alone at the end with his anger and uncertainty. In the cemetery scene, he literally gropes in the darkness toward understanding, attaining what Edmund Wilson has called "a gesture of indefinite revolt." It is this indefiniteness that places the interpretation of Amory's experience as a "completed education" in doubt. The themes that Fitzgerald would explore later are already present in *This Side of Paradise*—the wealth that nourishes romantic dreams, and then cruelly destroys them; the rich girl who loves and leaves the boy who does not "belong"; the recognition that social class in America may be as decisive as character in determining one's fate. But Fitzgerald has announced these themes without as yet having treated them with full understanding. One of the best critical judgments of *This Side of Paradise* is still that of Wilson, who noted that the novel does not develop into thematic clarity, and is therefore "really not *about* anything."[8] The sense of unresolved ideas involved in Amory's experience is felt in the novel's closing lines:

> He stretched out his arms to the crystalline, radiant sky.
> "I know myself," he cried, "but that is all."

The image conveys Amory's protest against the society into which he has come of age and is a gauge of the novel's realism. Yet notice the "loveliness" of the image, its highly stylized evocation of a romantic self-involvement. In this concluding image, Fitzgerald's realistic protest and his hero's romantic self-involvement seem to pull in opposing directions, or to be not fully integrated, as they are not fully in the novel as a whole.

This side of Paradise is sometimes callow, but there are redeeming things in it. Compared with Bishop's first volume of verse, *Green Fruit*, Fitzgerald's first novel shows a more uneven art, but a stronger individuality struggling to assert itself. Both Bishop and Fitzgerald are influenced by received literary models, but Fitzgerald manages to convey more of his uniqueness. He writes already as a stylist and here and there is capable of striking and inimitable phrasing. For an American writer, he shows an unusual awareness of class distinctions; and in Rosalind Connage, his strongest character, and her world, has indicated the existence of a social class relevant to the time when *This Side of Paradise* was published. The nervous pacing of the work has been used effectively by Fitzgerald to capture a great many diverse experiences—the life of the East Coast campus just before the war; tours in the Midwest with the Triangle show; weekend college sprees; undergraduate excursions into New York and Atlantic City; postwar New York, with its debutantes, coming-out parties, and young men finding their first jobs; the hero's disturbing postwar recognitions. Fitzgerald has managed to evoke the feeling of a particular time and place.

In assimilating so much of the contemporary moment as he does, Fitzgerald also manages to suggest what it is that makes that moment significant. In the movement from Fitzgerald's romanticized treatment of Amory's attempt to succeed in Princeton's undergraduate establishment just before the war to the chastened quality of his experiences after the war, Amory's life reflects a turning point in time—the country's entry into the postwar world, its disenchanted mood, the appearance of a "new generation . . . grown up to find all Gods dead, all faiths in man shaken" (p. 304). Fitzgerald's capturing of this mood is a prescient achievement. Published at the dawn of the decade of the twenties, *This Side of Paradise* initiated a period of imaginative writing in America whose overriding concern would be with the individual's alienated relation to society.

* * * * *

A number of the short stories Fitzgerald published in the period immediately after *This Side of Paradise* are of a commercial nature and do not reveal very much about his growth; but there is one, "May Day" (1920), which is more serious and comments further on the postwar world Amory discovered in New York. Published in *The Smart Set*, the story seems experimental in a number of ways, particularly in the way it develops in a series of disparate panels that by the end fit together to make a thematic statement. It reveals the influence of the American literary naturalists whom Fitzgerald had discovered "through a critic named Mencken," as Fitzgerald wrote of

Amory's discovery of them in a sentence added to the galley proofs of *This Side of Paradise*. His use of impressionistic naturalism in this story seems indebted, in particular, to Stephen Crane. Crane's abbreviated, two-dimensional characters, who seem depersonalized as they function in scenes of urban violence, might very well have inspired Fitzgerald's drawing of the returning soldiers Rose and Key. Indeed, Rose and Key are scarcely human at all. "They were ugly, ill-nourished, devoid of all except the very lowest form of intelligence, and without even that animal exuberance that in itself brings color to life . . . . tossed as driftwood from their births, they would be tossed as driftwood to their deaths."[9] They are borne along with crowds through the city until they eventually appear as part of a crowd at the newspaper office of Henry Bradin, where they give the impression of being vaudeville dummies, soldiers who have no names, one "short and dark, the other tall and weak of chin" (p. 115).

The scene is an extension of an earlier one in the street where a bearded Jew, delivering a speech about the war and the failure of capitalism to have improved the quality of life in the country, is senselessly beaten by a crowd of returning soldiers and patriotic citizens. "The Jew staggered to his feet, and immediately went down again before a half-dozen reaching-in fists. This time he stayed down, blood oozing from his lip where it was cut within and without" (p. 93). Cries of morality and patriotism cloak what is merely herd instinct and violence, and later that night the scene is reproduced in the office of Bradin's Socialist weekly, a mayhem acted out literally in the dark. The police who appear are as impersonalized as the rioters and are drawn with a naturalistic stylization:

Suddenly the lights were on and the room was full of policemen, clubbing left and right. The deep voice boomed out:

"Here now! Here now! Here now!" . . .

"Here now! This is no way! One of your own sojers got shoved out the back window an' killed hisself!" . . .

"They broke my leg. My God, the fools!"

"Here now!" called the police captain. "Here now! Here now!" (P. 116)

The victim in this passage, as it will be learned later, is Key, whose fall from the window "split his skull like a cracked cocoanut" (p. 118), an image that impersonalizes him in death, as he had been impersonalized in life.

The other characters of the story, however, not merely the rudimentary ones, have been sketched naturalistically. Gordon Sterrett's last name implies that as an artist, and a man, he is sterile; and his character is rigidly determined by the initial description of him as being "small, slender, and darkly handsome" and as having eyes with "unusually long eyelashes" underlined by "the blue semicircle of ill health" (p. 84). Philip Dean, who comes from a wealthy family and graduated with Gordon Sterrett from Yale a year before the war, is defined largely by his taste for expensive silk shirts and impressive ties and, since he is a huge consumer, by his prominent teeth. Edith Bradin wears a crimson, fur-trimmed opera cloak that is mentioned several times, so that it seems part of her identity. When she first appears, she has something of the quality of a hairdresser's dummy. She rebuffs her date, Peter Himmell, when he accidentally brushes his arm against her hair. "She had spent the afternoon at her hairdresser's; the idea of a calamity overtaking her hair was extremely repugnant" (p. 98). Her artificiality is implied in the description of her as "a complete, infinitely delicate, quite perfect thing of beauty, flowing in an even line from a complex coiffure to two small slim feet" (p. 99). The implication in this description is crystallized when Dean says of her that she is "still a sort of pretty doll—you know what I mean: as if you touched her she'd smear" (p. 85). She is indeed a doll—pretty and complete unto herself, with only a doll's likeness to fully dimensional humanhood.

The story is framed by its title, "May Day," with its historical connotations, suggesting both the rite of spring renewal celebrated in the dance around the maypole in earlier day England and the Marxist revolution, with its formulas of a perfect society in which the selfish principle has been eliminated. But personal and social renewal are shown here in the ironic terms of a spring exhaustion. The story begins with the quality of a fairy tale; the city to which the victorious troops return is at first specified only as "the great city" (p. 83), and the sense is given of a timeless and not yet particularized experience. "Never had there been such splendor in the great city. . . .and faster and faster and faster did the merchants dispose of their trinkets and slippers" (p. 83). It is apparently a victorious and happy world, in which the soldiers returning from the war are "pure and brave" and the young women waiting for them are "virgins." Then the great city becomes particularized as New York, the focused setting the Biltmore Hotel, the first-seen and exemplary character Gordon Sterrett, to whom Dean remarks: "You seem to be sort of bankrupt—morally as well as financially" (p. 87). The theme of moral bankruptcy is then explored in the lives of all the characters. In a demoralized state at the dance at Delmonico's, Gordon tells Edith Bradin that things "have been snapping inside me for four months like little hooks on a dress, and it's about to' come off when a few more hooks go" (p. 103), and the image of the dress reinforces the idea of a lack of masculine firmness in him, as well as in the world he reflects. For what has come in the wake of the war, the "something" Gordon says that he has lost, is a breakdown of belief, a loss of purpose.

Gordon's experience is paralleled by that of Dean and Himmell, who go off on a binge provoked by Edith's rebuff of Himmell. Himmell is about to graduate from Yale, but has been in the war, and is described as having a "hurt look"

(p. 100); his appearance also gives an impression that he is "humorous" (implying that he does not believe in anything, is cynical). When he meets Edith he makes an unusually low bow to her with "strained formality" (p. 100); the mockery implied in his gallantry comes out later when he is drinking upstairs at Delmonico's and repeats Kipling's lines that "any lady and Judy O'Grady" are the same "under the skin" (p. 107). He continues drinking with Dean all that night and into the morning, when they appear in a tipsy state at a Childs' restaurant, scattering hash like confetti over the patrons. Later they take a taxi to Delmonico's, where they take signs from a cloak room that read In and Out, and parade through the Biltmore lobby, as Mr. In and Mr. Out. In this way they become depersonalized, like a pair of vaudeville dummies; in effect, they are counterparts of the rudimentary characters Rose and Key. The signs In and Out—for which they have exchanged their personal identities—carry a number of suggestions. They suggest the prewar world that was, and the postwar world that has replaced it; and they suggest the idea of flux and emptiness, the common denominator of their world and that of the returning troops.

Early in the story, Fitzgerald describes Rose and Key, but comments on Key in particular. "The taller of the two was named Carrol Key, a name hinting that in his veins, however thinly diluted by generations of degeneration, ran blood of some potentiality. But one could stare endlessly at the long, chinless face, the dull, watery eyes, and high cheekbones, without finding a suggestion of either ancestral worth or native resourcefulness" (p. 92). This allusion to more illustrious, earlier-day Keys seems an indirect reference to Francis Scott Key and *The Star-Spangled Banner*, whose lines form a contrast between an earlier patriotism and impassioned belief and the present-day loss of belief:

O thus be it ever when free men shall stand
Between their lov'd home & war's desolation!

And the star-spangled banner in triumph shall wave
O'er the land of the free & the home of the brave.

Key and Rose delude themselves that they are patriots, with
courage and spirit, but they are both empty beings who are
herded like sheep either to death, in the case of one, or to arrest,
in the case of the other.

What is characteristic of this world, beneath the cheering and
slogans, is its materialism and self-concern. At the opening,
working-girls are seen in crowds loitering by windows of expensive shops, daydreaming of finery; and soon after, Dean is
shown in his Biltmore suite, with his piles of expensive shirts
and ties, as he is about to go out to an exclusive men's clothing
store. Edith Bradin is extraordinarily conscious of physical lux-
uries and is thus like the working-girls who stare avidly into
the windows of the Fifth Avenue shops at opera cloaks. Her
involvement with material things is part of her self-involvement
and her emotional superficiality. She has retained a romantic
picture of Gordon from the dance they attended at the Harris-
burg Country Club at the outbreak of the war; at Delmonico's,
at the first dance she has attended since then, she finds a different
Gordon, more grimly real than her romantic memory of him.
But finding him in tatters, she is merely repelled, does not try
to help him, and does not feel anything deeply. To her are given
the cruelest lines in the story, as she recognizes how much he
has changed: "Love is fragile—she was thinking—but perhaps
the pieces are saved, the things that hovered on lips, that might
have been said. The new love words, the tendernesses learned,
are treasured up for the next lover" (p. 104). Her selfishness
is complemented by that of Jewel Hudson, the lower-class girl
with over-rouged cheeks and "soft, pulpy lips" (p. 111) who,
like an empty sack that cannot stand upright, forces herself
upon Gordon, until he puts a bullet through his head. In this
way, the characters are all distinctly different from one another
and yet are all the same, are all symptomatic of the same environment. In *The Great Gatsby*, Fitzgerald's characters in the

Washington Heights apartment scene—Myrtle Wilson, her sister Catherine, the McKees—are all personally different and are yet all the same, versions of the same environmental psychology. In "May Day" Fitzgerald already began to explore this technique of characterization.

Anticipating *The Great Gatsby* in another way, Fitzgerald makes extensive use in "May Day" of color symbolism. Golden light at the opening has an association with morning light and renewing energy, but only ironically, since what it shines upon are store windows filled with purchasable goods: "The wealthy, happy sun glittered in transient gold through the thick windows of the expensive shops" (p. 89). With a similar irony, the city is depicted at the beginning in terms of fortunate festival, and flowers, the streets being "vivid with thrown flowers of white, red, and rose" (p. 183). These colors are used elsewhere in a way that debases their attractive associations. The merchants looking out at the celebration, estimating their sales, have "white-bunched faces" (p. 83); the superficial Edith Bradin is depicted in highlights of red—her crimson opera cloak, her "carmine" lips, her red hair swept in a haughty coiffure; the doughboy "Rose" lacks consciousness. In no way do they support the fruitful associations of the blooms.

At Delmonico's, dull yellow and blue are used to accentuate a character's inner state. Rose and Key are excluded from the larger, sensuous spectacle, the chandelier-glittering world of the dance, being cramped into a broom closet, which corresponds to their social status and outlook. The room is lit overhead by "one anemic electric light" (p. 106), which gives off a "dim" (p. 96) yellow glow, and this region they inhabit is said to be as "hot as hell" (p. 98). For Himmell, after he begins to lose himself in drink, the dance becomes a "paradise of violet blue" (p. 106), and later, asked for his floor by an elevator operator, he cries "Heaven," which is what the name of this escapist (Himmell, from the German word *Himmel*) means.

The climactic scene of the story has also been accented by

color imagery; it is the scene where Dean and Himmell are scattering hash at the Childs' restaurant:

> But the commotion upon his exit proper was dwarfed by another phenomenon which drew admiring glances and a prolonged involuntary "Oh-h-h!" from every person in the restaurant.
> The great plate-glass front had turned to a deep creamy blue, the color of a Maxfield Parrish moonlight—a blue that seemed to press close upon the pane as if to crowd its way into the restaurant. Dawn had come up in Columbus Circle, magical, breathless dawn, silhouetted the great statue of the immortal Christopher, and mingling in a curious and uncanny manner with the fading yellow electric light inside. (P. 120)

The statue of Columbus, against the astonishing blue moonlight of dream, forms an eerie contrast to the scene—of flat, drab, inadequate imagination—enacted within, under a "faded" yellow light. The sudden, impressionistic focusing upon the statue of Columbus expresses in more dramatic form what is implied obliquely in the names of two of the story's characters, Hudson and Key, discoverer and inspired patriot, respectively—namely, that an earlier vision of the new world has been emptied of its force. What has happened is emphasized further by the next view of the revelers and the soulless others who are blown in the wind like scraps of "gray" paper:

> In the car sat the souls of Mr. In and Mr. Out discussing with amazement the blue light that had so precipitately colored the sky behind the statue of Christopher Columbus, discussing with bewilderment the old, gray faces of the early risers which skimmed palely along the street like blown bits of paper on a gray lake. (P. 121)

"May Day" anticipates *The Great Gatsby* in a number of

ways—in its miniaturization of characters through dominant traits and the reflection they give of each other and the environment that formed them; in Fitzgerald's extensive use of color imagery to accent characterization and theme; and most of all, in the quality of moral fable that the story has, its implied contrast of an earlier vision of America and its present-moment inertia.

More immediately, as a study of Sterrett's disintegration in a postwar world of dissolving values, "May Day" forms a bridge to *The Beautiful and Damned*. *The Beautiful and Damned* is the most seriously flawed novel Fitzgerald wrote, but it is also a step forward in some important respects and deals with a larger, denser society than Fitzgerald treats in *This Side of Paradise*. It has the special interest, too, of revealing Fitzgerald's continuing assimilation of contemporary writers, particularly H. L. Mencken, whom Fitzgerald had begun to discover shortly before *This Side of Paradise* was published.[10] Mencken had, in fact, helped to launch Fitzgerald's career, having published his first professional stories in *The Smart Set*, and greeted *This Side of Paradise* with praise when it appeared, calling it "the best recent American novel" he had read.

Mencken, of course, played a special role at this time as an adversary of American culture; as a literary-social critic, he attacked American provincialism and popular myths on every front. The South, living in the afterglow of its myth of chivalry, was reduced in Mencken's pages to an arid wasteland, a cultural Sahara; the Northern businessman, supported by the myth of his enterprise and well-being, was revealed as a know-nothing, incapable of either reflection or deep feeling. In particular, he attacked our great national myth of "success," and the optimism that stood behind it. Carl Dolmetsch, in his history of *The Smart Set*, refers to "hundreds of variations of this anti-success theme" that appeared in the magazine in the early twenties—stories in which success is achieved at the sacrifice of integrity, romance, or artistic aspiration.[11] Mencken's concern with the illusion of national myth was to have an immediate and then a far-reaching effect on Fitzgerald's career in the twenties.

Mencken published his most influential volume of literary criticism, *A Book of Prefaces*, in 1917. Its chapter entitled "Puritanism as a Literary Force" explains the sources of American cultural stagnation in terms of a moribund Puritanism. In American letters, this surviving Puritanism takes the form of the "genteel tradition," which shrinks from a coarse exposure to life, and of literary censorship. The essays in the volume on Dreiser and Conrad are important in indicating the kind of literature Mencken endorsed and wished to encourage, a literature that is ruthless in exposing life in its tragic essentials. Dreiser is praised in the degree that his work is unlike most current American fiction, with its "infantile smugness and hopefulness"; his novels, instead, "arouse those deep and lasting emotions which grow out of the recognition of elemental and universal tragedy." Yet more even than Dreiser, Mencken admired Conrad, of whom he speaks as being "forever fascinated by the immense indifference of things, the tragic vanity of blind groping that we call aspiration, the profound meaninglessness of life."

By the time the *Prejudices: Second Series* (1920) Mencken had come into a position of exceptional prominence. Walter Lippmann referred to him as "the most powerful personal influence on this whole generation of educated people";[12] but his influence was felt particularly by a number of younger American writers. In a retrospective essay written later in his career, Fitzgerald remarked that Mencken had created a stimulating climate in which imaginative literature could be written, by which he surely meant his own. "I don't think many men of my age," he remarked, "can regard him without reverence."[13] A well-known instance of his influence may be seen in *Main Street* and *Babbitt*, as Mark Schorer, in his biography of Sinclair Lewis, has noted:

> In his review of Mencken's *Notes on Democracy* (1926),
> Edmund Wilson wrote that "Sinclair Lewis's Babbitt and the
> inhabitants of his Main Street are merely incarnations of the
> great American boob, evidently inspired by Mencken."
> Mencken's *A Book of Prefaces* (1917) may well have been
> the influence that gave Lewis the focus for *Main Street*. . . .
> but Lewis had already hit on his idea for *Babbitt* before
> Mencken publicly proposed it. Nevertheless, he was prepared
> to give Mencken credit. In January 1922, he wrote:

> > A year ago in a criticism of *Main Street* you said that what
> > ought to be taken up now is the American city—not NY
> > or Chi but the cities of 200,000 or 500,000—the Balti-
> > mores and Omahas and Buffaloes and Birminghams, etc.
> > I was startled to read it, because that was precisely what
> > I WAS then planning, and am now doing.

> > I think you'll like it—I hope to Christ you do. All our
> > friends are in it—the Rotary Club, the popular preacher,
> > the Chamber of Commerce, the new bungalows, the bunch
> > of business men jolliers lunching at the Athletic Club. It
> > ought to be at least 2000% American, as well as forward-
> > looking, right-thinking, optimistic, selling the idea of
> > success.[14]

The reflection of Mencken in *Babbitt* (1922) is seen as
clearly in *The Beautiful and Damned*, which appeared the same
year. Even at a glance the novel reveals the presence of
Mencken's American boob. In Mr. and Mrs. Gilbert, Fitzgerald
has depicted a couple who in their mutually reinforcing dullness
stand for middle America. The Gilberts are captured revealingly
in a protracted conversation about the weather:

> Mr. Gilbert with true masculine impassivity disregarded the
> awe he had excited in his wife. He returned to the two young

men and triumphantly routed them on the subject of the weather. Richard Caramel was called on to remember the month of November in Kansas. No sooner had the theme been pushed toward him, however, than it was fished back to be lingered over . . . and generally devitalized by its sponsor.

The immemorial thesis that the days somewhere were warm but the nights were pleasant was successfully propounded and they decided the exact distance on an obscure railroad between two points that Dick had inadvertently mentioned. Anthony fixed Mr. Gilbert with a steady stare and went into a trance through which, after a moment, Mrs. Gilbert's smiling voice penetrated:

> "It seems as though the cold were damper here—it seems to eat into my bones."[15]

The Gilberts' marriage suggests a gradual shriveling of romantic possibility, but they are not singular in this, having other counterparts in the novel. In a passage that comes not long after this one, two men are encountered, both newly married, who are versions of Mr. Gilbert in an earlier phase:

> After cocktails and luncheon at the University Club Anthony felt better. He had run into two men from his class at Harvard, and in contrast to the gray heaviness of their conversation his life assumed color. Both of them were married; one spent his coffee time sketching an extra-nuptial adventure to the bland and appreciative smiles of the other. Both of them, he thought, were Mr. Gilberts in embryo; the number of their "yes's" would have to be quadrupled, their natures crabbed by twenty years—then they would be no more than obsolete and broken machines, pseudo-wise and valueless, nursed to an utter senility by the women they had broken. (P. 55)

Mr. Gilbert and the young men at the University Club who will become versions of him indicate a social norm of conformity and inner emptiness, a further glimpse of which appears early in the work when Anthony and Gloria enter a midtown café:

> A tip circulates—and in the place knowingly mentioned, gather the lower moral classes on Saturday and Sunday night —little troubled men who are pictured in the comics as "the Consumer" or "the Public." They have made sure that the place has three qualifications: it is cheap; it imitates with a sort of shoddy and mechanical wistfulness the glittering antics of the great cafes of the theatre district; and—this, above all, important—it is a place where they can "take a nice girl," which means, of course, that everyone has become equally harmless, timid, and uninteresting through the lack of money and imagination.
>
> There on Sunday nights gather the credulous, sentimental, underpaid, overworked people with hyphenated occupations: book-keepers, ticket-sellers, office-managers. . . . With them are their giggling, over-gestured, pathetically pretentious women, who grow fat with them, bear them too many babies, and float helpless and uncontent in a colourless sea of drudgery and broken hopes. . . . This is where their docile patrons bring their "nice women," whose starved fancies are only too willing to believe that the scene is comparatively gay, and joyous, and even faintly immoral. (Pp. 69–70)

This social landscape clearly reflects Mencken's vision of American middle-class life as an unrelieved bleakness. But Mencken is present in the novel in many other ways as well, in part in the figure of Maury Noble (a composite of Mencken and Nathan) who toasts the fall of democracy, describes himself at one point as an "anti-Christ" (p. 43), and "a brilliantly meaningless figure in a meaningless world" (p. 23). The condescending tone of *The Smart Set* is pervasive in the work and can be noticed in Fitzgerald's slighting references to clergymen and public officials, but the satire crowning the work is that Anthony's grandfather is a vice crusader in the tradition of Anthony Comstock, whom Mencken had ridiculed. Fitzgerald describes old Patch in the following way:

> It was then that he determined after a severe attack of sclerosis, to consecrate the remainder of his life to the moral regeneration of the world. He became a reformer among reformers. Emulating the magnificent efforts of Anthony Comstock, after whom his grandson was named, he levelled a varied assortment of upper-cuts and body blows at liquor, literature, vice, art, patent medicines, and Sunday theatres. His mind under the influence of that insidious mildew which eventually forms on all but the few, gave itself up furiously to every indignation of the age. (P. 140)

In a later section old Patch speaks to Anthony about the "after-life" and in the same passage recalls, with maudlin emotion, his lost childhood; and his notion of the afterlife, and his childhood nostalgia, are made to seem equally sentimental:

> "I think a great deal about the after-life. . . . I was sitting here today thinking about what's lying in wait for us, and somehow I began to remember an afternoon nearly sixty-five years ago, when I was playing with my little sister Annie, down where that summer house is now." He pointed into the long flower garden, his eyes trembling of tears, his voice shaking.
> "I began thinking—and it seemed to me that *you* ought to think a little more about the after-life." (P. 140)

A moment later, however, his conversation suddenly takes an ominous turn:

> "—Why, when I was just two years older than you," he rasped with a cunning chuckle, "I sent three members of the firm of Wrenn and Hunt to the poorhouse."
> Anthony started with embarrassment. (P. 140)

Patch (whose first name, Adam, suggests man's original sin) has his cultural origins in American Puritanism. During the industrial expansion following the Civil War he had risen to power ruthlessly, and then in his later years redirected his aggressions toward policing art and other people's possible enjoyment of life. There are a number of amusing, understated moments in the novel when Adam Patch's name is mentioned before the stolid Joseph Bloeckman, who always remarks soberly: "A fine example of an American."

Set off against old Patch, the Gilberts, and others who represent the suppression of individuality are Anthony and Gloria, who, at least as they first appear, have a sense of personal style and of romantic possibility. They belong to a circle that includes the sophisticated Maury Noble and Richard Caramel then writing his first novel, and life seems to stand expectantly before them. But as the novel progresses, they become estranged, in both a social and a spiritual sense. This movement is part of Fitzgerald's attempted study of human deterioration, which draws from the work of the American naturalists—from Stephen French Whitman (whose novel *Predestined* is a minor classic that has only recently been rescued from oblivion),[16] and from Norris and Dreiser, who were admired particularly by Mencken. In his essay entitled "The National Letters," Mencken outlined what he considered the "superior," pessimistic novel, in contrast to the common run of contemporary American fiction, in which a hero succeeds in a conventional way and is regarded as a "success" by his peers:

> Here is one of the fundamental defects of American fiction—perhaps the one character that sets it off sharply from all other known kinds of contemporary fiction. It habitually exhibits, not a man of delicate organization in revolt against the inexplicable tragedy of existence, but a man of low sensibilities and elemental desires yielding gladly to his environment and so achieving what, under a third-rate civilization passes for success.

The man of reflective habit cannot conceivably take any passionate interest in the conflicts it deals with. . . . What interests this man is the far more poignant significant conflict between a salient individual and the harsh and meaningless mandates and vagaries of God. His hero is not one who yields and wins, but one who resists and fails. A superior man's struggle . . . is with the impulses, weaknesses, and limitations that war with his notion of what life should be. . . . Nine times out of ten his aspiration is almost infinitely above his achievement. The result is that we see him sliding downhill—his ideals breaking up, his hope petering out, his character in decay. Character in decay is thus the theme of the great bulk of superior fiction. One has it in . . . Balzac, in Hardy, in Conrad, . . . in Sudermann, in Bennett, and, to come home, in Dreiser.[17]

In some essentials, Anthony's deterioration resembles Vandover's in Norris's *Vandover and the Brute*. Both Anthony and Vandover have an aesthetic attitude toward life, were born into wealth, and attended Harvard; in time they drift into self-indulgence and descend to the bottom rungs of society, with the loss even (although for Anthony not permanently) of their reason. But Anthony's deterioration has an even stronger relation to Hurstwood's in Dreiser's *Sister Carrie*. The character of Hurstwood, in fact, had made a strong impression on Fitzgerald, who described him in a letter to Maxwell Perkins as "one of the three best characters in American fiction in the last twenty years."[18] In his review of *The Beautiful and Damned*, Mencken himself called attention to the resemblance between Hurstwood's decline and Anthony's,[19] and Perosa has enlarged on it further:

The deterioration of Hurstwood, in Dreiser's novel has many points in common with Anthony's deterioration and decay; the lack of a regular job, the sordid rooms in which both men waste away their lives, the friends who become shabbier and shabbier, the inner dejection and helplessness, the want of cash, and then the mean arguments, the hopeless drinking, and newspapers read in a gloomy half-light, the drifting along empty streets, an so on. Hurstwood himself is represented as a "pilgrim adream"—his dream, too, becomes a lethargy and then a nightmare. But in Hurstwood's case, many important economic and social factors are responsible for his ruin. If his destiny is determined by his own weakness—his hamartia, his tragic flaw—it is also the result of the concurrence of external circumstances, such as the ruthless laws of the business world. . . . His destiny is therefore tragic, not merely pathetic, as is the destiny of Anthony and Gloria, whose weaknesses are not matched by a corresponding conflict of forces.[20]

Perosa describes quite well the correspondence (and also the difference) in the deterioration of Hurstwood and Anthony, but it should be added that they are also part of a larger pattern of meaning and movement in the two novels. Dreiser and Fitzgerald have in common an extraordinary consciousness of money and its effect upon the lives of their characters. It is a determining force in *Sister Carrie*, one which either condemns to drabness and stultification, or makes possible a larger, freer life. The characters in Dreiser's novel may be schematized according to those who possess money and those who do not. The "haves," however, may become the "have nots," and the "have nots" may become the "haves"—especially in America, where society is less rigidly stratified than in Europe. A preoccupation with social mobility is of central importance in *Sister Carrie*, and it is again in *The Beautiful and Damned*, with a similar formal design.

Because the middle section of the novel sprawls, it has sometimes been said that *The Beautiful and Damned* lacks structure, but a close look at the work reveals that Fitzgerald did give thought to the structure, at least in the early and later parts of the novel. Consider the passage at the opening of the coming-out season in New York:

Every morning now there were invitations in Anthony's mail. Three dozen virtuous females of the first layer were proclaiming their fitness, if not their specific willingness, to bear children unto three dozen millionaires. . . . Five dozen virtuous females of the second layer were proclaiming not only this fitness, but in addition a tremendous undaunted ambition toward the first three dozen young men, who were of course invited to each of the ninety-six parties—as were the young lady's group of family friends, acquaintances, college boys, and eager young outsiders. To continue, there was a third layer from the skirts of the city, from Newark, and the New Jersey suburbs up to bitter Connecticut and the ineligible suburbs of Long Island—and doubtless contiguous layers down to the city's shoes: Jewesses were coming out in a society of Jewish men and women, from Riverdale to the Bronx, and looking forward to a rising young broker or jeweller and a kosher wedding; Irish girls were casting their eyes, with license at last to do so, upon a society of young Tammany politicians, pious undertakers, and grown-up choir boys.

And, naturally, the city caught the contagious air of entré —and working girls, poor ugly souls wrapping soap in the factories and showing finery in the big stores, dreamed that perhaps in the spectacular excitement of this winter they might obtain for themselves the coveted male—as in a muddled carnival crowd an inefficient pickpocket may consider his chances increased. And the chimneys commenced to smoke and the subway's foulness was freshened. (Pp. 31–32)

In this passage, aspiration is graduated according to a monetary scale. On all levels, the mating season (suggested as a kind of "pickpocket" activity) has the connotation of acquisition, but as one goes down the social scale longings become increasingly diminished. Those who are ineligible are described in terms of "skirts" and "shoes," images that imply the lack of a head, or of intelligent awareness. Even worse, the dream of a poor Irish

girl that she may catch an undertaker seems merely a preparation for death. It is a season of expectation, but the transitory is
emphasized, even in the image of the subway, a means of urban
transit. The subway's foulness is freshened—but presumably not
for long, because none of the longings transcend the money
from which they originate.

Shortly after this passage, Anthony and Gloria stop by at
what Fitzgerald calls a "brummagem cabaret," a place of cheap
flashiness, a crossroads of democracy, and here a curious scene is
observed. At a table next to them, they notice a young woman
with violets on her hat:

> The manner of the girl was a study in national sociology. She
> was meeting some new men—and she was pretending des-
> perately. By gesture she was pretending and by words and by
> the scarcely perceptible motionings of her eyelids that she
> belonged to a class a little superior to the class with which
> she now had to do, that a while ago she had been, and
> presently would again be, in a higher rarer air. She was almost
> painfully refined—she wore last year's hat covered with
> violets no more yearningly pretentious and palpable than
> herself. . . .
> ——And the other women passionately poured out the im-
> pression that though they were in the crowd they were not of
> it. This was not the sort of place to which they were accus-
> tomed, they had dropped in because it was near by and
> convenient—every party in the restaurant poured out that
> impression . . . who knew? They were forever changing class,
> all of them—the women often marrying above their oppor-
> tunities, the men striking suddenly a magnificent opulence.
> . . . Meanwhile, they met here to eat. (Pp. 70–71)

The yearning of the young woman with violets on her last
year's hat to seem refined, and to belong to a higher social class
than she does, provides a humorous moment in the narrative.
But, as the next paragraph shows, she is exactly like all the

others in the room, is symptomatic of the upward aspiration of the urban middle class.

This upward aspiration glimpsed in the cabaret scene appears elsewhere in a more ominous context. At the opening, Anthony attends the theater, where he moves easily in an ambience of sophistication and wealth, described in a fluid imagery. "There were jewels dripping from arms and throats and eartips of white rose; there were innumerable broad shimmers down the middles of innumerable silk hats. . . . Most of all there was the ebbing, flowing . . . slow-rolling wave effect of this cheerful sea of people as to-night it poured its glittering torrent into the artificial lake of laughter" (p. 24). Then as Anthony proceeds through Times Square, he enters another world. "Two young Jewish men passed him, talking in loud voices and craning their necks here and there in fatuous and supercilious glances" (p. 25). They wear gray spats and carry gray gloves on their cane handles and suggest a parvenu urbanity reminiscent of the social pretending at the cabaret. Above them is the glare of neon, and most particularly mentioned, more than once, is the Chariot Race sign. The Chariot Race sign may merely imply an urban splendor of a garish kind, but it may also hint at a grueling contest for place, the reason why Anthony begins to find the spectacle disquieting. It suddenly comes over him that there is a "loneliness here." Back at his apartment, Anthony has another impression that is both strange and memorable:

The elevated, half a quiet block away, sounded a rumble of drums—and should he lean from his window he would see the train, like an angry eagle, breasting the dark curve at the corner. He was reminded of a fantastic romance he had lately read in which cities had been bombed from aerial trains, and for a moment he fancied that Washington Square had declared war on Central Park and that this was a north-bound menace loaded with battle and sudden death . . . but his own street was silent and he was safe in [his apartment] from all the threat of life. (P. 27)

He is "safe," but only temporarily; the impression foreshadows events that will confirm the warlike nature of life.

In the course of his steady deterioration, he comes to make his recognitions of the harshness of existence. His lodgings, which grow progressively shabbier, are used to fix, or pinpoint, his decline. The changing nature of his friendships and associations has the same effect. Near the end, he has become friendly with Parker Allison, "who had been exactly the wrong sort of rounder at Harvard, and who was running through a 'yeast' fortune as rapidly as possible. Parker Allison's notion of distinction consisted in driving a noisy red-and-yellow racing car up Broadway with two glittering, hard-eyed girls beside him" (p. 415). Anthony's other friend at this time is Pete Lytell, described in a phrase that seems to sum him up—the phrase that he "wore a gray derby on the side of his head." Fitzgerald's "placing" of Allison and Lytell with Anthony at this stage of his decline is, of course, very calculated. At the opening, Anthony's two constant companions were Maury Noble and Richard Caramel, who had some association with intellect and perspective. They are replaced, in the course of Anthony's changing fortunes, by two others who indicate the debasement of his mind, since they are wholly materialistic and see nothing clearly.

By the end, Anthony is to sink further still, until he wanders drunkenly past a row of pawn shops, which have by that hour closed, and then attempts to obtain a loan, first from Maury Noble, who cuts him in the street, and finally—and disastrously —from Bloeckman. The encounter between Anthony and Bloeckman, forming the great ironic scene of the novel, is part of a similar diagram of social mobility in *The Beautiful and Damned* and *Sister Carrie*. In *Sister Carrie,* Dreiser's characters do not remain stationary, but move either upward or downward socially. Mrs. Hurstwood and her daughter, who marries into wealth, move upward; and in time the drummer Drouet moves upward too. Carrie Meeber, who comes to Chicago with little more than her train fare eventually becomes successful in the theater and is established in an expensive tower suite at the Waldorf. On the other hand, Hurstwood, originally the most highly placed, moves steadily downward; his descent to the dregs of society forms a movement in counterpoint to the rise of the other characters. At a point near the end these lives, pointed in different directions, intersect ironically in or near the impersonal metropolis of New York. Mrs. Hurstwood and her daughter, "turned supercilious by fortune," are arriving by express train, on their way to spend the winter in Rome. At the same moment, Hurstwood is seen desolate in a skid-row district: "He stood before a dirty four story building in a side street quite near the Bowery, whose one-time coat of buff had been changed by soot and rain. He mingled with a crowd of men." Just before this episode, Hurstwood had gone to the Waldorf in an attempt to beg money from Carrie. Lola Osborne, the companion of Carrie in her hotel suite, happens to look out the window at that moment, and remarks that a man (it is Hurstwood) has just fallen in the street below. "How sheepish men look when they fall, don't they?" she says.

There is a quite striking similarity between Dreiser's contrasting of altered fortunes at the end of his novel and Fitzgerald's diagram of changed fortunes at the end of his. Heir to a large fortune at the beginning, apparently having a brilliant future before him, Anthony loses his inheritance and his footing, sinking lower and lower in society. With Bloeckman, his counterpart, it is the reverse. As he first appears in the novel, he is an awkward parvenu, condescended to by Anthony and Gloria; later, however, he begins to acquire confidence and polish:

It seemed to Anthony that during the last year Bloeckman had grown tremendously in dignity. The boiled look was gone, he seemed "done" at last. In addition he was no longer overdressed. The inappropriate facetiousness he had affected in ties had given way to a sturdy dark pattern, and his right hand, which had formerly displayed two heavy rings, was now innocent of ornament and even without the raw glow of a manicure.

This dignity appeared also in his personality. The last aura of the successful traveling-man had faded from him, that deliberate ingratiation of which the lowest form is the bawdy joke in the Pullman smoker. One imagined that, having been fawned upon financially, he had attained aloofness; having been snubbed socially, he had acquired reticence. But whatever had given him weight instead of bulk, Anthony no longer felt a correct superiority in his presence. (Pp. 207-8)

Anthony's encounter with him at the Boul' Mich' completes the reversal of their original roles, with Bloeckman (his name now changed to Black, to correspond to his changed social status) a member of the American establishment and Anthony a shabby outsider. In his drunken confusion, Anthony abuses Bloeckman, and there is a scuffle in which Bloeckman strikes him to the ground. He is then thrown out onto the sidewalk by waiters who treat him as a derelict:

> The shock stunned him. He lay there for a moment in acute distributed pain. Then his discomfort became central-ized in his stomach, and he regained consciousness to discover that a large foot was prodding him.
> "You've got to move on, y'bum! Move on!"
> It was the bulky doorman speaking. A town car had stopped at the curb and its occupants had disembarked—that is, two of the women were standing on the dashboard until the obstacle should be removed from their path. (P. 438)

It is, of course, deeply ironic that Anthony's humiliation should be suffered at the hands of Bloeckman. Bloeckman had begun life in his native Munich as a peanut vendor with a traveling circus; later, he is the manager of a side show, and then of a vaudeville house, until—still a young man—he enters the business end of motion pictures, a thriving young industry that bears him up with it. By the end of the novel, like Simon Rosedale at the end of Mrs. Wharton's *The House of Mirth,*[21] he has become part of the social upper crust. In his treatment of Bloeckman's "arrival," Fitzgerald is conscious, and intends the reader to be, of the exemplary role he plays. Midway in the work, as their train takes them into midtown Manhattan, Anthony and Gloria have a view of the far East Side:

> Down in a tall busy street he read a dozen Jewish names on a line of stores; in the door of each stood a dark little man watching the passers from intent eyes—eyes gleaming with suspicion, with pride, with clarity, with cupidity, with comprehension. New York—he could not dissociate it now from the slow upward creep of this people—the little stores, growing, expanding, consolidating, moving, watched over with hawk's eyes and a bee's attention to detail . . .
>
> Gloria's voice broke in with a strange appropriateness upon his thoughts.
>
> "I wonder where Bloeckman's been this summer." (P. 283)

The Jews of the Lower East Side are shown here in an unattractive stereotype, but Fitzgerald does not imply they are "different" from the rest of New York; they are part of the stirring energy of the lower and middle classes, people of every ethnic origin and background. Bloeckman embodies their upward striving, which was foreshadowed earlier—in the scene at Times Square, and at the cabaret, where the young woman with violets on her hat pretends to a class above her own, an image that suddenly expands to include all the others in the room.

Bloeckman's arrival by the end is part, moreover, of the novel's concern with "success" and what it means. Fitzgerald is not deeply antagonistic to Bloeckman; in fact, he is made to seem a reasonably decent sort of man. But it is obvious that he is not very "fine." He understands the common mind because he embodies it, and for that reason will succeed as a high-ranking executive with Films Par Excellence, producers of opiated movies for the masses. Other versions of those who have become successful have a similar point. Maury Noble repudiates philosophy for a socially advantageous marriage and the money that can be made in banking; and Richard Caramel, soft and pliable like his name, will write novels that are successful because they console shop girls with dreams of romance. Their success is money oriented, and their aspiration is defined by money.

There are other versions of success in *The Beautiful and Damned*, and they have the same implication. Midway in the novel, Anthony attempts working on Wall Street, in a beginning position with a brokerage house. His first conversation with another employee reveals what is required for advancement—a total immersion in business and selling, and its ideals. Anthony does not last long on Wall Street, but later he tries the business world again, attempting to sell "Heart Talks on Ambition," which ends in a clumsy debacle. Anthony's failure with the Heart Talks is symptomatic of his deepening alienation from the mainstream, since Mr. Carleton, the sponsor and purveyor of the Heart Talks, is in the American grain, a self-made entrepreneur who trains other self-made entrepreneurs in his craft, involving enthusiasm, optimism, and money. Anthony thus assumes a likeness to the protagonist whose experience Mencken believed had "significance," the man of superior aspiration who acts against the grain of his environment and suffers defeat. The society shown in *The Beautiful and Damned* is wholly materialistic. Money is, of course, essential to Anthony and Gloria, since it makes personal style possible, but Fitzgerald seems to say that they are committed to romantic possibility that transcends money itself and are in this way different from the other characters in the work.

One of the fatal weaknesses of the novel, however, is that Anthony and Gloria do not embody Fitzgerald's conception very well. They are too often like spoiled children whose ruin, while unfortunate, escapes seeming even deeply poignant. But

Fitzgerald does continually attempt to suggest that they represent something of importance, something that youth—uncorrupted as yet—can still feel, something like the life of the imagination, which is wholly absent elsewhere in their society. Early in their romance, Anthony's remarks that "only the romanticist preserves the things worth preserving" (p. 73), and the thrust of the novel is the contrast between romantic possibility and inert materialism. Both Anthony and Gloria are evoked in terms of radiance and light. Fitzgerald says of Anthony at an early point, for example, that he "was handsome then if never before, bound for one of those immortal moments which come so radiantly that their remembered light is enough to see by for years" (p. 128). The image is an early anticipation of the light and radiance later associated with Gatsby. And like Daisy Fay later, Gloria is described in the imagery of flowers. Her kisses had been "flowers" (p. 117), and she appears in a pink dress, "starched and fresh as a flower" (p. 138). She eclipses all the other young women she and Anthony know. "Promptly Gloria emerged from her bedroom and in unison every eye turned on her. The two girls receded into a shabby background, unperceived, unmissed" (p. 85).

Fitzgerald also uses the device, which he will again in *The Great Gatsby*, of playing the heroine off against a foil, in this case Muriel Kane, "a woman with wide hips" (p. 95). Muriel is said to have originated in "a rising family in East Orange" (p. 83), and is described at one point in the following way: "Her fingernails were too long and ornate, polished to a pink and unnatural fever. Her clothes were too tight, too stylish, too vivid, her eyes too roguish, her smile too coy. She was almost pitifully over emphasized from head to foot" (p. 84). She reads "Town Tattle" and imagines a resemblance between Theda Bara and herself; her notion of "romance" comes from movie magazines. Like the other characters who are "rising" socially, she finds an easy accommodation with her commercial environment and takes her form from it, as Anthony and Gloria do not.

At least as they appear early in the work, Anthony and Gloria are dedicated to the young, romantic moment, which, by its nature, cannot last, and their fate is therefore dark, as Fitzgerald has suggested in the symbolic scene in which they visit the Lee mansion at Arlington on their honeymoon. Here Gloria remarks that "there's no beauty without poignancy and there's no poignancy without the feeling that it's going, men, names, books, houses—bound for dust" (p. 167). The Lee association is evocative because Lee's cause was lost, its brief incandescence irrecoverable. The house has known its moment of "youth and beauty" (p. 167), but it is now a modernized, tourist version of what it once was. On the wall of the room where Lee was married, they notice a large sign that reads Ladies Toilet, and outside while Gloria speaks of the romantic past, a boy hurls banana peels in the direction of the Potomac. The scene comments upon the marriage of Anthony and Gloria at its outset, with the intimation that it, too, is doomed, that its glimpsed radiance will be cheapened in time, like the national monument that is strewn with tourists' garbage. Their married life forms a lengthy history of corruption by the world in which they had sought to keep alive their sense of romantic possibility. At the end, Anthony is seen in a "vinous" and quasi-romantic reverie of Wall Street, which is meant to suggest the final debasement of his mind, for it is Wall Street, and the culture it represents, that has defeated his romantic aspiration. This irony is repeated in the shipboard scene of the last pages, when Anthony comes into his inheritance but only after both he and Gloria have become "unclean," have lost their light and radiance, and their souls.

In his conception of Anthony's defeated aspiration, Fitzgerald appears to have been influenced by a novel referred to earlier— Stephen French Whitman's *Predestined: A Novel of New York Life* (1910). How highly Fitzgerald regarded Whitman's novel may be seen by his letter to Charles Scribner in 1922, in which he proposed that the firm establish a Scribner Library of eighteen books, with Mrs. Wharton's *Ethan Frome* (or alternatively, *The House of Mirth*) placed first on his suggested list, and Whitman's *Predestined* second.[22] A work of artistry and intelligence, *Predestined* has for years been almost forgotten. It obviously made a strong impression on Fitzgerald, however, and its hero, Felix Piers, creates a precedent for Anthony Patch. Felix is born into a wealthy family and attends an Eastern college (based on Princeton, which Whitman attended), but by the time he comes of age loses his patrimony and is on his own as he attempts to become a "famous writer" in New York. At this point, he is full of confidence. "How good, how valuable life was; how dazzling its promises. . . . Exalted by superb aspirations, he dreamed of the future, which appeared before him like a bright mist."

In New York, he meets Oliver Corquill, who produces a bestseller every year, his latest being *The Rainbow*, which expresses a pervasive optimism calculated to ensure its sale. Corquill is the man against whom Felix is measured, the man who is able to accommodate himself to his environment and succeed brilliantly in it. But Felix cannot. His books do not come together, and he drifts into self-indulgence, drinks too much, and finally becomes involved in an affair that causes his well-to-do fiancée, together with all of her friends, to cast him off. As he sinks lower socially, he supports himself by working for shoddy newspapers, and spends his lunch hours with a young man named Johnny Livy, whose aspirations are no higher than a marriage to a lower-class girl and a cottage in the Bronx. Felix's view of Livy is worth quoting since it is relevant to *The Beautiful and Damned:*

"An elementary soul," thought Felix, his lip curling. "A mind without metaphysical sense, without ability for introspection and observance, for great doubts or great sins. A man who can deny that pain and ruin exist, who always sees the world as does a child on a clear day. What immense regions of experience are closed to him! Better to suffer, than to be half alive, like that!"

Felix continues to sink lower and lower in society and at one point lies drunkenly in an alleyway like a derelict, while neighborhood Negroes go through his pockets, or attempt to, before he is rescued by an Irish policeman, who takes him to his brother-in-law's bar, Quilty's, where Felix drinks with shabby associates. His employment becomes more and more marginal, and then nonexistent, and the sense is given of the indifference of the city and the harshly competitive nature of its life. "Did not the conqueror," Whitman remarks here, "invariably have to drive his chariot to victory over prostrate bodies?" Felix's early life now forms an ironic contrast to his present, spent in the stale atmosphere of Mrs. Snatt's rooming house and Quilty's saloon.

At this late point he meets another, older man of culture and aesthetic sensibility, Monsieur Pierre, an émigré from Paris, and a familiar of its *fin-de-siècle* café world. Together they talk of the rare, delicate, aesthetic imaginings of the poets and of old civilizations: "Arm in arm, they wandered at random through the darkness, striving to find the unattainable." There is an intensification in this section between appetency and rich visionary longing and the increasingly constricted nature of Felix's life. His mind corrodes; his sense of the ideal fades in "the inadequacy of the actual world," as he thinks "what a mockery is aspiration." He commits suicide by an overdose of drugs, and as he waits for them to take effect his thoughts are recorded by Whitman, who remarks: "The ideal! He could not recollect in what it had consisted. It was as if a guiding beacon had gone out." The final section of the novel is suffused with twilight, and it is in twilight that Felix dies alone.

The model Felix establishes for Anthony is quite striking—his aesthetic ideals at the beginning, the loss of his patrimony, his drinking, which accompanies his sinking lower and lower in society, the steady corruption of his mind, the mockery of his aspiration at the conclusion. Whitman's picturing of New York is also relevant, since it is almost wholly materialistic, a background against which Felix's failed aspiration becomes credible. *Predestined* and *The Beautiful and Damned* are both studies in irony, although the irony is ineffective in Fitzgerald's novel, because he has not drawn Anthony with the cold, even glacial, objectivity with which Whitman has studied Felix Piers. He has, instead, identified himself subjectively with Anthony and produced a figure blurred and out of focus, like the irony that is supposed to surround him.

Fitzgerald is more successful in the work with a minor character like Bloeckman, who is observed objectively, and in the sketching of social surfaces. Mencken's attitudes give outline to these surfaces and also help to bring out Fitzgerald's developing gift for caustic satire. With sharp, deft strokes he begins to explore the banality of the contemporary scene and can at times be lethal, as in the brief scene at a Childs' restaurant in New York, where there is a waitress who is characterized succinctly. She wears shell-rimmed eyeglasses attached to a long, dangling black cord:

"Order, please!" . . .
"You wanna order or doncha?"
"Of course," he protested.
"Well, I ast you three times. This ain't no restroom." . . .
The waitress bent upon him a last disgusted glance, and, looking ludicrously intellectual in her corded glasses, hurried away. (P. 117)

The waitress's looking "intellectual" in her corded glasses brings together with an unexpected suddenness the bathos of her world and the idea of intellectual order, with an effect that is like a glimmer of hallucination.

A sense of something approaching hallucination occurs also

in another scene, as Anthony and Gloria return to New York by train and have a glimpse of the Bronx:

> The Bronx—the houses gathering and gleaming in the sun, which was fallen now through the wide refulgent skies and tumbling caravans of light down into the streets. New York, he supposed, was home—the city of luxury and mystery, of preposterous hopes and exotic dreams. Here on the outskirts absurd stucco palaces reared themselves in the cool sunset, poised for an instant in cool unreality, glided off faraway, succeeded by the mazed confusion of the Harlem River. (P. 282)

In this brief image, Fitzgerald implies the illusion of New York, with its "preposterous hopes" that become garish reality and end in the "mazed confusion" of the East Side ghetto. This foreshortened image reveals that Fitzgerald has begun to grasp a subject and theme—the spiritual emptiness of the great City and its suburbs. *The Beautiful and Damned* may ultimately fail as a work of art, but it reveals a great deal about Fitzgerald's development and the large literary background from which he drew and attempted to assimilate. It is a transitional work, published during the same year as *Babbitt* and *The Waste Land* and one that begins to approach their desolate social vision.

✠ ✳ ✳ ✠ ✳

Other anticipations of *The Great Gatsby* during this period can be noted in Fitzgerald's short stories. They appear even in his least important stories written for popular magazines,[23] but primarily can be seen in a group of tales of that time that are better known and that include "The Diamond as Big as the Ritz." Written shortly after *The Beautiful and Damned*, "The Diamond as Big as the Ritz" (1922) was published in *The Smart Set* and pleased Mencken especially. It shares with "May Day" the quality of a moral fable of America. Its youthful hero,

John Unger (for which read *hunger*), comes from a small town in the South called Hades, which "has the earnest worship and respect for riches as the first article of its creed" (p. 9). Unger's father plays golf and his mother plays politics, and they are both, like all the other inhabitants of the town, out of touch with culture. Young Unger is sent North to be educated at St. Midas', the most expensive boys' preparatory school in the world. As he leaves, his father presents him with "an asbestos pocket-book stuffed with money" (p. 5) and tells him to remember the ideals he has learned in Hades, and no harm will come to him. But up North, outside of Boston, the cradle of the republic, Unger is to find that the creed of the St. Midas school has much to do with the West—and the dream of El Dorado. Fitzgerald refers to El Dorado more than once, and by this and other means creates a sense of fable, suspending a strict realism in order to reveal the underlying reality of reality.

Historically, El Dorado was located in South America, a sacred and secret place where natives cast gold and jewels of great cost into a holy lake, a reverential offering to their gods—until the treasure was discovered and seized by Spanish conquerors. Their seizure of this fabulous treasure led to legends of other treasure as yet undiscovered, other El Dorados. Young Percy Washington, a classmate of Unger's at St. Midas', is connected through his family with an American El Dorado in Montana and invites Unger to spend the summer with him there, where he will meet his father, who owns a diamond as big as the Ritz Carlton Hotel. They travel westward by train and alight at night at a forsaken place called Fish:

> The Montana sunset lay between two mountains like a gigantic bruise from which dark arteries spread themselves over a poisoned sky. At an immense distance under the sky crouched the village of Fish, minute, dismal, and forgotten. There were twelve men, so it was said, in the village of Fish, twelve sombre and inexplicable souls who sucked a lean

milk from the almost literally bare rocks upon which a mysterious populatory force had begotten them. They had become a race apart, these twelve men of Fish, like some species developed by an early whim of nature, which on second thought had abandoned them to struggle and extermination.

Out of the blue-black bruise in the distance crept a long line of moving lights upon the desolation of the land, and the twelve men of Fish gathered like ghosts of the shanty depot to watch the passing of the seven o'clock train, the Transcontinental Express, through some inexplicable jurisdiction, stopped at the village of Fish, and when this occurred a figure or so would disembark, mount into a buggy that always appeared from out of the dusk, and drive off toward the bruised sunset. The observation of this pointless and preposterous phenomenon had become a sort of cult among the men of Fish. To observe, that was all; there remained in them none of the vital quality of illusion which would make them wonder or speculate, else a religion might have grown up around these mysterious visitations. But the men of Fish were beyond all religion—the barest and most savage tenets of even Christianity could gain no foothold on that barren rock—so there was no altar, no priest, no sacrifice; only each night at seven the silent concourse by the shanty depot, a congregation who lifted up a prayer of dim, anaemic wonder. (Pp. 7–8)

This passage, one of the most extraordinary in Fitzgerald's early fiction, is expressionistically rendered, is like a dream that has become diseased and incoherent. The place named Fish and the twelve men who are like disciples have Christian associations, but with Christian connotations reversed. They are "those Godforsaken fellas in Fish" (p. 9), who have not even the capacity for wonder and illusion. If the Christian church had been founded upon the rock of faith, the men of Fish have been begotten upon barren rock, with no prospect for them (they cannot reproduce) other than extermination. They are seen in darkness, their eyes lifted to the lights of a passing train in the form of an inadequate prayer. It is a moral darkness in which they exist, and they prefigure what is to come. They guard the entranceway, as it were, to the mountain of diamond inhabited by the very rich, who are a "race apart."

The arrival of Unger and Percy Washington has even some suggestion of a night journey to Hades, with Percy Washington acting as Unger's mythic guide. They are transported to the Washington estate in a jewel-encrusted car, and soon afterward Unger meets Washington's people and learns their family history. The mother, "a Spaniard," has an appropriate association with the Spanish conquerors of El Dorado. Percy's father, Braddock Tarleton Washington, is the son of Fitz-Norman Washington and is descended from the stock of Washington and Lord Baltimore. All the family names have connotations of power and class assumption, beginning with the Norman conquerors who brought with them a system of steep class differences. Lord Baltimore, of a later period of English history, necessarily implies a charter-holding proprietor of a large tract of early America who held absolute and supreme power. Tarleton and Braddock belong to the same English tradition of lordship as it descends to the period of eighteenth-century colonialism. Both were noted for their presumptuousness—Tarleton for the barbaric cruelty of his campaigns, Braddock for his obstinacy and arrogance. Washington himself was not personally like Braddock, his commanding officer in the early colonial wars, but as a Southern, slave-owning plantation owner, he was at least implicated in proprietary interests, as they passed from England to America. Like Washington, Braddock Washington is a plantation owner; he has, in fact, transferred his plantation intact, together with his Negro slaves, to the top of the mountain composed of solid diamond. Through Braddock Washington, who has "intelligent eyes" set in a "proud, vacuous face"

(p. 30), John Unger comes to learn what this luxurious world means. It means luxury that cannot and will not be shared and that rests upon a foundation of nightmare.

Fitzgerald's evocation of the plantation, buildings, and grounds has been heightened by a number of significant allusions. At the center of the estate, for example, is a lake, suggestive of the holy lake of El Dorado, from which the Spanish plunderers wrested the natives' sacred treasure, converting it into millions of dollars. The chateau where the Washingtons live suggests a place of fable; one tower, dark at its base but illuminated at top, seems like a "floating fairyland" (p. 11). The architecture of the chateau itself has a Middle Eastern appearance, which suggests the *Arabian Nights* and their fabulous tales that frequently end with the attainment of great wealth and the fulfillment of all desire. Inside the chateau the mosaic of rooms, window panels, and color combinations make Unger think of "some mosque on the Adriatic sea" (p. 13), an allusion surely to Venice, the wealth-oriented capital of a great mercantile empire.

In this section too, and indeed throughout the story, there are continual references to the opposing colors of black and white. Unger's experience at the Washingtons' estate begins and ends in darkness, and in between he is conscious of the glitter of diamonds, including those that line one room in an unbroken mass and "dazzled the eyes with a whiteness that could be compared only with itself, beyond human wish or desire" (p. 12). The imagery of brilliant light (sometimes white light) and darkness occurring in the story conditions the reader to feel that a struggle is taking place, in some Manichean way, between two opposing and, as it were, moral forces.

For there is a great darkness beneath the great brilliance. In order to preserve the secrecy of his diamond mountain, Braddock Washington has had to corrupt whole departments of state surveyors, and federal officials, as well as foreign powers, and has covertly manipulated the international financial market.

Those who have accidentally strayed into his preserve are placed in a below-ground "cage," where they await Braddock Washington's decision as to what he will do with them. Most treacherously of all, since the Washingtons cannot very well live in total isolation, the family invites guests for summer visits, from which they do not return, being put to death—usually in August or September. "It's only natural for us," young Kismine Washington explains, "to get all the pleasure out of them that we can first" (p. 27). Their invited guests provide some "pleasure" for them, but they cannot share in the spoils, or let the outside world know that the Washington fortune exists. Such is the dream of great wealth!

The material form this paradise of wealth takes, with its jeweled corridors, cloudlike beds of down, and incensed pools, is like a dream of bad taste. The man who designed all the reception rooms and halls was, in fact, "a moving picture fella" (p. 25), who could neither read nor write, but was "used to playing with an unlimited amount of money" (p. 25). Before long, however, the Washington preserve is threatened by outsiders, since one of the captured aviators, an Italian, has managed to slip away, and returns with other pilots who bomb the mountain. Washington at this point addresses his words arrogantly to the heavens, offering up a fragment of the diamond mountain as a bribe to God if his treasure is spared. But it is not, and Washington detonates the mountain, rather than share it. Before this happens, John Unger manages to flee with young Kismine, but the world to which they flee at the end of the "dark and glittering reign of the Washingtons" (p. 32) is as tainted as the one they have left. At the rim of the mountain, they look back upon "the ruins of a vista that had been a garden spot" (p. 32), and an impression is given of them as Adam and Eve leaving a blasted Eden and entering a corrupt world.

The world without has been suggested in part by the twelve men of Fish who are affiliated with religion, but of a malignant kind—the worship of wealth. But the men of Fish, shut out from the temple of worship, are doomed to live in a visionless and unending night. They stumble "blindly" in the darkness, with "bleak, joyless eyes" (p. 30) and thus anticipate a future Fitzgeraldian terrain, the valley of ashes. The implication of Unger's own hot Southern town of Hades culminates in the Washingtons' diamond mountain that is ultimately consumed by fire as an abomination. The estate has a large golf course, where Braddock Washington is seen, when he is not corrupting government officials, and the reader may recall that Unger's father plays golf and his mother concerns herself with politics, versions in small of the Washingtons. The name Washington itself necessarily implies a national experience, a national ideal and dream.

The liberators of the diamond mountain, the captured aviators, are also relevant to the Washingtons' dream. Called "middle-class Americans of the more spirited type" (p. 21), they are a moronic crew, the fittest to survive among them a slippery Italian who has deceived the Washingtons as they have deceived everyone else. They are consigned to a black pit that, in its suggestion, is not unlike Hades, and the dark night of Fish; from the bottom of this dark pit, in fact, they call up: "Come on down to Hell!" (p. 21). In the conversation that takes place between them and Braddock Washington, Washington remarks that it is not in his interest to be fair-minded:

> "You might as well speak of a Spaniard being fair-minded toward a piece of steak."
> At this harsh observation the faces of the two dozen steaks fell. (P. 22)

If Washington's carnivorous nature is suggested in this exchange, the nature of the crew in the "cage" is evoked in a surprisingly similar way. After Washington snaps out the light illuminating the pit, "there remained only *that great dark mouth* covered dismally *with the black teeth* of the grating" (p. 22, emphasis added), an image implying a lower-class voraciousness.

The sense of the absoluteness of illusions lost at the diamond mountain is reinforced by the insinuation that the world without holds no alternatives or compensations, being only a meaner version of the Washingtons' dream. The revelation of this paradise as spurious is equivalent to an Eden lost, an idea supported by the lonely figures of Unger and Kismine as they prepare to enter the world, and the contrast between the white radiance of the diamond and the darkness into which they are now plunged:

> At any rate, [Unger tells Kismine] let us love for a while . . . that's a form of divine drunkenness that we can all try. There are only diamonds in the whole world, diamonds and perhaps the shabby gift of disillusion. . . . Turn up your coat collar, little girl, the night's full of chill. . . . His was a great sin who first invented consciousness. Let us lose it for a few hours. (P. 38)

"The Diamond as Big as the Ritz" anticipates *The Great Gatsby* in its concern with the national ideal of wealth, as well as in its form as a fable or modern morality. It also prepares for the novel in a number of ways specifically—in its expressionistic projection of Fish, weirdly evocative of a God-forsaken world, like the valley of ashes; in its use of history to give factual underpinning to fable; and in its focusing of national aspiration through the American West. Moreover, the Washingtons, a fantasy version of arrogant aloofness formed by wealth, will be embodied with more concrete realism in the Buchanans of East Egg. Braddock Washington, seen at one point in "a pair of riding boots" (p. 30), proprietor of the plantation, will be refocused as Tom Buchanan, the polo player.

More immediately, "The Diamond as Big as the Ritz" belongs to a group of stories written after *The Beautiful and Damned* that show a preoccupation with illusion. In "Winter Dreams"

(1922), a story of the same year, a young man is brought into contact with the very rich in the Midwest while acting as a golf caddy. The golf course is located on Sherry Island, set apart from the village of Black Bear, a "footstool," as Fitzgerald calls it, of the wealthy resort. The youthful hero, Dexter Green, comes into contact in particular with Judy Jones, the beautiful, spoiled girl who is the product of substantial wealth. Like Gatsby, Green is immoderately hopeful, as his name implies, and is associated with two seasons, summer and fall, the first in which his romance takes place, the second where it is anticipated and then remembered in a dying fall. The late autumns of the early part of the story "filled him with hope" (p. 127); he senses "something gorgeous" (p. 127) about the weather; his dreams are "raised to an ecstatic triumph" (p. 127). The words *ecstasy* and *ecstatic* keep recurring through the story:

> The sound of the tune precipitated in him a sort of ecstasy and it was with that ecstasy he viewed what happened to him now. It was a mood of intense appreciation, a sense that, for once, he was magnificently attune to life and that everything about him was radiating a brightness and a glamour he might never know again. (P. 133)

As a village boy, Dexter Green comes into contact of an accidental kind with the rich, but he is not part of their world. That world, or rather Judy Jones, becomes the focus of his "winter dreams"; and when he grows up, and is in his early twenties, he meets her again at Sherry Island, and they have a romance. He has now begun to make money, but it is new and not as yet really substantial money, and her remoteness from him is emphasized by the island on which she lives, by her distant house, and by its dock. Confident, impulsive, and much courted, she tells him that she had suddenly become disillusioned with one of her beaux when she learned that he had once been poor. In a certain sense, not having been born into wealth,

Green will remain a "caddy"; he is now the owner of a chain of laundries, which have succeeded through their specialty of cleaning the golf garments of the rich, and he is to share the fate of the other young man who had once been poor. In time, he will be thrown over.

Judy resembles Daisy Fay physically, since she has an "exquisite sadness" or "wanness" in her beauty, and is associated, like Daisy, with flowers. Her front porch is banked by "garden arbors" (p. 137), and Fitzgerald says of her at one point that "the fragile glow of her face seemed to blossom as she smiled at him" (p. 140). And like Daisy, again, she lives in a protected, self-contained, and privileged world that places her a little beyond sincerity, a quality about her that fascinates the hero. Her smile is "radiant, blatantly artificial—convincing" (p. 128). He cannot tell if she is sincere or playacting, but at one point he finally learns. When he becomes engaged to another girl, she renews her interest in him, possibly, it occurs to him, to see if she can take him away from his fiancée, which she does. After that, the romance lasts only a short time. He has sacrificed his honor for her, hurting his fiancée and her family—and provided her with a diversion. Yet his fascination with her remains and is involved in the fascination for him of her class, which her psychology reflects. She is framed by paradox in the scene in which Dexter drives her to her family's "great white house"; it is here that, asking him into her house, she tempts him away from the obligation to his fiancée. The paradox suggested here is that such massive wealth should be necessary to create such delicacy, that anything so sturdily planted should be so romantically elusive:

> The dark street lightened, the dwellings of the rich loomed up around them, he stopped his coupé in front of the great white bulk of the Mortimer Joneses's house, somnolent, gorgeous, drenched with the splendor of damp moonlight. Its solidity startled him. The strong walls, the steel of the girders, the breadth and beam and pomp of it were there only to bring

out the contrast with the young beauty beside him. It was sturdy to accentuate her slightness—as if to show what a breeze could be generated by a butterfly's wing. (P. 142)

After their breakup, he goes into the army and enters officers' training school, and after the war comes East, to New York. In New York he becomes very successful, and ten years after their romance, he hears of her again. She has married a man of her own class named Simms, who not only dominates her, as Green had never been able to do, but is unfaithful to her, "runs around" (p. 144). He had continued to imagine her as she was at Sherry Island, inhabiting a romantic world apart, and is now confronted by a totally different reality—a woman who has been subdued by time, delimited by the commonness of her situation. He had, of course, always overdreamed her (her common name, Judy Jones, undercuts his romantic picture of her), an illusion having to do with the original difference in their class. But there is an additional irony of illusion at the end, because his ability to feel, once so sharp, has been blunted by time. His "winter dreams" have expired, together with his ability to feel anything deeply at all, so that in a sense, he loses her twice—once in fact and again in memory. Gatsby's illusions are longer enduring than Green's, but Green seems a preliminary sketch for Gatsby —his youthful love affair with a rich girl; her family mansion drenched romantically with moonlight; her interest in him that falls somewhere elusively between sincerity and acting; his leaving for the army and the war, and then settling in New York, where in time he comes into money; his continuing to dream of her as she once was for him; her marriage in the meantime to a man of her own class who "runs around."

A variation on the theme of "Winter Dreams" can be seen in another story of that same time, " 'The Sensible Thing' " (1924), in which George O'Kelly is desperately in love with a girl named Jonquil Cary. (Like Daisy, Jonquil has a flower name and is evoked in the imagery of flowers, has "lips half

open like a flower" [p. 157].) During the summer in which
the story opens, Jonquil breaks off their engagement, or at least
postpones doing anything until he is financially secure. When
he returns in the fall, a year later, he has established himself in
his career, but as they meet again they find that they have both
lost the vitality of illusion. They visit the house of a lady who
has an extremely large garden full of chrysanthemums, and they
go out into her garden, an experience that is like "a trip back
into the heart of summer" (p. 156). But these are only the
flowers of memory; the intensity of their romantic feeling for
each other has irrecoverably passed. "There are all kinds of love
in the world," Fitzgerald remarks at the end, "but never the
same love twice" (p. 158).

But a much superior story is "Absolution" (1924), in which
romantic illusion is focused forward in time, rather than back-
ward into the past, as it is in "Winter Dreams" and " 'The
Sensible Thing.' " "Absolution" centers upon an eleven-year-old
boy named Rudolph Miller who lives in a small Dakota town
and is seen against the immediate background of a fearsome
father and a frightening priest. In its setting of a small town in
the Midwest where people's lives have a narrow scope, the story
is reminiscent of Sherwood Anderson; but it seems influenced
more importantly by Joyce—partly in Fitzgerald's projection of
the boy's inner confusion and fright over the violation of the
sacrament, and the fierce, unwarranted beating he receives;
partly in the dingy, oppressive atmosphere like that of the *Dubliners* stories, with their sense of constriction and entrapment, of
things run to decay like the priest gone odd.

In narrating the story, in fact, Fitzgerald uses Joyce's technique in *Dubliners*, working naturalistic detail and symbol
tightly into the fabric of the tale. The first sentence, with compressed implication, begins: "There was once a priest with cold,
watery eyes who, in the still of the night, wept cold tears"
(p. 159). The priest's watery eyes call attention to his failing
vision and to vision itself as a theme to be explored in the story.

His weeping implies inner torment, which will concern not the priest alone, although it concerns him particularly at the beginning, as he weeps at night, and a buried part of him is expressed that has not been expressed as fully in the light of day. Finally, his weeping "cold" tears implies that the priest's inner life has suffered some dislocation, has become unnatural, since tears are warm, never cold. Fitzgerald then continues:

> He wept because the afternoons were warm and long, and he was unable to attain a complete mystical union with our Lord. Sometimes, near four o'clock, there was a rustle of Swede girls along the path of his window, and in their shrill laughter he found a terrible dissonance that made him pray aloud for the twilight to come. At twilight the laughter and the voices were quieter, but several times he had walked past Romberg's Drug Store. . . . He passed that way when he returned from hearing confessions on Saturday nights, and he grew careful to walk on the other side of the street so that the smell of the soap would float upward before it reached his nostrils as it drifted, rather like incense, toward the summer moon.
>
> But there was no escape from the hot madness of four o'clock. From his window, as far as he could see, the Dakota wheat thronged the valley of the Red River. The wheat was terrible to look upon and the carpet pattern to which in agony he bent his eyes sent his thought brooding through grotesque labyrinths, open always to the unavoidable sun. (P. 159)

The first paragraphs introduce the controlling images of the story—the sun and the wheat, light and darkness, the moon. The intensity of the imagery—"a terrible dissonance," "the hot madness," the wheat that is "terrible to look upon"—suggests the priest's overwrought state, emphasized further in the carpet patterns that form "grotesque labyrinths" through which his mind wanders hopelessly, for they always open upon "the unavoidable sun." Only later in the story does Fitzgerald enlarge upon the carpet patterns upon which the sunlight falls, bringing out "the swastikas [sun insignias] and the flat bloomless vines and the pale echoes of flowers" (p. 169). The story concludes with a Joycean epiphany, as the controlling images suddenly expand into completed revelation:

> Outside the window the blue sirocco trembled over the wheat, and girls with yellow hair walked sensuously along roads that bounded the fields, calling innocent, exciting things to the young men who were working in the lines between the grain. Legs were shaped under starchless gingham, and rims of the necks of dresses were warm and damp. For five hours now hot fertile life had burned in the afternoon. It would be night in three hours, and all along the land there would be these blonde Northern girls and the tall young men from the farms lying out beside the wheat, under the moon. (Pp. 171–72)

At the very end, reinforcing the sense of the boy's liberation, there is an evocation of release from constriction into intense life.

Father Schwartz (whose name in German means "black" or "dark," the color also of his clerical garments) is always presented in images of enclosure, contrasted with the "open world of wheat and sky" (p. 163). The two places where he is seen are his "haunted room" (p. 159) and the confessional booth, where his spiritual state is suggested through a small, naturalistic detail: "The plush curtain of the confessional rearranged its dismal creases, leaving exposed only the bottom of the old man's shoe" (p. 160). The desolate priest cannot avoid the heat, even in the church, which is "muggy" (p. 163), or in his "ugly room" (p. 169), where his deepening crisis is evoked through intense physical details. "The priest's nerves were strung thin and the beads of his rosary were crawling and squirming like snakes" (p. 169). Into his presence at this point comes the boy, Rudolph Miller, described as "intense" (p. 159) and presented in the imagery of brightness, which contrasts with the dark figure of the priest. In particular, Rudolph's eyes are a contrast with the priest's cold, watery eyes suggesting two kinds of vision, one almost unnaturally bright, the other almost unnaturally faded. The boy sits down before the priest "in a patch of sunlight" (p. 159), where his eyes seem silver-white, like cobalt, "two enormous, staccato eyes, lit with gleaming points of cobalt light" (p. 159). Elsewhere Rudolph is called "the beautiful little boy with eyes like blue stones, and lashes that sprayed open from them like flower-petals" (p. 169), suggesting his affiliation with the natural rather than the supernatural world, where the priest with faltering faith attempts to live. The opening meeting is intensely dramatic because of its sharp focus upon experience as it is perceived from different angles and time perspectives, and has a sense of expectant encounter.

But Rudolph is seen against the adult figure not only of the priest but also of his father, who is distinctly different from the priest and yet not unlike him, since he too has suffered a phychic dislocation in his life and lives at the edge of torment. The father is described in the following way:

> Rudolph's father, the local freight-agent, had floated with the second wave of German and Irish stock to the Minnesota-Dakota country. Theoretically, great opportunities lay ahead of a young man of energy in that day and place, but Carl Miller had been incapable of establishing either with his superiors or his subordinates the reputation for approximate immutability which is essential to success in a hierarchic industry. Somewhat gross, he was, nevertheless, insufficiently hard-headed and unable to take fundamental relationships for granted, and his inability made him suspicious, unrestful, and continually dismayed.
>
> His two bonds to the colorful life were his faith in the Roman Catholic Church and his mystical worship of the Empire Builder, James J. Hill. Hill was the apotheosis of that quality

in which Miller himself was deficient—the sense of things, the feel of things, the hint of rain in the wind on the cheek. Miller's mind worked late on the old decisions of other men, and he had never in his life felt the balance of any single thing in his hands. His weary, sprightly, undersized body was growing old in Hill's gigantic shadow. For twenty years he had lived alone with Hill's name and God. (P. 164)

The father's oddness is that he could have confused two such different entities as God and James J. Hill, the spiritual calling and the worldly life. Like Father Schwartz, divided between inward and outward life, the father searches ineffectually for transcendence, which he finds nowhere, not in the freight office, where he is merely a servant of Hill's greater, more powerful, and realized dream, or in his home, which seems as constricted and haunted as the priest's study. Moreover, like the priest, he seems about to break down. He is depicted in his isolation even at home, and significantly sleeps in a separate bedroom from his wife, from whom he has apparently become estranged. The mother appears only peripherally in the story, and then to underscore her husband's psychological disturbance. She is mentioned in "the other bedroom" (p. 164), where she "lay nervously asleep" (p. 164), and she appears only once, at a doorway, in the weird imagery of exhausting tension: "He was aware of his mother standing at the doorway in a wrapper, her wrinkled face compressing and squeezing and opening out in new series of wrinkles which floated and eddied from neck to brow" (p. 167). In the kitchen, the father's frustration finally explodes into violence as he beats the boy fiercely. The ostensible reason that he beats him is that he has smashed a glass; in throwing it into the sink, he has shown disobedience. But the real reason is that the boy has demonstrated defiant boldness, the quality that he himself fears and so fatally lacks.

The inwardly divided figures of the priest and the father are used by Fitzgerald to accentuate the inner conflict of the boy.

Skillfully, Fitzgerald does not reveal the real nature of the boy's conflict at once. It seems at first to have to do only with his anxiety over his violation of the sacrament and its consequences to his soul. But as the story progresses, it becomes clear that he has an inner dream life of garish splendor, and a romantic double with the unlikely name of Blatchforth Sarnemington. It is said of him that he "slept among his Alger books" (p. 164), implying that the Alger stories have also nourished his dreams. He cannot believe that he is the son of his parents. In the strange scene that ensues, the priest eventually lays bare what has preyed upon his own mind so long and harrowingly. "When a lot of people get together in the best places," he exclaims startlingly, "things go glimmering" (p. 169). Only a Fitzgeraldian priest perhaps would use quite these words, but they do communicate what has been coming to a head and evoke the future direction of the boy. The priest "fixes" his violation of the sacrament with an opaque phrase of learned argument, but the boy's absolution is really that the exposure of the priest's own fascination with the worldly life has dispelled the guilt with which the boy has been struggling, his inner conviction that there was "something ineffably gorgeous somewhere that had nothing to do with God" (p. 171). The story has moved suspensefully toward this moment, when the inner lives of the boy and the priest are revealed at once.

The unusually rich texture of the story is achieved in part through Fitzgerald's use of time, which has been handled impressionistically, the story beginning in the middle of a central action, then moving back in time through a flashback, and then forward to the present. This movement back and forth in time complements the important role of time—future, present, and past—in the story. The priest focuses a consciousness of time-present as compared to an increasingly receding time-past; and time-present and time-past or "lost" are played off against each other. Haunted by time "lost," the priest is restricted to "this lost Swede town" (p. 169) and to his study, where clocks seem always to be heard ticking. When he is first seen, his mind is running down "like an old clock" (p. 159), and outside his study door "the hall-clock ticked insistently toward sunset" (p. 169). As he struggles to remember something that recedes further and further from him, "the clock ticked in the broken house" (p. 169). The strange stillness of the Miller house suggests time in temporary suspension, with a muted implication of expectancy. In the kitchen, the center of the house, "the sunlight . . . beat on the pans and made . . . the table yellow . . . as wheat" (p. 165). On the cupboard, tins are said to fit into tins "like toys," an image that implies imagination at play. A pot on the stove simmers (like Rudolph), "and the steam whistled all day on a thin pastel note" (p. 165). At the edge of a faucet water beads form and drip "with a white flash into the sink below" (p. 165). The periodic white flash of a water bead evokes a consciousness of time, like the ticking of a clock (and the syncopated beating of the sunlight on the pans and Rudolph's "stacatto eyes"), and in an understated way suggests the boy's time expectancy. By the end the priest's dream-past flows into the boy's dream-future, and it is toward the future that the story looks at the end. But there is an irony involved in this future in which things go "glimmering," since the priest warns Rudolph not to "get up close because if you do you'll only feel the heat and the sweat and the life" (p. 171). The gorgeousness of the world, which has nothing to do with God, is more ominous than the boy yet understands.

Fitzgerald's apprenticeship fiction, as I have considered it, reveals a great many anticipations of *The Great Gatsby*—even very early in *This Side of Paradise*, in its concern with a rich girl and the poor boy she discards, his illusions of wealth and romance; and in Fitzgerald's modern fable "May Day," in which Columbus the visionary discoverer is placed in sudden juxtaposition with the dim postwar scene enacted in the Childs' restaurant under a dim yellow light. In *The Beautiful and Damned*, an important transitional work, Fitzgerald begins to conceive of a world in which romantic commitment is so incompatible with the norm of contemporary society that it can lead only to radical alienation. In "The Diamond as Big as the Ritz," Fitzgerald reexplores the possibilities of the moral fable as a literary form, this time in connection with the national dream of wealth that is imagined as a malignant nightmare and at times projected expressionistically. In "Winter Dreams," he examines the rich in a realistic mode, sketching the hero's illusionist involvement with them, particularly with a beautiful and elusive young woman formed by their world, a story whose plot has many specific points of resemblance with Gatsby's career in *The Great Gatsby*. In "Absolution," he creates the prototype of the poor boy in his Midwestern youth, who dreams of a romantic double who "glimmers" out in the world, a story with an impressionistic time framework and a compression and intricacy that are characteristic of *The Great Gatsby*.

This early fiction leads up to *The Great Gatsby* and enters into its conception. But if one were to conclude that it provides a full explanation, in itself, of the imaginative process that brought *The Great Gatsby* into being, one would be wrong. For there is another aspect of the novel's conception that needs to be considered—the intervening imagination of Joseph Conrad.

2

The Great Gatsby and Conrad

In the autumn following the publication of *The Beautiful and Damned* the Fitzgeralds returned east from their stay in St. Paul and settled in Great Neck, within commuting distance of New York City. Nearby, overlooking Long Island Sound, were many of the palatial homes of the very rich, but Great Neck itself was largely upper-middle rather than upper class. During the year and a half they lived in Great Neck (from autumn 1922 until spring 1924), Fitzgerald's writing time was taken up with his play *The Vegetable*, which failed before reaching Broadway, and with a large number of stories, but there he also began the first draft of *The Great Gatsby*. In April 1924 the Fitzgeralds left for France, where, during five months of uninterrupted work, the manuscript of *The Great Gatsby* was completed.

His sixteen months in Great Neck provided Fitzgerald with the social background for his novel and even clues for certain characters. Some of the details for Gatsby, for example, were furnished by a scandal of that period (Fitzgerald consulted newspaper accounts of it) that involved E. M. Fuller, head of the New York investment house of E. M. Fuller & Co. Fuller was a thirty-nine-year-old bachelor and man-about-town who owned an estate at Great Neck and lived in an expensive style, commuting weekly to Atlantic City by private plane during the horse-racing season. The shortages at E. M. Fuller & Co. resulted from large sums Fuller lost on sport and gambling (and spent on women). There was even some question as to whether he was also involved in the improper sale of bonds and the negotiation of fraudulent securities. Fuller stood trial four separate times, in the course of which his association with the underworld figure Arnold Rothstein came to light. Rothstein was believed to have "fixed" the World Series in 1919, although nothing conclusive had been proved. The Fuller scandal contributed to Fitzgerald's sketching of Gatsby's situation, his shadowy dealing in "bonds," and his association with Wolfsheim, who has fixed a World Series.[1]

The Long Island setting also contributed, in a number of other ways, to the background of *The Great Gatsby*. Robert Sklar, in his examination of the Fitzgerald papers, noted Fitzgerald's own attribution of his sources.[2] On the back inside cover of his copy of Malraux's *Man's Fate*, Fitzgerald listed people or incidents he had used. Sklar comments: "For the opening chapter's scene in Tom Buchanan's East Egg mansion, Fitzgerald recalled the 'glamor of the Rumsies and Hitchcocks'; Tommy Hitchcock was a wealthy polo player whom the Fitzgeralds met on Long Island. Gatsby's first party in Chapter III was drawn, he wrote, from 'Goddards, Dwans, Swopes.' Herbert Bayard Swope was a well-known journalist, Allen Dwan a movie director, who lived at Great Neck in the early twenties." In addition, Mizener has noted that Fitzgerald once met on Long Island a certain Max Fleischman, a young bootlegger whose garish, new-money style of life impressed him as appalling, a figure who may have provided an early idea for Gatsby.[3]

But apart from these specific personalities, the community of Great Neck gave Fitzgerald a special suburban life-style to absorb and analyze. A sharp sense of an immediate scene had been one of Fitzgerald's strengths as a writer, and now Great Neck, sometimes called "the suburban Riviera," offered itself as material to be given imaginative shape. By the early twenties, it had become popular with many artists, writers, and people in the theater. Fitzgerald's fellow townspeople included Ring Lardner, the columnist Franklin P. Adams, Jane Cowl, Lillian Russell, George M. Cohan, Samuel Goldwyn, and Florenz Ziegfeld. Fitzgerald, in particular, formed a close friendship at this time with Ring Lardner, whose next-door neighbor was Herbert Bayard Swope, executive editor of the New York *World* and well known for his parties. In one of Fitzgerald's biographies, for example, one reads of Swope's croquet course at night, where "illumined by car headlights, games were played for $2,000 stakes."[4] In his biography of Lardner, Donald Elder describes Great Neck in the following way: "Long Island society was somewhat stratified, but in the twenties the social barriers were breaking down. There were the old rich who belonged to the social register and entertained in a decorous atmosphere of intellectual conversation—and croquet by gaslight; there were the new rich who did nothing but drink and play bridge and golf; there were people of talent who worked hard and made a lot of money but were not rich—theatrical people, writers, and journalists, composers, and artists. There were probably a few hosts like Fitzgerald's Gatsby, but mysterious bootleggers were not typical of Long Island society. But the stratifications were not rigid. The Swopes entertained everybody, although not all at the same time. . . . They gave parties for celebrities and also for high society."[5]

Lardner himself had a very wry attitude toward Great Neck and the American "success" ideal it seemed to represent. In an interview, he described its diversions with tongue in cheek, but in a way that made its life seem opulently empty:

> The peace and quiet of Great Neck is a delusion and a snare, I can assure you. . . . There is a continuous round of parties in progress here, covering pretty nearly twenty-four hours a day. It is almost impossible to work at times and still more difficult to sleep. Mr. Swope of the *World* lives across the

way and he conducts an almost continuous house party. A number of other neighbors do the same; there are guests in large numbers roaming these woods all the time. Apparently they become confused occasionally and forget at whose house they are really stopping, for they wander in at all hours demanding refreshment and entertainment at the place that happens to be nearest at the moment. . . . Scott Fitzgerald ran away to Europe, hoping to get some work done over there.[6]

In the seclusion of their villa at St. Raphael, Fitzgerald wrote to Maxwell Perkins: "I feel I have an enormous power in me now, more than I've ever had. . . .in my new novel I'm thrown directly on purely creative work—not trashy imaginings as in my stories but the sustained imagination of a sincere yet radiant world."[7] Later in his life, he remarked that he had never kept his imagination as pure as in that period in which he wrote *The Great Gatsby*. The novel is, indeed, so large an act of assimilation that no amount of reference to Long Island suburban life in the early twenties could begin to account for it. For some explanation of it one must search in the work itself, in its art, in the forces that helped to shape it.

One might begin by noting Mencken's continuing influence on Fitzgerald. As soon as Fitzgerald finished correcting the proofs of *The Beautiful and Damned* he began work on *The Vegetable*, a satire of Washington politics and national success worship. *The Vegetable* is a dramatization of the life and times of a henpecked civil servant who is satisfied being a postman, working out of doors. He is nagged by his wife Charlotte for not wanting to be rich and famous like the heroes of the popular fiction she reads. In a second-act dream sequence, the hero, Jerry Frost, is president of the United States, ineptly presiding over Washington scandal and corruption, until he is finally impeached. By the third act, Frost runs off, and is later reconciled with his wife, who is now ready to have him back on his own terms—as a postman. One of his weaker efforts, *The Vegetable* is nevertheless evidence that Fitzgerald was still fascinated by the social and political criticism of Mencken. Perosa remarks of *The Vegetable* that "it was still a way of burning incense before Mencken's disdainful frown, and in fact, Fitzgerald joined Mencken again in the denunciation of the vulgarity and ridicule of the contemporary popular myths. He offered Mencken a tribute of great esteem and possibly a form of alliance. This coincidence with Mencken's crusade, however, is a passing one."[8] Perosa is right that *The Vegetable* reflects Mencken's attack upon such marketplace idols as the worship of "success"; but he is certainly mistaken when he says that Fitzgerald's alliance with Mencken was to end with *The Vegetable*.

Fitzgerald's letters establish that he was reading a group of writers at this time—Edith Wharton, Willa Cather, Stephen Crane, Joseph Conrad—who shared a concern with form and craft; of these the most important for Fitzgerald was Conrad, who was also the enduring favorite of Mencken. In *A Book of Prefaces*, in his lengthy chapter on Conrad, he refers to Conrad as the greatest of all modern novelists. "My own conviction," he wrote, "sweeping all those reaches of living fiction that I know, is that Conrad's fiction stands out from the field like the Alps from the Piedmont plain. He not only has no masters in the novel; he has scarcely a colourable peer. Perhaps Thomas Hardy and Anatole France—old men both, their work behind them."[9] Mencken was particularly impressed by Conrad's austere vision, the continuing theme in his work of cosmic cruelty; his heroes "one and all . . . are destroyed and made a mock of by the blind, incomprehensible forces that beset them." Conrad's situation—aloof, aristocratic, and ironic—to this spectacle is to Mencken the measure of his greatness. "The lures of facile doctrine do not move him. In his irony there is a disdain which plays about even the ironist himself."

Mencken was in the habit, in much of his writing, of invoking Conrad's name as a standard of quality and of offering him as a model for other writers. In an essay on Conrad in the December 1922 issue of *The Smart Set*, Mencken referred to *Lord Jim* as quite possibly the finest novel in English and of *Almayer's Folly* as the most remarkable first novel of any writer of whom he knew:

> Nor is *Lord Jim* a chance masterpiece, an isolated peak. On the contrary, it is but one unit of a long series of extraordinary and almost incomparable works—a series sprung suddenly and overwhelmingly into full dignity with *Almayer's Folly*. I challenge the nobility and gentry of Christendom to point to another Opus I as magnificently planned and turned out as *Almayer's Folly*. The more one studies it, the more it seems miraculous. If it is not a work of absolute genius then no work of absolute genius exists on this earth.[10]

The article provoked a letter from Conrad to an English friend, in which he acknowledged his gratitude to Mencken:

> This outburst is provoked, of course, by dear Mencken's amazing article about me, so many-sided, so brilliant and so warm-hearted. For that man of a really ruthless mind, pitiless to shams and common formulas, has a great generosity. My debt of gratitude to him has been growing for years, and I am glad to have lived long enough to read the latest contribution. It's enough to scare anyone into the most self-searching mood. It is difficult to believe that one has deserved all that. So that is how I appear to Mencken![11]

On the occasion of Conrad's death in 1924, Mencken published a tribute in *The Nation*, in which he praised Conrad once again for his detachment and irony, for his vision that rejected optimistic formulas:

> Men no longer believed in an anthropomorphic Deity, half amiable grandpa and half prohibition-enforcement officer, but

they still believed that they knew the purpose of human life, the destiny of man—they were still full of a new and pseudo-scientific cocksureness, as idiotic at bottom as the worst dog-matism of a Calvin. . . . It was against this dogmatism that Conrad launched himself, and against whatever was left of the older brand. Upon it he played the hose of his irony. Against it he patiently arrayed his devastating facts. His execution was excellent. Certainties dissolved into doubts, and then into absurdities. A whole theory of knowledge went to pieces, and with it a whole cannon of ethics. There emerged at last his own aloof skepticism—not complacent and atti-tudinizing, like Anatole France's, nor bitter and despairing, like Thomas Hardy's or Mark Twain's, but rather the more serene skepticism of the scientist, with no room in it for any emotion more violent than curiosity.[12]

It was Mencken, indeed, who brought Conrad to Fitzgerald's attention originally, as can be seen in Fitzgerald's first reference to Conrad in his letters, a paraphrase from Mencken. He wrote to President Hibben of Princeton in June 1920 that his view of life was "the view of the Theodore Dreisers and Joseph Con-rads—that life is too strong and remorseless for the sons of man,"[13] a phrase Mencken used more than once in *A Book of Prefaces*, which Fitzgerald was then reading.[14] Interestingly, too, Mencken's review of *This Side of Paradise* appeared in the latter section of an article that began with a review of Conrad's *The Rescue*. Mencken began by remarking that a new book by Conrad naturally took precedence over any other. "It is amazing, indeed, how the melancholy and sinister Pole holds his high and lonesome place. There is not only no living novelist in active practice who challenges him; there is not even one who respect-ably follows him." He conceded that *The Rescue* did not belong on the "top row" of Conrad's works, "not to the class of *Al-mayer's Folly* and *Lord Jim*," but he nevertheless used the appearance of the book as an occasion to praise Conrad again for his power of reducing life "to its stark and tragic elementals."

References in Fitzgerald's letters indicate that he habitually associated Conrad with Mencken. His review of Mencken's *Prejudices: Second Series*, for example, concludes with the statement: "One is inclined to regret a success so complete. What will he do now? . . . Will [he] find new gods to dethrone. . . . Or will he strut among the ruins, a man beaten by his own success, as futile, in the end, as one of those Conrad characters that so tremendously enthrall him?"[15] If Mencken had become an idol of Fitzgerald's, Mencken's idol, as he well knew, was Conrad.

In the five-year period before *The Great Gatsby*, Conrad's name keeps appearing in Fitzgerald's correspondence, and references to him seem to echo Mencken. In his introduction to *The Great Gatsby*, written in 1934, Fitzgerald explained that before beginning to write the novel, he reread Conrad's preface to *The Nigger of the 'Narcissus,'* which sets forth the terms to be fulfilled by "a work which aspires to the condition of art." In the same paragraph and obviously with Conrad in mind, he says that he thought of his novel as "an attempt at form."[16] Fitzgerald had also compared the novel to Conrad's fiction when it was first published. In a letter to Mencken in 1925, he defended *The Great Gatsby* by remarking: "Despite your admiration for Conrad you have lately become used to the formless. It is in protest against my own formless two novels . . . that this was written."[17] During the same summer, he wrote to Mencken again, citing Conrad once more, and even more pointedly:

> By the way, you mention in your review . . . that Conrad had only two imitators. How about
>
> O'Neill in *Emperor Jones* (*Heart of Darkness*)
> Me in *Gatsby* (God! I've learned a lot from him)[18]

Mencken's review of *The Great Gatsby* was strangely unperceptive, and these two letters from Fitzgerald seem like an attempt to point out to him that there was a whole dimension of *The Great Gatsby*, closely related to Conrad's art, that he had failed to see.

James E. Miller has commented on Conrad's relation to *The Great Gatsby* in his pioneering study, *The Fictional Technique of F. Scott Fitzgerald* (1957). His discussion, stated briefly, places Fitzgerald's growth as a novelist within the framework of the James-Wells controversy, still being discussed in the 1920s, over the most satisfactory form for the novel. In "The New Novel," James made the distinction between two genres of fiction: the novel of "saturation" (exemplified by Compton Mackenzie and H. G. Wells), which he associated with discursiveness and "the affirmation of energy, however directed or undirected," and the novel of "selection" (exemplified by Conrad), which he associated with a controlling idea and theme and a clear center of interest. Using illustrations from Fitzgerald's writing, Miller argues that Fitzgerald's career formed an arc from the time of *This Side of Paradise* (indebted to the "saturation" novelists, Mackenzie and Wells) to *The Great Gatsby* (indebted to the "selection" novelist Conrad). He concludes by citing specific evidence in *The Great Gatsby* of Conrad's "narrative technique": the use of a Conradian narrator, the fragmentation of time, the dominance of irony in the novel. His argument that Fitzgerald's novels in the twenties move from discursiveness to selection has generally been accepted, although with the reservation that the term *discursive* does not account with complete critical accuracy for all of the different tendencies found in Fitzgerald's early writing.[19]

But Miller's argument does not say all that might be said about the Conrad relation. His discussion is limited solely to what he calls "technique" and does not consider other substantive matters, such as characterization and structural and thematic relationships. Since his study Robert Stallman, in a seven-page note, has reviewed some similarities in plot and characterization between Fitzgerald's novel and three of Conrad's works—*Nos-*

tromo, Lord Jim, and *Heart of Darkness.*[20] Stallman draws a number of interesting parallels: the loyalties of the Fitzgerald and Conrad narrators to their heroes in *Heart of Darkness* and *The Great Gatsby,* and the pride they both take in their personal honesty; the time motif in *Lord Jim* and *The Great Gatsby;* the common subject of isolation and illusion. The note suffers from the absence of a single idea unifying its observations, but in raising the subject of structural similarities, it will serve as a point of departure for my own examination of structural similarities that exist between *The Great Gatsby* and Conrad's early fiction. Extraordinary parallels and similarities *do* exist, and I will outline them as fully as I can see them. Some of these parallels may merely be coincidental, but in other cases there is a strong suggestion of Conrad's influence on Fitzgerald. Collectively, they lead to the conclusion that Fitzgerald was aided in his understanding of the experience he treats in his novel by Conrad's example. In his early period, Conrad gave authoritative expression to the theme of romantic illusion, and in *The Great Gatsby* one sees Fitzgerald treating this theme again, in a novel of a different kind, with a different setting and different characters, but in respect to many essentials in a strikingly similar way.

∗ ∗ ∗ ∗ ∗

Almayer's Folly and *The Great Gatsby* have never, as far as I know, been compared, and yet they have a very striking affinity in plot and theme. The epigraph of *Almayer's Folly* (from Amiel) announces the subject that is to be explored in both novels: "Qui de nous/ n'a enterre promise,/ son jour d'extase/ et sa fin exile?" Both Almayer and Gatsby have an exalted dream that is to be realized in the future, its realization seeming very near; their obsessive, future-oriented dreams are even described in the same vocabulary. Almayer's future is repeatedly imagined to be "splendid"; Conrad insists upon his "dream of a splendid future"[21] and his "gorgeous future" (p. 10) to be realized in Europe with his daughter, Nina. These characterizing phrases are used so often that they have, as it were, the function of a recurring motif. The vocabulary occurs again in *The Great Gatsby.* Carraway says of Gatsby, for instance, that "there was something gorgeous about him,"[22] and the quality of his life is evoked in capsule form in his "gorgeous car" (p. 49), and the "gorgeous pink rag of a suit" (p. 117) that he wears. Gatsby's house, closely identified with Gatsby himself, is described with sunlight playing across the whole front of it in a dazzling brilliance, and Carraway has to agree with Gatsby that "the sight is splendid" (p. 68) There are differences, of course, in the heroes themselves; for one thing, Gatsby comes to share in the nature of his life something of the wondrous quality of the epithets with which he is described, while Almayer never does. Yet they are strikingly alike in this essential of their lives: both envision a splendid destiny, about which they are misled by their naiveté. The naiveté of Almayer is focused in the moment when the Dutch naval officers visit his house and he tells them of his ambitious plans: "They listened and assented—amazed by the wonderful simplicity and foolish hopefulness of the man" (p. 36). The phrase later echoes ominously in Gatsby's "extraordinary gift for hope" (p. 4).

In both *Almayer's Folly* and *The Great Gatsby* the heroes' illusions are embodied in their houses. Almayer's house becomes synonymous with his dream as early as the opening page of *Almayer's Folly,* where he meditates on his future, on the verandah of "his new but already decaying house—that last failure of his life" (p. 4). On the occasion of the naval officers' visit, the half-finished house built for the reception of Englishmen and in the short-lived expectation of the renewing of his fortunes becomes the joke of the seamen as they leave their host. The house "received on that joyous night the name of 'Almayer's Folly' by the unanimous vote of the lighthearted seamen" (p. 37). Almayer's folly is both his house and his dream, the one symbolic of the other.

Similarly, in *The Great Gatsby* the history of Gatsby's house at West Egg is a prophecy of Gatsby's own life. It had originally been built by a brewer with the impractical notion of establishing a feudal estate; his children later sold the house while the funeral wreath was still on the door. The "feudal silhouette" of the house reflects ironically upon Gatsby's impractical dream, just as its windows, in a dazzling burst of sunlight, evoke the wondrous quality of Gatsby's imagination. On the evening before the reunion of Gatsby and Daisy the house is lit up from top to bottom; its illumination along the highway casts streaks of light on electric wires that, blowing in the wind, seem to flash on and off in an impressionistic effect of grand illusion. After Gatsby's death, his father produces for Carraway some papers that had belonged to his son, among them a crumpled photograph of Gatsby's house—a mirage of success. Appropriately, summing up Gatsby's strange life, Nick Carraway goes over to look "at that huge incoherent failure of a house once more" (p. 137).

The two houses, moreover, are located near water, across which may be seen, or glimpsed, the houses of the heroes' more securely established opponents. The establishment of Abdullah, the native Rajah of Sambir, is part of the monolithic opposition to Almayer:

> From the low point of land where he stood he could see both branches of the river. The main stream of the Pantai was lost in complete darkness . . . but up the Sambir reach his eye could follow the long line of Malay houses . . . with here and there a dim light twinkling through bamboo walls, or a smoky torch burning on the platforms built out over the rivers. Further away . . . founded solidly on a firm ground with plenty of space, starred by many lights burning strong and white . . . stood the house and godowns of Abdulla bin Selim, the great trader of Sambir. . . . The buildings in their evident prosperity looked to him cold and insolent and contemptous of his fallen fortunes. (P. 15)

Almayer, who dreams of becoming a self-made millionaire in the manner of Captain Lingard and had come to the tropics to "woo fortune . . . ready to conquer the world, never doubting that he would" (p. 5), finds that very harsh and intractable realities (such as those represented by Abdulla) lie in his way.

In *The Great Gatsby*, the Buchanan house is located across the bay from Gatsby's and is visible at night only by its dock light; the two houses are in a position of confronting one another, though distantly. The estates are not as closely situated as the houses in *Almayer's Folly*, nor could Gatsby's fortunes at this point be said to be fallen. Yet even the Georgian Colonial architecture of the Buchanan house suggests its solid associations and its essential difference from Gatsby's, with its evocations of fantasy. The proximity of the houses ·dramatizes the conflict between the actuality represented by one and the quixotism of the solitary outsider represented by the other; in their exclusion and defeat, Almayer and Gatsby share a similar fate. As a lone white man in that part of the East where he has come to find himself, Almayer will be frustrated in his ambitions by the material realities of Sambir; Gatsby is an outsider also, and his strange estate at West Egg is as close as he will ever come to the established society of the Buchanans.

In the backgrounds of Almayer and Gatsby—in the progression of events bringing them to Sambir and West Egg, with their belief in a "splendid future"—there is a remarkable parallel. Almayer is "adopted " by Lingard, "the old adventurer" (p. 11) who takes him as a young man aboard his yacht, the *Flash*, on a cruise in which every island of the archipelago is visited. Vinck had first spoken of Lingard to Almayer, and his words, "He has lots of money. . . . You know, he has discovered a river" (p. 7), give Lingard a fabulous background. The cruise aboard the *Flash* is Almayer's initiation into life and into his dream. In *The Great Gatsby*, the role of Lingard is played by Dan Cody, who brings young James Gatz aboard his yacht, the *Tuolomee*, for a voyage that takes them three times around the

continent. Dan Cody is, like Lingard, "an old adventurer" of a
former age who has made his fortune from slender beginnings,
and he poses for Gatsby the same possibility. In each of the
novels the figure of the older man stands in the background of
his protégé's dreams. Cody's yacht, the *Tuolomee*, is named after
the gold fields in northern California and underlines the idea of
grandiose promise betrayed by harsh reality; Lingard's yacht,
the *Flash*, is symbolic of a brief and illusory grandeur.

Similar as these initiations are, they are followed by events
that are also similar, for both Almayer and Gatsby come to fix
their conception of the future upon the idealization of a girl.
For Almayer it is his daughter, Nina, toward whom he appears
to feel more nearly the emotions of a lover than a father. "His
faith in Nina had been the foundation of his hopes, the motive
of his courage" (p. 192). He has fantasies of a life in his
mother's native Amsterdam, with Nina accepted and admired
by all, and vindicating his life. "I myself have not been to
Europe," he tells her, "but I have heard my mother talk so often
that I seem to know all about it. We shall live a—a glorious
life, You shall see" (p. 18). Without Nina, Almayer's dream
cannot be realized, and in this respect it is like Gatsby's, which
Daisy Fay must necessarily share. Nina and Daisy both, however, repudiate by the end the promise with which they have
been identified. They had seemed to the heroes to belong to their
visions; yet they reveal, finally, prior and stronger commitments
to the forces that oppose and overcome the heroes.[23]

In *Almayer's Folly*, Almayer is opposed by a difference in
race between himself and the entire community of Sambir.
Nature, too, seems massed menacingly against Almayer's dream,
and ironically, he is frequently seen laying plans against a background of nature's capricious violence. In the opening scene, he
is shown standing on his verandah at night, pondering his
grandiose future, while in the darkness a storm rages and the
river is swollen ominously by rain: "The tree swung free of the
obstruction began to move down the stream again, rolling slowly

over, raising upwards a long, denuded branch, like a hand lifted in mute appeal to heaven against the river's brutal and unnecessary violence" (p. 4). As the only "civilized" man in Sambir, Almayer is most alien to nature, while Mrs. Almayer and Dain are more closely associated with the "triumphant savagery of the river" (p. 28). Nina is Almayer's own child, but she is also the daughter of his Sambir wife, who reverts to her native character not long after their marriage. The child Nina is sent to live with the Vincks in the capital of Singapore for several years, but becomes unwelcome in the "white nest" of the Vincks when she deflects the attention of suitors from their own daughters. Captain Ford, who brings Nina back to Sambir, offers Almayer good advice: "You can't make her white. It's no use swearing at me. You can't" (p. 31). In the course of time, Nina is won over to her mother. "She had little belief and no sympathy for her father's dreams; but the savage ravings of her mother chanced to strike a responsive chord" (p. 151). The suit of the young nephew of Abdulla is refused by Almayer with barely concealed fury, but Nina is obviously moved by the possibility of love with one of her own race; and it is not long after that Dain Maroola appears. At their first meeting, Dain feels "the subtle breath of mutual understanding passing between their two savage natures" (p. 63). At the end Nina chooses Dain, destroying her father's dream. "I am not of your race," Nina tells Almayer, "between your people and me there is a barrier that nothing can remove" (p. 179).

Like Almayer, who sees Nina not as she is but as he would have her be in his vision, Gatsby understands little of Daisy or of the social realities she embodies. Although of a different kind, the forces that oppose Gatsby's vision are as invincible as those that overcome Almayer. While Gatsby, as a young officer during the First World War, is stationed at Camp Taylor in Louisville, he is brought into contact with Daisy's circle; it is possible for him momentarily, in the social mobility that the war brings about, to pass as one of Daisy's own class. "In various unrevealed capacities he had come into contact with such people, but always with indiscernible barbed wire between" (p. 113). Daisy's large house, its corridors redolent of gaiety and excitement, opens before Gatsby exalted romantic dreams, centering upon Daisy herself; the actual, as opposed to the romantic, intimations of wealth Gatsby does not grasp. Fitzgerald's insight into the nature of wealth in *The Great Gatsby* is that while wealth ought to heighten romantic possibilities of life, it may, in fact, merely harden the sensibilities of those who possess it. The wealth of the Buchanans has not been recently acquired, like Gatsby's; they have grown up with wealth, and their sense of superiority, molded by it, prevents a genuine relationship with other people. Moreover, boundary lines have already been firmly drawn in the minds of the Buchanans between those who "belong" and those who do not, and when Gatsby attempts to cross these boundaries he finds only a ruthless exclusion. In this respect, that of the heroes' deception about the realities they face, Almayer and Gatsby are not vastly different. Both are outsiders at the beginning and, even more firmly, at the end.

The moment of defeat for Almayer and Gatsby occurs near the end of the novels in a scene that has been constructed in such a way as to be symbolic. In *Almayer's Folly*, the scene takes place at an island beyond Sambir. Nina, Dain, and Almayer are brought face to face in a critical moment of decision, and Nina, forced to choose between the two men, chooses Dain. It is here that she announces to Almayer that a barrier of race divides them; it is Almayer's great moment of recognition and awakening, the defeat of a lifetime's hopes. The defeat of Almayer occurs at the moment of Nina's repudiation. A parallel confrontation scene in *The Great Gatsby* occurs at a rented suite at the Plaza Hotel. Compelled to choose, in effect, between Gatsby and Tom, Daisy makes it clear that her loyalties are, after all, with Tom's world. Gatsby's illusion that nothing can violate the integrity of their romance is shattered in Daisy's admission that since her affair with Gatsby, she has loved Tom. Tom drives a final wedge between Gatsby and Daisy when he reminds the group that Gatsby's new and suspect money is hardly the same as theirs. As in *Almayer's Folly*, it is in this confrontation scene that the hero's dream is actually destroyed. "Only the dead dream fought on as the afternoon slipped away, trying to touch what was no longer tangible, struggling unhappily, undespairingly, toward the lost voice across the room" (p. 103). These scenes mark a sudden reversal in the novels, for just before they occurred the hopes of the heroes had seemed to them close to fulfillment. Almayer cries of Nina (it could be said more justly of Daisy) that her betrayal comes "cruelly, treacherously, in the dark; in the very moment of success" (p. 192).

The houses in *Almayer's Folly* and *The Great Gatsby*, which had earlier been identified with the heroes' dreams, are reintroduced at the end to heighten the sense of the dreams' having now come apart. Almayer goes to live in the half-finished house known along the river as "Almayer's Folly," where he attempts vainly to find peace amid the confusion and disorder of decaying planks and half-sawed beams. Assuming the total isolation that had always been his destiny, he is like "an immense man-doll broken and flung there out of the way" (p. 204). He dies unmourned, hardly even an object of curiosity. At the end of *The Great Gatsby*, Gatsby's house has a similar quality of disorder and incoherence; it is described as "ghostly" when Nick and Gatsby roam through its empty rooms looking for cigarettes, and with Gatsby relating the last fragments of his late-summer romance with Daisy Fay. An autumnal motif rises up through the narrative, and evocations of Gatsby's dream become autumnal too. With the death of Gatsby, only Carraway and a few others trudge through the rain to attend his funeral, joined later by the man whose enormous spectacles had evoked a sense of "wonder" and who now, in a sense, sees the end of wonder in death. The careers of Almayer and Gatsby thus come full cycle from their early visions of a transcendent future, to the isolation, death, and oblivion that their actual futures hold.

The preoccupation with time, the yachts aboard which the heroes are initiated into their dream, the young women who represent the dream only to repudiate it, the passage from vision to oblivion, the irony that plays continually over the expectations of the future-oriented heroes—all these things *The Great Gatsby* shares with *Almayer's Folly*. But there are also other works of Conrad in which striking parallels occur and that are of a nature that suggests, perhaps even more strongly, Conrad's immediate influence.

✳ ✳ ✳ ✳ ✳

Between *Almayer's Folly* (1895) and *Lord Jim* (1900) a new type of hero begins to appear in Conrad's fiction; in place of Almayer, and Willems of *An Outcast of the Islands*, who are straw figures toppled by their harsh fates, there is an anticipation of the young man who in his initiation into life is deceived by romantic illusion. Conrad's "Youth," about a first command at sea, commemorates youthful illusion, the promise that grows dim with every year of experience. "But for me," says Marlow, "all the East is contained in that vision of my youth. It is all in that moment when I opened my young eyes on it. I came upon it from a tussle with the sea—and I was young—and I saw it looking at me. And this is all that is left of it! Only a moment; a moment of strength, of romance, of glamour—of youth!"[24] Marlow's discovery in "Youth" becomes incorporated into the theme of both *Lord Jim* and *The Great Gatsby*; it is that the "glow in the heart" belongs not as it appears with the future, but with the past—with the unattainable dreams of youth.

Fitzgerald introduced his review of Thomas Boyd's war novel *Through the Wheat* (1923) with the following quotation from "Youth":

I did not know how good a man I was till then. . . . I remember my youth and the feeling that will never come back any more—the feeling that I could last forever, outlast the sea, the earth, and all men . . . the triumphant conviction of strength, the beat of life in a handful of dust, the glow in the heart that with every year grows dim, grows cold, grows small, and expires too soon—before life itself.[25]

"So in part," Fitzgerald began the review, "runs one of the most remarkable passages of English prose written these thirty years. . . . Since that story I have found in nothing else even the echo of that life and ring." In fact, a number of Fitzgerald's own stories between *The Beautiful and Damned* and *The Great Gatsby* reflect the theme of "Youth." In "Winter Dreams," when Dexter Green loses Judy Jones, he also loses his winter dreams, and therefore his youth:

Even the grief he could have borne was left behind in the country of illusion, of youth, of the richness of life, where his winter dreams had flourished.

"Long ago," he said, "long ago, there was something in me, but now that thing is gone. . . . I cannot cry. I cannot care. That thing will come back no more."

In "The Diamond as Big as the Ritz," Fitzgerald remarks that youth can never live in the present, "but must always be measuring up the day against its own radiantly imagined future . . . prophecies of that incomparable, unattainable young dream." At the end, Kismine says that the diamond mountain has begun to seem like a dream, even though it had been where she had spent all of her youth, and the hero, John Unger, tells her that it *was* a dream: "Everybody's youth is a dream."

But not until *Lord Jim* for Conrad, and *The Great Gatsby* for Fitzgerald, does there appear the conception of a hero who embodies the youthful imagination. Unlike the heroes of the short stories that immediately precede *The Great Gatsby*, and unlike Marlow in "Youth," Jim and Gatsby know nothing of the disenchantment experience brings; with their great naiveté, they will not allow that the dream of youth *is* unattainable. Their conceptions of themselves and their destinies have, indeed, a godlike character. Marlow says of Jim that he "must have led a most exalted existence" (p. 96), and later he comments that "the point about him was that of all mankind Jim had no dealings but with himself."[26] He is so alone in his Platonic and elusive self-conception that Marlow finds nothing whatever with which he can compare him. When Gatsby says that Daisy's love for Tom was "just personal" (p. 116), Carraway can only wonder at "some intensity in his conception of the affair that couldn't be measured" (p. 116). Gatsby seems to have "sprung from his Platonic conception of himself" (p. 75).

The careers of Jim and Gatsby begin alike, with boyhood dreams. Jim is sent from the country home of his clergyman father at an early age, and from the foretop of a training ship, he looks out over the scene of departing ships. The sea, shining with a hazy splendor, seems to stir with intimations of romantic fulfillment: "He loved these dreams and the success of his imaginary achievement. They were the best part of life, its secret truth, its hidden reality. They had a gorgeous virility, the charm of vagueness. . . . They carried his soul away with them and made it drunk with the philtre of an unbounded confidence in itself" (p.20). Young Gatsby also lives in his dreams; the son of unsuccessful farm people in North Dakota whom his imagination cannot accept as his parents, he lies in bed at night imagining his transcendent future. The boy is so immersed in dreams that he comes to regard them as (in Marlow's phrase) "the greater part of reality." Gatsby's early reveries were "a satisfactory hint of the unreality of reality, a promise that the rock of the world was founded securely on a fairy's wing" (p. 75). As Jim and Gatsby grow older, they do not leave their boyhood dreams behind them, but attempt to live them out in the years of their young manhood.

As young men, they have certain similarities even in their appearance and manners. They are described as immaculate and as having chivalrous manners, and there is a suggestion of boyish restlessness about each of them. Gatsby is an "elegant young roughneck" (p. 38), and Marlow speaks of Jim's boyishness repeatedly—his eyes that looked straight into his, "his artless smile, his youthful seriousness" (p. 78). Gatsby's character has also been evoked by his smile. Carraway says that Gatsby's "was one of those rare smiles with a quality of eternal reassurance in it, that you may come across four or five times in your life" (pp. 37–38). The last time Nick sees Gatsby alive, he tells him that he is worth the whole crowd at East Egg, and Gatsby again breaks into a smile that is at first merely polite and then suddenly radiant. While Jim is talking about his plans, Marlow notices that "a strange look of beatitude overspread his features. . . . He positively smiled! . . . It was an ecstatic smile that your face—or mine either—will never wear, my dear boys" (p. 84). The smiles and other details of their appearance are perhaps expressions of a single quality. Fitzgerald uses the phrase "romantic readiness" to describe Gatsby, and the same idea is conveyed in Marlow's saying of Jim that "he had the faculty of beholding at a hint the face of his desire and the shape of his dream" (p. 175). "It was extraordinary," Marlow says, "how he could cast upon you the spirit of his illusion" (p. 109).

The naiveté of Jim and Gatsby has the same large scale as their visions. Musing over Jim's situation, the scholarly Stein sighs: "Yes, he is young," and Marlow replies: "The youngest human being now in existence" (p. 219). Marlow calls him "fabulously innocent" (p. 94), and the insidious Cornelius, intriguing with "Gentleman Brown" against Jim, cries that Jim is, after all, vulnerable: "He's no more than a little child . . . like a little child" (p. 327). One of Jim's employers, a friend of Marlow's, gathering from what has been said that Jim may have been guilty of some offense, writes to Marlow that he is "unable to imagine him guilty of anything much worse than robbing an orchard" (p. 188). Gatsby's whole conception of Daisy, his mansion and elaborate lawn parties that exist merely as a possible means of meeting her again, suggest innocence of an extraordinary kind.

As young men, both Jim and Gatsby meet with a stunning defeat that threatens their visionary conceptions of themselves; in both cases the crucial incident in which the defeat is suffered has the form of a central symbolic occurrence.[27] In *Lord Jim*, it is Jim's jump from the *Patna*; in *The Great Gatsby*, it is Daisy's marriage to Tom Buchanan. Jim's jump from the *Patna* is the focal point of the novel, for it is here that his destiny is revealed, that the discord between his imagination and his performance is fixed. In *The Great Gatsby*, the wedding of Tom and Daisy takes place before the novel opens, but it is always present in the reader's mind as the reality Gatsby cannot explain away, the occurrence that has settled his fate. But neither Jim nor Gatsby can accept the finality of these occurrences; their conceptions of themselves threatened, they still believe that the past can be reclaimed. Carraway says that Gatsby had "talked a lot about the past, and I gathered that he wanted to recover something, some idea of himself perhaps, that had gone into loving Daisy" (p. 84).

Following these decisive incidents, the careers of Jim and Gatsby proceed on the belief in a "second chance," or, as Jim puts it, the possibility of beginning with a "clean slate." "A clean slate, did he say?" cries Marlow. "As if the initial word of each [*sic*] our destiny were not graven in imperishable characters upon the face of a rock" (p. 196).[28] Carraway advises Gatsby that "you can't repeat the past." " 'Can't repeat the past?' he cried incredulously. 'Why of course you can! . . . I'm going to fix everything just the way it was before' " (p. 84). Jim believes that "some day one's bound to come upon some sort of chance to get it all back" (p. 179). It would be for him, as it would for

Gatsby, as if the past had never existed. " 'Never existed—that's it, by Jove!' Jim murmured to himself" (p. 232).[29]

In their attempts to recover the past Jim and Gatsby begin a second career that brings them to a pinnacle of apparent success. Patusan, according to Marlow, is a land without a past, and in Patusan, with his past disguised or seemingly effaced, Jim achieves the stature of a hero. The time comes when Marlow sees him "loved, trusted, admired, with a legend of strength and prowess around his name as though he had been the stuff of a hero" (p. 175). Jim seems to lead a charmed life and tells Marlow that he feels nothing can touch him now. Indeed, he becomes practically a mythic figure in Patusan, where he is known as Tuan Jim, or Lord Jim. When Marlow comes to Patusan, he meets a native on the coast who speaks of Jim. "He called him Tuan Jim," says Marlow, "and the tone of his references was made remarkable by a strange mixture of familiarity and awe" (p. 242). Fabulous stories circulate about him, one about a priceless emerald that is supposed to be concealed on the person of Jewel, the native girl who loves and is protected by Jim. Jewel, too, Marlow comments, "was part of this amazing Jim-myth" (p. 280).

Jim's later career has its parallel in the second career of Gatsby, which leads him to a mansion in West Egg and to the kind of glamour and success he may have dreamed about as a boy. The parties he gives are on an epic scale: his garden glows with colored lights, and film stars and financiers arrive from New York to add to the variety and gaiety of life. In the midst of this spectacle Gatsby stands alone, dominating the scene around him. Like Jim, Gatsby appears to have come out of nowhere, to have no past, and also like Jim, he is the subject of rumor and apocryphal legends. Even the speculation that he is the nephew of the Kaiser, or that he was a German spy during the war, merely adds to Gatsby's mystery.

In Patusan and West Egg, where their real pasts are unknown, Jim and Gatsby live out a dream life of their own making; their identities, like their names, are assumed. Conrad uses the word *incognito* in connection with Jim. Jim's last name is never specified in *Lord Jim*, and after the Patna incident, when Jim drifts from one obscure job to another, not wishing to be recognized, he goes only by his first name. "His incognito," Conrad remarks, "which had as many holes as a sieve, was not meant to hide a personality but a fact. When the fact broke through the incognito he would leave suddenly the seaport where he happened to be at the time and go to another—generally farther east" (p. 4). When he works for the ship chandlers, Egstrom and Blake, he is called Mr. James; the title *Tuan Jim*, or *Lord Jim*, is the last of his assumed identities, and it is never clear whether this identity is a disguise for a vulnerable Jim merely, or a fantasy self that becomes the genuine selfhood he achieves. In a similar way, Jay Gatsby is the creation of James Gatz, a fictional identity or incognito that is always threatened by reality; yet in the end, James Gatz comes to seem less real than Jay Gatsby.

Involved in the problem of identity relating to Jim and Gatsby are two mutually exclusive selves and a pattern of behavior that might be called schizophrenic. Neither is able to accept that part of reality that contradicts, or menaces, his imaginative identity. Jim cannot believe, despite his intense consciousness of lost honor, in the reality of his desertion of the *Patna*; it is to him as if only his *physical* self had jumped, his imaginative self remaining uncompromised. Gatsby's wealth derives from his association with "Wolfsheim's crowd," and from various kinds of illegal activity, yet he does not regard these shady dealings as having anything to do with himself. The same impulse that causes him to reject his origins, and even his name, also prompts him to see in Daisy Fay qualities that are proportionate to his vision.

The problem of identity and the romantic will is diagnosed by Stein in chapter 20 of *Lord Jim*, one of the most brilliant scenes in the novel. "So fragile!" says Stein, "and so strong! And so exact! This is nature—the balance of colossal forces. Every star is so—and every blade of grass stands *so*—and the mighty Kosmos in perfect equilibrium produces—this . . . this masterpiece of Nature" (p. 208). Man, however, is an imperfect creature, and it seems to Stein that he has come where he is not wanted, where there is no place for him. "We want in so many different ways to be. . . . This magnificent butterfly finds a little heap of dirt and sits still on it; but man he will never on his heap of mud keep still. He want [*sic*] to be so, and again he want to be so. . . . He wants to be a saint, and he wants to be a devil—and every time he shuts his eyes he sees himself as a very fine fellow—so fine as he can never be . . . in a dream" (p. 123).

The romantic will resolves itself, for Stein, into the question of "how to be, or become." Because of the nature of human limitations, Jim's case is hopeless, and it might be better for him if he were buried and underground; the next best thing is to submit to the "destructive element," or to find in action as near an approximation of one's dream as possible. "To follow the dream, and again to follow the dream—and so—ewig— *usque ad finem*" (p. 214). Jim in Patusan, and Gatsby in West Egg, take the course Stein prescribes, enter into the "destructive element," attempting to become "so fine" as they can never be.

In this attempt, in the second careers of Jim and Gatsby— despite the apparent success they achieve—the limitations they cannot accept reassert themselves. The past breaks in upon them, in the form of recurrences of the central symbolic incidents, and this time dooms them irrecoverably. The implication of reenactment is apparent even in the name *Patusan*, an approximate anagram of *Patna*; in Patusan Jim has the entire community in his trust, as before he had been entrusted with the lives of eight hundred passengers aboard the *Patna*, bound toward Mecca on a "mission of faith." In the incident where Jim, at the height of his success, is confronted by the renegade Brown, the central symbolic scene of the novel is reproduced. Brown at once searches out Jim's weak spot and fastens upon it. "And there ran through the rough talk a vein of subtle reference to their common blood, an assumption of common experience; a sickening suggestion of common guilt, or secret knowledge that was like a bond of their minds and of their hearts" (p. 287). Jim is again immobilized in the moment of crisis and decision, this time by a psychic identification with Brown. He releases Brown, with the result that he slaughters a party of natives, including Dain Waris, the faithful friend of Jim and the idol of his father, the old chief Doramin. Jim's facing death at the hands of Doramin is his last attempt to recover what is left of his dream—too late, because the dream has already been devastated. In *The Great Gatsby* the wedding of Tom and Daisy is reenacted in the scene at the Plaza Hotel. The stifling heat of New York introduces the wedding motif, calling to mind the heat of June, in Louisville, when Daisy married Tom; the music of Mendelssohn's "Wedding March" is heard from the apartment below as Daisy tells Gatsby that she cannot say she has never loved Tom. Her statement comes like the crush of reality against the fragile fantasy of James Gatz, and it is at this moment that Gatsby's dream shatters.

But in addition to these parallels in the conception of the heroes and the sequence of events, there is also a parallel in the narrative frame. The first-person narrators, Marlow and Carraway, are themselves characters in the novels; they find themselves reluctantly but unavoidably drawn into the lives of the heroes and observe them with a sense of their having some possible relevance to themselves personally. They both complain that they have always been singled out as (in Marlow's words) "the recipient of confidences" (p. 324). Carraway protests that "most of the confidences were unsought" (p. 3) and had come about as the result of his reserving judgment, "a habit that has opened up many curious natures to me" (p. 3). Something about Marlow makes the same appeal to men with "hidden plague spots . . . and loosens their tongues at the sight of me for their infernal confidences" (p. 34).[30]

The ambivalence of Marlow and Carraway toward the heroes creates much of the ironic tension in the novels. Carraways says in the opening pages of *The Great Gatsby* that Gatsby represented everything for which he has an unaffected scorn, and his account of Gatsby's career reveals a sympathy that is always seriously qualified by his awareness of Gatsby's gaudy illusion. Marlow's sympathy for Jim is continually undercut by his referral of Jim's intentions back to his evasion of moral responsibility. He speaks of Jim's "high-minded absurdity of intention" (p. 197), and when Jim tells him of his boyhood dreams, Marlow remarks that "with his every word my heart, searched by the light of his absurdity, was growing heavier in my breast" (p. 95). This ambivalence, however, also complicates the judgment of the heroes that the narrators attempt to make. Marlow speaks of the "subtle unsoundness" of Jim, yet he affirms that he had achieved genuine greatness!

The heroic stature of Jim and Gatsby is evoked in the great tableaux that occur in the two works. In the most memorable tableau scene in *Lord Jim*, Marlow sees Jim as a solitary, enigmatic figure against a somber and darkening sea:

> He was white from head to foot, and remained persistently visible with the stronghold of the night at his back, the sea at his feet. . . . For me that white figure in the stillness of coast and sea seemed to stand at the heart of a vast enigma. The twilight was ebbing fast from the sky above his head, the strip of sand appeared no bigger than a child—then only a speck, a tiny white speck, that seemed to catch all the light left in a darkened world. . . . And, suddenly, I lost him. (P. 336)

In the tableau of Gatsby calling forth the promise of the green light, Gatsby is a solitary figure observed in the darkness by Nick, and he vanishes from sight suddenly and strangely. In a

second tableau, Gatsby is contrasted with the chaos of a procession of stalled cars on his drive: "A sudden emptiness seemed
to flow now from the windows, and the great doors, endowing
with complete isolation the figure of the host, who stood on the
porch, his hand up in a formal gesture of farewell" (p. 43).
The tableaux serve to heighten the sense of Jim and Gatsby as
heroes of, as it were, mythic stature, distancing them from the
lives and purposes of ordinary men. The aura that surrounds
them is evoked mythopoeically, with a fusion achieved between
the felt presence of the heroes and the mood conjured up in
the physical world.[31]

But their heroic role is precarious, threatened by the darkness against which they are seen in representative tableaux and
by the material world from which their Platonic imaginations
divorce them. The "destructive element" in *Lord Jim* includes
an extraordinary number of vicious and warped characters,
among the first in Conrad's gallery of grotesques. There is, for
example, the strange pair of Chester and Robinson, who have
no use for idealism or for men who take things to heart; old
Robinson, who shrugged off the notoriety of an incident in
which he had been guilty of cannibalism, conforms to Chester's
idea of what a man ought to be like. Robinson "sees things as
they are" (p. 162). They form a company to exploit a guano
deposit and would like to engage Jim as an overseer of impressed
coolie workers. Jim's remorse over lost honor makes him, in
their view, "not much good . . . too much in the clouds" (p.
168), and consequently suitable for such a repulsive assign-
ment. The German captain who had been the chief officer aboard
the *Patna*, and the first to desert the ship, flees a court inquiry,
his conscience untroubled. And in Patusan, Jim is confronted
by the malevolence of "Gentleman Brown" and Cornelius, so
abject and immoral "that a simply disgusting person would
have appeared noble by his side" (p. 286). Jim's idealism is
challenged by a world peopled by such characters, who measure
him scornfully. Cornelius indicts Jim in the name of them all:

"He throws dust into everybody's eyes; he throws dust into your eyes, honourable sir, but he can't throw dust into my eyes" (p. 327). Tom Buchanan makes a similar indictment of Gatsby: "He threw dust into your eyes just like he did in Daisy's, but he was a tough one" (p. 136).

At the end of *Lord Jim* and *The Great Gatsby*, the callous characters triumph, and the heroes are defeated in worlds far from idealistic. Yet they alone of the characters possess vision. "The sheer truthfulness of [Jim's] last three years of life," Conrad says, "carried the day against the ignorance, the fear, and the anger of men" (p. 393). Taking up the romantic position at one point, Conrad remarks that it is only through imagination that anything exists, that Jim exists. It is the final irony of the two novels, and the distinguishing feature of their resemblance, that although Jim and Gatsby pursue illusion and are defeated, their "exuberant imagination" (*Lord Jim*, p. 176) gives them both heroic stature and, in a certain sense, exemplary truthfulness.

✷ ✷ ✷ ✷ ✷

In 1898 Conrad interrupted his work on *Lord Jim* to write the much briefer *Heart of Darkness*, completed that year and published in the "Youth" volume in 1902. The two works may seem quite different but are actually companion volumes. Marlow reappears as the narrator in *Heart of Darkness* and identifies reluctantly with the central character; his mind is divided once more between imagination on the one hand and the ethics of conduct on the other. Both Jim and Kurtz are "isolates," illusionist heroes whose imaginations set them apart from other men. Jim is isolated from others by his Platonic ego, while Kurtz is isolated by his knowledge of "unexplored regions," by his vision of horror in existence, which comes to him in the remote interior of the Congo. The great difference between *Lord Jim* and *Heart of Darkness* in this respect is that in *Heart of Darkness* the hero's experience is directed back much more specifically to the failure of contemporary society. It is this juxtaposing of the "isolate" hero's imagination with the moral failure of modern society that gives *Heart of Darkness* its special relevance to *The Great Gatsby.*

The themes of *Heart of Darkness* and *The Great Gatsby* are worked out on two distinct levels: one, the drama of a spiritually alienated hero; the other, the gradual exposure of a society with which his life places him in opposition. The two levels impinge upon one another. Though different, the societies in *Heart of Darkness* and *The Great Gatsby* are both described impressionistically, the use of distortion giving them something of the atmosphere of waking dreams. In *Heart of Darkness,* the "mournful and senseless delusion"[32] of the Company's enterprise takes the form of the incomprehensible in the series of images presented at each stage of Marlow's journey overland and up the river. The ship that takes Marlow into the interior discharges custom-house clerks to levy toll in the middle of a forsaken wilderness. Soldiers are landed, too, and some of them drown in the surf; yet no one seems particularly to notice, or to care. One day a man-of-war is sighted shelling the bush, with no object in sight: "There she was, incomprehensible, firing into a continent" (p. 62). At the outer station, Marlow comes upon a ravine where blasting can be heard and a railway is apparently being built; the odd thing, however, is that the cliff being destroyed is not in the way of anything. This pointless blasting is the only work going on. Walking into the shade of the ravine (for relief from what he has seen), Marlow has the sudden sensation that he has wandered into "the gloomy grove of some Inferno" (p. 66). It is the Grove of Death, where natives, dehumanized by the forces of "progress," are dumped like damaged cargo and left to die. They have the appearance of unearthly apparitions, "black shadows of disease and starvation lying confusedly in the greenish gloom" (p. 66).

While the world of *The Great Gatsby* is not as radically irrational as the Congo milieu of *Heart of Darkness*, it nevertheless shares with Conrad's novel an incongruity and grotesqueness of atmosphere. Carraway says that "even when the East excited me most . . . even then it had always for me a quality of distortion" (p. 134). Fitzgerald's valley of ashes is both real and fantastic: "Ashes take the form of houses and chimneys and rising smoke, and, finally, with a transcendent effort, of men, who move dimly and already crumbling through the powdery air" (p. 19). The latter part of chapter 2 is devoted to the apartment scene in New York, which is prepared for and grows out of the earlier scene and communicates a similar sense of spiritual emptiness. The distortions of the apartment scene are predominately optical and begin almost unnoticeably. An overenlarged photograph on the wall seems to have the blurred indistinctness of an ectoplasm, at first appearing to be a picture of a hen sitting on a large rock, and at a distance focusing into a view of a stout old woman wearing a bonnet. Myrtle's sister, Catherine, has eyebrows that have been plucked, with the eyebrow line redrawn at an acute angle, so that her face seems blurred like a photograph. By the end of the scene—with the room as hazy as the valley of ashes, Myrtle moaning on the bloodied couch, and people stumbling about confusedly—Fitzgerald has presented a world that is morally unintelligible.[33] In the progression of effect in *Heart of Darkness* and *The Great Gatsby*, Conrad uses broad, bold images, while Fitzgerald works with images that are more subtle. But the effect is similar insofar as it creates a lingering sense of the "actual" as hallucinatory.

The heroes, too, Kurtz and Gatsby, are shown in atmospheres that have a quality of the bizarre. The approach to Kurtz is a "weary pilgrimage amongst hints for nightmares" (p. 62), but when he is actually found the final nightmare takes shape. Marlow's party first encounters a young Russian, who prepares for the sensation of being "captured by the incredible" (p. 82). The Russian youth—the "harlequin," as he is called—is characterized by his uncritical wonder and awe, continually expended in the direction of Mr. Kurtz. "I tell you," he proclaims enthusiastically of Kurtz, "this man has enlarged my mind!" (p. 125). At this point Marlow comments: "He opened his arms wide, staring at me with his little blue eyes that were perfectly round" (p. 125). The harlequin prepares the reader for the incredible reality of the hero, a function assumed in *The Great Gatsby* by Owl Eyes, who appears in Gatsby's library just before Nick's first meeting with him. The enormous spectacles worn by Owl Eyes give him, like the young Russian, a quality of wonder, and it is in this wondering attitude that he is discovered, marveling at the real books in the library.

The dreamlike meeting with the "harlequin" in *Heart of Darkness* is merely a prelude to the actual meeting with Kurtz. The view of Kurtz borne on a stretcher is conveyed by a phantasmagoric optical effect: "The stretcher shook as the bearers staggered forward again, and almost at the same time I noticed that the crowd of savages was vanishing without any perceptible movement of retreat, as if the forest that had ejected these beings so suddenly had drawn them in again as the breath is drawn in a long aspiration" (p. 134). Kurtz is seen at this point with an El Greco–like distortion: "He looked at least seven feet long. His covering had fallen off, and his body emerged from it pitiful and appalling as from a winding sheet. I could see the cage of his ribs all astir, the bones of his arm waving. . . . I saw him open his mouth wide—it gave him a weirdly voracious aspect, as though he wanted to swallow all the air, all the earth, all the men before him" (p. 134).

Kurtz's particular experience in the Congo has no parallel in Gatsby, but the "dream sensation" of his experience, or a variation of it, also surrounds Gatsby's life at West Egg. Gatsby's mansion and the parties he gives are described with a grotesque foreshortened effect that has been described as nearly surrealistic, an effect that underscores the quality of fantasy in Gatsby. Even his automobile is described as if it were an optical illusion, with windshields reflecting a dozen suns. Crossing the bridge into Manhattan, the automobile is chimerical: "With fenders spread like wings, we scattered light through half Astoria" (p. 52). In the Plaza Hotel scene, when Tom is triumphant, Gatsby seems to vanish like a phantom: "They were gone, without a word, snapped out . . . like ghosts" (p. 103).

Part of the structural similarity, then, between *Heart of Darkness* and *The Great Gatsby* consists of the confrontation of two "nightmares," one of the hero and the other of society, and of the reluctant choice finally made by the narrator in favor of the hero. "It was strange," comments Marlow, "how I accepted this unforseen partnership, this choice of nightmares forced upon me in the tenebrous land invaded by these mean and greedy phantoms" (p. 147). Gatsby's gaucherie and illusion are preferred at last by Carraway to the confusion of the inhabitants of the valley of ashes and the Buchanans. If the aberrations of Kurtz and Gatsby are described with the quality of a strange dream, the "normal" world also, seen from a higher perspective, is hallucinatory, almost insane. In this way, the case for Kurtz and Gatsby is stronger than it might at first seem.

But in addition to this similarity, there is also a similarity in the relationship between the narrators and the heroes. As in *Lord Jim*, the relationship of narrator and protagonist in *Heart of Darkness* is ambivalent. Kurtz is a "hollow sham," and the heads drying on the stakes before his hut seem to Marlow symbolic. "They only showed that Kurtz lacked restraint in the gratification of his various lusts, that there was something lacking in him—some small matter which, when the pressing need arose, could not be found under his magnificent eloquence" (p. 131). Yet Marlow also finds Kurtz "remarkable" and his defeat a kind of triumph. "He had summed up—he had judged. . . . After all, this was the expression of some sort of belief" (p. 151). Carraway says of Gatsby late in the novel that he had always disapproved of him, and yet he is loyal to Gatsby at the end, as Marlow had been to Kurtz, because he alone has stood for some sort of belief.

There is a likeness, too, in the personal honesty both narrators profess in introducing themselves. "Everyone," Carraway says, "suspects himself of at least one of the cardinal virtues, and this is mine; I am one of the few honest people that I have ever known" (p. 46). Marlow, too, prides himself on his honesty. "You know I hate, detest, and can't bear a lie. . . . There is a taint of death, a flavour of mortality in lies" (p. 82). Both, however, compromise their honesty in the course of the novels. Carraway drifts into an affair with Jordan Baker, thinking apparently that he can accept her while disregarding her values. His honesty is not as perfect as he had at first thought, although he reaffirms it at the end when he breaks with both Jordan and the East. Marlow finds himself involved in a lie to Kurtz's Intended; to tell her the truth would have been "too dark—too dark altogether" (p. 162). The complications that challenge the narrators' honesty are merely part of larger questions of value illuminated by their meetings with Kurtz and Gatsby.

The meetings do not take place immediately; Marlow and Carraway approach the heroes very gradually, hearing of them first by rumor. Marlow hears of Kurtz even on the coast, and at points thereafter asks information about him, receiving peculiar answers. On his asking who "this Kurtz" is, the bookkeeper at the Outer station replies factually that Kurtz is a first-class agent, and then, seeing that this answer is not satisfactory, adds that Kurtz is a "very remarkable person" (p. 69). Marlow, at the Central station, again asks about Kurtz, and the brickmaker tells him sarcastically that Kurtz "is an emissary of pity, and science, and progress" (p. 79). Kurtz is whispered about and conspired against by the manager and his uncle, who are displeased to learn that he is spoken of even on the coast. Gatsby's name is also mentioned well before he appears. He is "this man Gatsby," as Kurtz is "this Kurtz"; at the first of Gatsby's parties that Nick attends people whisper about Gatsby's "corruption," and Gatsby, like Kurtz (whose corruption is real), is kept fascinatingly vague. Kurtz is encountered only near the end of *Heart of Darkness*, while Gatsby appears in the early part of *The Great Gatsby*, but in either case the actual meetings are delayed and come as the climax of mounting suspense. Once they appear, they dominate the scene as convincingly as they had previously by their absence.

The dramas Kurtz and Gatsby act out end with their deaths, but by this time the narrators have become seriously involved in their lives, and by the end of both novels the narrators finally make some sort of affirmation about the heroes. After the death of Kurtz, Marlow and the manager of the Central station talk together, and the manager is barely able to conceal his satisfaction, his "peculiar smile sealing the unexpressed depths of his meanness" (p. 150). He speaks of Kurtz's "unsound method" and of·his unfortunate duty of having to report it in the proper quarters. Marlow agrees that Kurtz has no method, but adds: " 'Nevertheless, I think Mr. Kurtz is a remarkable man,' I said with emphasis. He started, dropped on me a cold heavy glance, said very quietly, 'He *was*,' and turned his back on me. My hour of favour was over; I found myself lumped with Kurtz as a partisan of methods for which the time was not ripe. I was unsound!" (p. 138). In *The Great Gatsby*, when Gatsby's dream is disintegrating and his great house practically deserted, Nick Carraway makes a dramatic, because long-suspended judgment: " 'They're a rotten crowd,' I shouted across the lawn. 'You're worth the whole damned bunch put together' " (p. 117).

Marlow stays with Kurtz to hear his last words and to receive from him some personal papers and his report ironically entitled "The Suppression of Savage Customs." Kurtz dies alone in the cabin of the ship, scorned by the manager and company "pilgrims," and Marlow buries him along the bank of the river. "I remained to dream the nightmare out to the end," Marlow remarks, "and to show my loyalty to Kurtz once more" (p. 150). He says that it was preordained he should never betray Kurtz: ". . . it was written I should be loyal to the nightmare of my choice" (p. 150). Carraway also shows his loyalty to Gatsby, gathers up the broken fragments of his life, and attends to the arrangements for the funeral, which hardly anyone attends. At the conclusion of *The Great Gatsby*, Carraway remarks, "I found myself on Gatsby's side, and alone" (p. 124), and becomes the spokesman for Gatsby, as Marlow is for Kurtz. After Gatsby's death, "every surmise about him, and every practical question was referred to me" (p. 124).

It is in this "dying fall" with which both *Heart of Darkness* and *The Great Gatsby* end that many of the parallels in their plots are concentrated. One of the most noticeable of these concerns the packet of papers and photographs that Kurtz, just before his death, gives to Marlow. An official-looking man with gold-rimmed spectacles calls on Marlow after his return to the city and asks that the papers be given to him. They would no doubt be of great value to the company, because of Mr. Kurtz's "knowledge of unexplored regions." The phrase gives rise to Marlow's ironic reply that Kurtz's "knowledge of unexplored regions, however extensive, did not bear upon the problems of commerce or administration" (p. 153). To another man, calling himself Kurtz's cousin, Marlow gives the chief document among the papers—Kurtz's pathetic, unfinished report on the "Suppression of Savage Customs." The final scene, with Kurtz's Intended, contains the most pointed ironies of all; it reintroduces the illusion of the original Kurtz, who was to have been an emissary of light but dies in darkness, with the words, "the horror!" on his lips. Kurtz's Intended assures Marlow that it was she who "knew him best," and finally Marlow is unable to tell her Kurtz's actual last words; he says, instead, that Kurtz had died speaking her name, sheltering her from reality by the story of a death scene out of a shop girl's romance. She cries exultantly that she "knew it—was sure," as the room seems to darken around them. "They," Marlow says, "the women, I mean—are out of it—should be out of it. We must help them stay in the beautiful world of their own, lest ours gets worse" (p. 115).

In the "dying fall," in *The Great Gatsby*, Carraway has an

experience similar to Marlow's. Gatsby's father arrives from North Dakota for the funeral and produces for Carraway some papers that had belonged to his son. As with the packet of Kurtz's papers, there is a photograph (in this case, a crumpled picture of Gatsby's house), together with an old schedule and list of resolutions for self-improvement. The schedule and list of boyhood resolves have the same function of irony as the packet of papers that had belonged to Kurtz; they introduce again the illusions of the young Gatsby after the somber outcome of Gatsby's life is known. Henry C. Gatz—Gatsby's father—is like Kurtz's Intended, too, in his being so totally in the dark at the end:

> "If he'd of lived, he'd of been a great man. A man like James J. Hill. He'd of helped build up the country."
> "That's true," I said, uncomfortably. |P. 128)

In his optimistic reading of his son's career, Gatsby's father merely emphasizes its darker meaning ironically.

In the final summing up in *Heart of Darkness* and *The Great Gatsby*, the narrators have "visions" that, with great economy, bring the experiences they have lived through into focus. The visions are similar not only in being "fantastic dreams," but also in concrete details, such as their mournful city settings. Marlow's vision brings together in one image Kurtz's spiritual crisis and death in the Congo, and the life of the "sepulchral city":

> Between the tall houses of a street as still and decorus as a well-kept alley in a cemetery, I had a vision of him on the stretcher, opening his mouth voraciously, as if to devour all the earth, with all its mankind. He lived then before me; he lived as much as he had ever lived. . . . The vision seemed to enter the house with me—the stretcher, the phantom-bearers . . . the beat of the drum, regular and muffled like the beating of a heart—the heart of a conquering darkness. (P. 155)

Nick's "vision" also incorporates in a single image an earlier occurrence contained in the novel, and the life of the city; it reintroduces Daisy's state on the eve of her marriage to Tom (as related by Jordan) and projects it against a brooding urban background:

> West Egg, especially, still figures in my more fantastic dreams. I see it as a night scene by El Greco: a hundred houses, at once conventional and grotesque, crouching under a sullen, overhanging sky and a lustreless moon. In the foreground four solemn men in dress suits are walking along the sidewalk with a stretcher on which lies a drunken woman in a white evening dress. Her hand, which dangles over the side, sparkles cold with jewels. Gravely the men turn in at a house—the wrong house. But no one knows the woman's name, and no one cares. (P. 134)

The narrative structures of *Heart of Darkness* and *The Great Gatsby* are circular, their endings leading back to the beginnings of the narratives. Both end in the city where Marlow and Carraway, after the death of the heroes, feel a numbing lack of interest in the affairs of ordinary men. In *Heart of Darkness* an image of the city, overclouded by an unnatural darkness, is presented portentously in the opening pages; the scene is returned to at the conclusion and given new emphasis, the darkness of the Congo now directed back to the moral life of the city. There are actually two cities in *Heart of Darkness*—London, and another not named but obviously Brussels (the point of departure for the Congo adventure), which has always made Marlow think of a "whited sepulchre." He refers to it as the "sepulchral city," and the house in Brussels where he finds the company offices is "as still as a house in the city of the dead" (p. 57). In either case, the city becomes a focal point, a culture symbol of modern Europe.[34]

The contrast with Kurtz's death in the Congo brings into sharp relief the meanness and materialism of the city. Marlow sees its inhabitants "hurrying through the streets to filch a little

money from each other, to devour their infamous cookery . . .
to dream their insignificant and silly dreams" (p. 152). Marlow
tells his listeners aboard the yacht in the Thames estuary that
they could not even understand Kurtz. "How could you? . . .
surrounded by kind neighbors ready to cheer you or to fall on
you, stepping delicately between the butcher and the policeman.
. . . How can you imagine . . . that utter solitude, where no
warning voice of a kind neighbor can be heard whispering of
public opinion" (p. 116). The bourgeois life of the town is
"monstrous" in its absence of imaginative energy. Carraway's
repudiation of the "East" is, too, a rejection of its culture, which,
like that of the society in *"Heart of Darkness,* is characterized
by sterility and the failure of inward life.

As a result of their meetings with the heroes, the narrators
arrive at new understandings of their societies. The interest of
the novels centers steadily upon the heroes—until the end, when
it shifts to the reality underlying contemporary life that the
heroes' experiences have served to illuminate. This revelation,
in turn, becomes the theme of the two novels. In this respect,
Heart of Darkness and *The Great Gatsby* are like fables, or
modern moralities, which instruct. Their instruction, however,
is starkly pessimistic, and both works end in a literal darkness.
The final scene in *Heart of Darkness* shows the city shrouded
by a menacing darkness, and *The Great Gatsby* closes with the
image of a benighted continent, of a "vast obscurity beyond the
city, where the dark fields of the republic rolled on under the
night" (p. 137).

※ ※ ※ ※ ※

The perspective of Conrad's early fiction reveals how closely
The Great Gatsby follows Conrad's treatment of romantic illusion and how much Fitzgerald's novel belongs to Conrad's
ironic mode. My comparison has involved examination in considerable detail, but I have been more interested in sketching
main outlines and essentials. The theme of Conrad's "Youth,"
for example, is essential to the theme in *The Great Gatsby* of

the radiantly imagined future as belonging, in fact, to the past and the illusions of youth. *Almayer's Folly* contains a number of striking parallels with *The Great Gatsby*: the hero's futuristic dream set in an ironic time perspective; his apprenticeship aboard the yacht of an old adventurer who has become rich, which marks his initiation into his dream; the young woman who seems to embody, but then repudiates, the dream; the ghostliness of his house, embodying his "folly," at the end; the movement from vision to oblivion. *Lord Jim* and *The Great Gatsby* share the unusual conception of a young man who incarnates the youthful imagination, who suffers an initial defeat threatening his Platonic selfhood, yet still believes in the possibility of a "second chance." and is defeated a second time in an incident that reenacts the original defeat. *Heart of Darkness*, with its hallucinatory effects and its "dying fall" echoing with ironies, contrasts the central figure's experience with the spiritual emptiness of contemporary society and is thus what *The Great Gatsby* is also, a moral parable.

The textual evidence is persuasive that in certain essential respects—involving incident, characterization, and theme— Fitzgerald was indebted directly to Conrad in his conception of his novel. Parts of the conception of *Almayer's Folly* and *Lord Jim* suggest this influence, but *Heart of Darkness* argues for it very strongly. Fitzgerald's assimilation of Conrad is part of a pattern of his assimilation of other writers' work that I traced earlier in the fiction of Fitzgerald's apprenticeship. Fitzgerald's adaptations from Conrad come as the culmination of this tendency in his earlier career, but *The Great Gatsby* is a culmination also in the sense that Fitzgerald was able to realize his greatest work, one with its own uniqueness and integrity, and that cannot be accounted for exclusively in terms of influence, however important. The creative act that brought *The Great Gatsby* into being was large and complicated, and to understand it more fully it will be necessary to consider the novel's "intricate art."

3

The Great Gatsby—the Intricate Art

After finishing *The Beautiful and Damned*, Fitzgerald wrote to Maxwell Perkins: "I want to write something *new*—something extraordinary and beautiful and simple and intricately patterned."[1] He did not then have his conception for *The Great Gatsby*, but it was at its completion everything Fitzgerald had written he hoped to achieve in his next novel. *The Great Gatsby* has an apparently simple, pellucid surface, but its patterning is intricate, so much so that the novel comes to seem, on examination, like a large structure of interwoven detail and nuance in the tradition of Flaubert. It makes extensive use of iterative imagery, leitmotivs, character doubles, parallel and symbolic scenes, and has been given an intense visual focus that contributes to the novel's scenic and dramatic form.[2]

The Great Gatsby develops in a series of sharply focused scenes, like Mrs. Wharton's *Ethan Frome*, but Fitzgerald's scenes are more intricately modeled than Mrs. Wharton's. Beneath the enamel of their realistic surfaces there is an elaborate play of implication and suggestion. The first three of Fitzgerald's "scenic" chapters work together, particularly, as a novelistic unit. All of the principals appear in these chapters, and the reader is introduced to their backgrounds and situations as they are defined by the three distinctly separate social spheres to

119

which they belong—East Egg, with its affluence and perogatives; the valley of ashes, where the lower middle class has a hazy existence; and West Egg, an upper middle class suburb inhabited, in part, by the newly rich. By the end of these opening chapters, the several social worlds to be explored have been presented to the reader distinctly, and it remains, suspensefully, to be seen how they will interact.

These three opening chapters also reveal a common pattern, since a party or social gathering takes place in each.[3] In the first chapter it is a social call by invitation; the occasion is exclusive and limited to a single individual who qualifies. Carraway is not a member of the Buchanan's set, having nothing like their wealth, but his background makes him acceptable. He is a second cousin, once removed, of Daisy, and was a classmate of Tom's at Yale and a member of the same senior society. The time is established by Daisy's remarking that "in two weeks it'll be the longest day of the year" (p. 11), so that it must be nearly the middle of June, the time of the year when, as it will come out later, Daisy married Tom Buchanan. As Carraway arrives, the sense of place is established immediately. He finds a red and white Georgian Colonial mansion, which Tom has acquired from the oil man, Demaine; its architecture suggests an early America, but the ownership of the estate passing to Demaine ("of main force") to Buchanan intimates the big money it now represents. The substantial nature of Buchanan's wealth is indicated in the opening pages in Carraway's remark that Buchanan casually brought with him to East Egg a string of polo ponies from Lake Forest. ". . . it was hard to realize," he adds, "that a man in my own generation was wealthy enough to do that" (p. 6). When Carraway reaches their estate, he is greeted by Buchanan, shown in a proprietary posture as he stands, in the swank of a riding outfit, "with his legs apart on the porch" (p. 7).

Inside there is an atmosphere that is both gracious and disturbing. Upon his arrival in their living room, under "the frosted wedding cake of the ceiling" (p. 8), Carraway finds Daisy and Jordan Baker seated on a sofa, both wearing white dresses that stir in a breeze moving through the room, creating an idyllic impression. As soon as Tom appears, however, shutting the windows with a bang, the vision is immediately deflated, and the young women appear to balloon down from their cloudlike couch. This opening impression—the sense of a beguiling vision and its deflation—is in small what the chapter will be in large. Impressions of Daisy and Jordan that follow are conveyed through "gestures" almost entirely, as, for example, in Daisy's enchantment-promising voice and in Jordan's elaborate attitude of self-sufficiency, her appearance of balancing an invisible object on her chin. "At any rate," Carraway remarks facetiously of their introduction, "Miss Baker's lips fluttered, she nodded at me almost imperceptibly, and then quickly tipped her head back again—the object she was balancing had obviously tottered a little and given her something of a fright" (p. 9). Both Daisy and Jordan have about them an aura of private understandings, inaccessible to an outsider, which underscores the special world of wealth to which they belong. At one point Daisy tells a story about their butler, who had previously cleaned a wealthy family's silver until at last the silver cleaning affected his nose, and he was forced to leave their employment. There is an implication in this brief account of something malodorous about the rich— something relevant to the world of the Buchanans, which is not without charm but is also disquieting.

For the "superior" world in which they live is filled with tensions, communicated by gestures that do not belong to real emotions and by innuendoes of a vaguely disturbing kind. At one point, Tom says: "Oh, I'll stay in the East, don't you worry," and then glances at Daisy, and back at Carraway, "as if he were alert for something more" (p. 10). An impression is given (and later confirmed) that the Buchanans left Chicago over some unpleasantness involving Tom's infidelity. His infidelity comes out later that afternoon with a "shrill, metallic" (p. 14) ring of the telephone, and at this point Carraway learns that Tom keeps a mistress. In one passage it is implied, comically, that Tom, a horseman, has this woman "in his stable." As he refers to his stable, the telephone rings again, and the group is frozen in a tense silence. The earlier gracious appearances dissolve into discord and are replaced by a sense of a deep unease, as Carraway leaves with a feeling of disgust and "confusion." He returns to his cottage, from the lawn of which he detects the figure of the man he will later know as Gatsby, his arms outstretched worshipfully toward a point somewhere across the darkness and the bay. He is as yet a shadowy figure, but Fitzgerald has already hinted at some depth of emotion in him that is antithetical to the group Carraway has left at East Egg, particularly that figure of chronic unfaithfulness, Tom Buchanan.

The first chapter leads into the second by the telephone call from Myrtle, but otherwise the transition is a study in contrasts, from great wealth to bare subsistence—to a land of ashes and powdery shapes, which may be buildings or men, but are all equally indistinct. It is an area in which "the only building in sight [is] a small block of yellow brick, sitting on the edge of the waste land, a sort of compact Main Street ministering to it" (p. 20), a description linking the valley of ashes, and its spiritual condition, to the middle-class world pictured by Sinclair Lewis and T. S. Eliot. Presiding over this exhausted acreage is George Wilson, who runs a garage–filling station and is called colorless, spiritless, and anemic. When his wife, Myrtle, appears, she seems to walk "through her husband as if he were a ghost" (p. 21), and when Wilson enters the garage, he mingles "immediately with the cement color of the walls" (p. 21). This valley of ashes is a dumping ground where "ashes grow like wheat" (p. 19), but ashes are not fertile like wheat (as in "Absolution"), and the phrase merely reinforces the implication of infertile life. Ironically, it is close to Independence Day when Carraway enters this forsaken area, as his own words make clear: "It was a few days before the Fourth of July, and a gray, scrawny

Italian child was setting torpedoes in a row along the railroad track" (p. 21). The valley of ashes, at the approach of the Fourth of July, is the novel's second comment on the new republic and the society it has fostered.

Myrtle's name has a number of associations that confirm her role as a character double of several others in the work. With her green name, she is a double of Gatsby, and her aspiration is played off, in a horrible way, with his, heightening Gatsby's stature by contrast. At the same time, she is a double of Daisy, for she, too, has a floral name. But if the daisy is a flower with a bright, petite, and particular distinctness, myrtle is an ivy, growing close to the earth, with no individual distinctness at all. There is, furthermore, nothing of the "fay" or elfin quality in Myrtle—nothing of the slight, beguiling, and graceful. She is captured with comic effect in her first appearance: "In a moment the thickish figure of a woman blocked out the light from the office door" (p. 20). It is noted that she has "rather wide hips" (p. 21), and in a sense, she is the heavy-hipped Venus of the valley of ashes. "Her face . . . contained no facet or gleam of beauty, but there was an immediate perceptible vitality about her as if the nerves of her body were continually smouldering" (p. 21). She boards the train at the same time as Tom and Carraway, joining them when they arrive at the station in New York, and there, before leaving for the Washington Heights apartment, she buys a puppy "of an indeterminate breed" (p. 22), an incident that suggests the idea of Tom's "buying" the mongrel Myrtle for his amusement.

The Washington Heights apartment has an atmosphere that is quite strange. "The living-room," Carraway comments, "was crowded to the doors with a set of tapestried furniture entirely too large for it, so that to move about was to stumble continually over scenes of ladies, swinging in the gardens of Versailles" (p. 23). These Watteauesque tapestried scenes set the tone of the "love nest," of Myrtle's movie-magazine notion of romance. The strangeness of the apartment, however, is also reflected in the characters encountered in the scene. Myrtle's sister, Catherine, for example, has a "solid, sticky bob of red hair, and a complexion powdered milky white" (p. 24), and has thus something of a clown's appearance (part of the motif of mockery that runs through the scene). There are, too, many oddly blurring impressions, which are part of the concern in the chapter with seeing, or with being unable to see, with vision and sightlessness. Figuring appropriately in the scene is Chester McKee, a photographer who tells Carraway that he is in "the artistic game" (p. 24). If the role of the artist is to achieve a vision underlying the inchoate material of reality, McKee is an artist *manqué*, who records only surfaces. Of his wife, called "shrill, languid, handsome, and horrible" (p. 24), he has taken one hundred twenty-seven photographs, a figure that, in its exactness, emphasizes the hopeless literalness of his mind.

Myrtle's personality, as it is brought out by Fitzgerald, has special interest in respect to the scene. What she is like has been suggested on her first appearance, in the fact that she wears "a spotted dress of dark blue crepe-de-chine" (p. 21) at the Wilson garage. A woman might wear a sheer crepe de chine dress at an early evening cocktail party, or at formal occasions, but she would not normally wear crepe de chine in the afternoon, or at a garage. Her wearing the crepe de chine dress at the garage suggests that she pretends to, or has some vulgar notion of, social distinction. At the station in New York, she lets four cabs pass before selecting one that is painted lavender, and when they reach the apartment building in Washington Heights, Fitzgerald remarks that she "went haughtily in" (p 23). "The intense vitality that had been so remarkable in the garage," he comments, "was converted into an impressive hauteur" (p. 24). Myrtle is reminiscent, indeed, at this point, of the young woman with violets on her hat, in the "brummagem cabaret" scene in *The Beautiful and Damned*, who pretends to belong to a higher social class than she does, a figure who suddenly expands into a whole roomful of people who are pretending in the same way.

An impression is given, through her, and again through Myrtle, that the middle-class imagination can aspire toward the ideal no further than, say, the possession of a showier dress or house. In the course of this brief chapter, in fact, Myrtle wears three different dresses, and speaks of going out the next day to buy another. "Her laughter, her gestures, her assertions became more violently affected moment by moment," until she seems to be "revolving on a noisy creaking pivot" (p. 24)—an image that suggests something on public show, something wooden and overburdened. "The room rang full of her artificial laughter" (p. 28).

Myrtle's pretensions, however, are shared by the other women at the apartment. Fitzgerald remarks that Myrtle's elaborate chiffon dress "gave out a continual rustle as she swept about the room" (p. 24); but the sense of a too obtrusive showiness is also conveyed in Fitzgerald's description of Myrtle's sister, Catherine, of whom he says that when she moved about "there was an incessant clicking as innumerable pottery bracelets jingled up and down her arms" (p. 24). And like Myrtle, Mrs. McKee has social pretensions, the baselessness of which her own words betray. " 'I almost made a mistake, too' [Mrs. McKee] declared vigorously. 'I almost married a little kike who'd been after me for years. I knew he was below me. Everybody kept saying to me: 'Lucille, that man's 'way below you!' But if I hadn't met Chester, he'd of got me sure' " (p. 27).

Myrtle, however, remains the presiding figure, and she queens it over Mrs. McKee as she announces that she is going to give her the dress she is wearing—when she is ready to discard it. There is an extremely comic moment when, in referring to menials, Myrtle remarks that "all they think of is money" (p. 24). It is particularly comic because at that moment Myrtle is imagining herself as an aristocrat, a big consumer whose day is taken up with purchases at various shops. "I'm going to make a list," she says, "of all the things I've got to get. A massage and a wave, and a collar for the dog, and one of those cute little ash trays where you touch a spring, and a wreath with a black

silk bow for mother's grave that will last all summer. I got to
write down a list so I won't forget all the things I got to do"
(p. 29). (At the height of her pretending to largeness, the shop-
ping list also comments tersely on her narrow scope—the ash
tray, her valley of ashes background; the dog collar, her relationship with Tom Buchanan; the cemetery wreath, her fate.)

Myrtle's pretensions collapse suddenly when, with "a short
deft movement" (p. 29), Tom breaks her nose. The scene had
been building steadily toward this climax, the room growing
dimmer with a heavy haze of cigarette smoke, insinuating again
the "fatal" region of the valley of ashes. People now stumble
confusedly about through the cigarette haze while there is heard
"high over the confusion a long broken wail of pain" (p. 29).
Myrtle is seen lying on a couch, bleeding profusely, while the
others attempt to spread copies of "Town Tattle" over the
tapestry scenes of Versailles. In this telescoped detail, a contrast
is implied between the court of Versailles, with its formal ele-
gance and aristocratic associations, as well as its court romance
and love intrigues, and the "love intrigue" that has just been
witnessed. This kind of detail, emphasizing through historical
contrast the banality of the present moment, is reminiscent of
The Waste Land, and may have been inspired by it; but not even
in Eliot is the detail worked in more tellingly.

The apartment sequence "freezes" a moment of time, and its
implications. Its implications are several, for Tom's affair with
a married woman will be played off against Gatsby's with
Daisy. But it is already apparent that Tom's affair has a purely
physical nature, is imaginatively vacant, while Gatsby's affair
with Daisy is of quite another kind. The whole scene at the
apartment evokes the idea of vacancy, as well as failure and
casualty, not the least of these casualties being Chester McKee,
the wife-dominated photographer hinted to be more homosexual
than heterosexual. As he first appears, an impression is given
that he has just been shaving, for he has a "white spot of lather
on his cheekbone" (p. 24), a detail that makes Chester seem

like an ineffectual little man. Ironically, he is shown again near the end of the scene "asleep on a chair with his fists clenched in his lap, like the photograph of a man of action" (p. 29). Carraway sees him to his apartment and practically tucks him into bed. Sitting up in bed, rather like a child, McKee shows Carraway samples of his photographs, with titles like *Loneliness* and *Brook'n Bridge*, which suggest his own painful failure. Failed as artist and as man, McKee is a small figure in relief, set against the figure of Gatsby, who is to dominate the following chapter.

The dinner party at East Egg was exclusive and limited to a few, but Gatsby's party at West Egg has a vast scale and is open to "the world and its mistress" (p. 47). Gatsby's house, a "factual imitation of some Hotel de Ville in Normandy" (p. 6) also indicates Gatsby's nature; as a Hotel de Ville, it is a town or city hall, and implies Gatsby's inclusiveness rather than exclusions. (His inclusiveness is also underlined quietly in the volumes of *Stoddard's Lectures*, the travel books taking in the entire world, which are found on Gatsby's book shelves.) Although the interior of the house is shown, the scene is set for the most part at night in Gatsby's "blue gardens [where] men and girls came and went like moths among the whisperings and the champagne and the stars" (p. 31). Gatsby and his moonlit world of festival are at the very furthest remove from the valley of ashes, noted immediately before, in the previous chapter.

Gatsby's "enormous garden" (p. 21) is strung with colored lights and is the scene of a "spectroscopic gayety" (p. 35); is a night world where magic and reality mingle. People come uninvited from everywhere, crowding onto his lawn, enjoying his apparently endless supply of champagne, his buffets of pastry pigs and turkeys bewitched to a dark gold, and dinners served at different times of the night, while a large orchestra plays the "Jazz History of the World." To Carraway, the party has an incredible gaudiness; yet he remarks: "I had taken two fingerbowls of champagne, and the scene changed before my eyes into something significant, elemental, and profound" (p. 37). *It is exactly at this moment* that he meets Gatsby, the creator of this raw splendor. Gatsby is "placed" here as having creative energy; he has the power to make others share in his own vision, to make them participate in something outside of and larger than themselves. From the raw material of reality, he produces wonder, but his wonder-making imagination, in which discrimination is in abeyance, is also his tragic flaw. For this reason, it is reasonable that Owl Eyes should be found in Gatsby's library, expressing amazement at Gatsby's world and its doubtful relation to reality. Owl Eyes inspects the library shelves, surprised to find that the books are authentic, and then compares Gatsby with Belasco, who used real props to heighten stage illusion. Gatsby's implications, his inner self, are evoked through setting and scene in a way that is similar to Fitzgerald's presentation of his characters in the preceding chapters.

But these first three chapters do more than introduce Fitzgerald's characters and their social settings; they also intimate what is to follow. The Buchanans are shown first at their great shorefront estate, which, partly by its appearance at the opening, has primacy as solid fact. The time of the scene is also important, since it initiates a time sequence in the first three chapters. In the opening scene at the Buchanans' home, sunset is approaching, but the late afternoon sunlight is still strong. The New York apartment scene begins in the afternoon and fades into evening. It is late at night, however, past midnight, when Gatsby is shown and his party observed. There is thus a continuance in time, although the parties occur on different days, from afternoon to midnight, that binds the opening chapters together and adumbrates the novel's movement from day into night, from light into darkness.

The chapters are given internal unity, also, by the motif of confusion that runs through them. Its source originates, significantly, with the Buchanans, who establish the theme of money at the outset. In the opening section, the telephone call shatters brittle appearances, and the scene ends with a feeling of confusion and disgust on the part of Carraway, which will later be enacted on a larger scale. In the apartment scene, a sordid confusion follows the love tryst that leaves Myrtle broken and bleeding, prefiguring her role in the novel as victim, her life to be violently extinguished by Daisy, as Gatsby's is to be, through Wilson, by Tom. The third version of confusion appears again in the chapter devoted to Gatsby, in the procession of stalled cars and the honking of their horns, on Gatsby's drive; but from this scene, Gatsby himself is aloof, as he stands under the moon in an imposing isolation, gesturing farewell, that is like a signaling of the role he is to play in the novel. The theme of a deepening confusion is insinuated in the first three chapters, even before the novel has well begun.

The dominant strategy of the opening chapters is exactness and sharpness of definition, and such definition continues on into the following chapters, marking out the progressive stages of Gatsby's experience. Chapters 4 and 5 build to the reunion of Gatsby and Daisy, occurring in chapter 5, at the exact center of the novel. They meet on the "neutral ground" of Nick's cottage, and from there go over to Gatsby's house. The emotion of Daisy's arrival is evoked importantly through scenic effect. On the day she arrives it rains, the rain letting up half an hour before she appears in a dewy mist. "Under the dripping lilac-trees," Carraway relates, "a large open car was coming up the drive. It stopped. Daisy's face, tipped sideways beneath a three-cornered hat, looked out at me with a bright ecstatic smile. . . . A damp streak of hair lay like a dash of blue paint across her cheek, and her hand was wet with glistening drops" (p. 65). At this moment she belongs to a world heightened by the imagination; the dew in which she appears has the suggestion of a dew of dawn, the promise of a fresh beginning, which is what the reunion does mean to Gatsby.

The sense of promise evoked in this chapter, however, is undercut by many of Fitzgerald's allusions. When Daisy is about to arrive, for example, Fitzgerald remarks that "Gatsby

looked with vacant eyes through a copy of Clay's *Economics*"
(p. 64),[4] which, in a very muted way, contrasts Gatsby's ideal-
ized vision of Daisy with the reality of capital. There is a further
undermining of Gatsby's hopefulness when Daisy arrives and
asks Carraway, "Why did I have to come alone?" and he replies
facetiously, "That's the secret of Castle Rackrent" (p. 65).
Maria Edgeworth's *Castle Rackrent* (1800) describes the decline and fall of an Irish estate that had been founded in an
expectation of prosperity. The last of the line, Sir Condy Rackrent, marries an undowried daughter of a wealthy family, who
contributes to the extravagance that leaves him ruined at the
end, borne practically alone to a pauper's grave where, as Thady,
the narrator, remarks: "He had but a poor funeral, after all."
Fitzgerald's oblique allusion to *Castle Rackrent* is thus an ill
omen, implying not only that Gatsby's grasp on reality is weak
and that his hopes will not flourish, but even foretelling a lonely
grave. The reunion begins at Carraway's cottage, after the little,
comic sequence of Gatsby's nervous anticipation; soon Carraway
leaves them together, allowing the reader to imagine for himself
Gatsby's "unimaginable" state of mind. But it is also an occasion
for Carraway, standing alone under a tree in the rain that has
resumed, to study Gatsby's house. It is at this point that the
reader learns the history of the house for the first time; the improbable and soon extinguished dream of a "brewer," the house
comments ironically, like the allusion to *Castle Rackrent*, on
the reunion taking place.

When Carraway rejoins them half an hour later, they go over
to Gatsby's mansion, and no one is more impressed by the house
at this moment than Gatsby himself. "See," he cries ingenuously,
"how the whole front of it catches the light" (p. 68). Inside,
the house is "splendid" (p. 68) too ". . . as we wandered," says
Carraway, "through Marie Antoinette music-rooms and Restoration salons, I felt that there were guests concealed behind every
couch and table, under orders to be breathlessly silent until we
had passed through. . . . We went upstairs, through period bed-

rooms swathed in rose and lavender silk and vivid with new flowers, through dressing rooms and poolrooms, and bathrooms, with sunken baths" (p. 69). But Gatsby's lyric mood is undercut in small but telling ways—by the picture of Dan Cody that looks down ominously upon Gatsby and Daisy in their reunion, and by the unreality of Gatsby's house, with its "Restoration salons" and "Merton College" library, associated with Gatsby's "wonder." "I could have sworn," Carraway says, as Gatsby shows his house to Daisy, "[that] I heard the owl-eyed man break into ghostly laughter" (p. 69). Leaving them together, Carraway "went out of the room and down the marble steps into the rain" (p. 73). The rain falling over the house may be a blessing on the reunion, may suggest that Gatsby and Daisy have a fertile and promising future, but as water, it more likely implies illusion.

In the next section, comprising chapters 6 and 7, there are a great number of incidents and short scenes, giving an impression of continual movement. But each of these chapters has a scene that is like a still center through which meanings are communicated. The first is the party at Gatsby's that Daisy attends with Tom and at which she admires only an actress who, with her director at her side, is seated under a white plum tree, affecting a lovely pose. "But the rest," Carraway says, "offended her—and inarguably, because it wasn't a gesture but an emotion" (p. 81). The different things Daisy and Gatsby see in the party are symptomatic of the gulf that now begins to open between them. For Gatsby, the party represents the raw vigor out of which dreams are born, but to Daisy, the party is disturbing in what it says to her of an openness, and therefore vulnerability, to experience.

In the pivotal scene of chapter 7, which takes place at the rented suite of the Plaza Hotel, the gulf dividing Daisy and Gatsby becomes complete. It becomes clear even to Gatsby, in a reluctant and hardly admitted way, that her romantic attachment has not, after all, been the same as his. Tom calls attention to Gatsby's new money, which might vanish or involve Daisy in scandal; and it is here that Daisy breaks, that she begins to draw back into a world of lovely surfaces, which are protected by absolutely solid wealth. And as she does, there rises up a motif of heat and confusion, which continues through the second crossing of the valley of ashes, where Myrtle is senselessly run down. Terrain of haze and death, the valley of ashes becomes the scene of death in fact.

The last section of the novel (chapters 8 and 9) is a "dying fall," in which Gatsby's dream is ending, and ends. At his house in West Egg, Gatsby waits for Daisy's telephone call, which never comes; all that comes, sent by Tom Buchanan, is the gray shape of George Wilson, scattering death. In the last chapter, Gatsby's house, now deserted, is viewed again under moonlight, an obscenity scrawled by some boy with a piece of brick on its front steps. Festival ends with Gatsby's death and is replaced by the rites of burial. The funeral is attended only by Carraway, a few servants, and—by an inspired touch—Owl Eyes. That Owl Eyes should appear at the funeral is improbable, and yet in another way is not, since all of his appearances have been improbable; moreover, alone of Gatsby's guests, Owl Eyes was aware of what Gatsby and his parties were actually about. At the first party, he announced Gatsby's affiliation with wonder; and it is fitting that he should be present at the burial of wonder, should be at the graveside to deliver Gatsby's obsequies. "The poor son-of-a-bitch," Owl Eyes comments simply, summing up Gatsby's naive misreading of his world. This last section has the form of a coda and brings the novel to a conclusion with the formal precision of a fugue.

The scenic and dramatic development of *The Great Gatsby* helps to give the work its sharply defined immediacy, but it is only one of the strategies of Fitzgerald's art. The novel develops, as importantly, through an elaboration of imagery, often as motif, in patterns of recurrence. Sharply focused images appear, only to reappear in a later scene, in a way that comments on the image initially. In the opening scene, for example, Daisy and

Jordan are shown seated on the Buchanans' cloudlike couch, like goddesses of wealth who seem to invite devotion. The image is reproduced in chapter 7, when Carraway arrives with Gatsby at the Buchanan house to find Daisy and Jordan on the same couch, like sirens, their "white dresses against the singing breezes of the fans" (p. 88). Yet from the moment Gatsby steps over the *solid* threshold of the Buchanan house, his dream begins to be destroyed, and *is* by the end of that afternoon. In another instance, recurrence is seen in the opening impression of Gatsby, keeping his night vigil on his lawn, as he faces out longingly toward Daisy's dock light, and at the end of chapter 7, when Gatsby is alone under the moonlight by the Buchanan house, his affair with Daisy ended, Gatsby an "outsider" once again, now keeping a night vigil "over nothing" (p. 111). Recurrence appears in Fitzgerald's early, and then late, imagery of rainfall—in the rain that falls over Gatsby's house, as if in blessing, when Gatsby and Daisy are reunited, and again in the rain in which Gatsby is buried, at the funeral almost no one attends. In each case, an initial image recurs in the form of a denial of the romantic possibilities it seemed to forecast.

There is, indeed, a large system of reiterated imagery in the novel, which has a leitmotiv function. One example is the recurrence throughout the work of bird and flower imagery. "There's a bird on the lawn that I think must be a nightingale," Daisy says, "come over on the Cunard or White Star line. He's singing away" (p. 14). She asks Tom if the nightingale's singing isn't romantic, and Tom, thinking of his stables, replies tersely: "Very romantic." But the nightingale's song is the love motif, developed more fully in the reunion scene, where as Daisy and Gatsby enter Gatsby's house the air is described as being full of "bird voices in the trees" (p. 69). And that day is evoked again at the end, when Gatsby's dream has ended, and the shadow of a tree "fell abruptly across the dew and ghostly birds began to sing" (p. 115). Bird imagery is used sparingly and discreetly, but floral imagery is prominent in the work.

Daisy has a flower name and is first seen against a background of a sunken Italian garden in bloom by her porch. Inside the house, Carraway describes Daisy as "opening up" to him "in a flower-like way" (p. 17). Later, flowers are associated with Gatsby, through the night gardens where his dream life is lived. On the afternoon when Daisy is to arrive at Nick's, Gatsby sends over a "greenhouse" of flowers; and when Gatsby and Daisy enter Gatsby's grounds by the front postern, his gardens are fragrant with "the sparkling odor of jonquils and the frothy odor of hawthorne and plum blossoms and the pale gold odor of kiss-me-at-the-gate" (p. 69). Later, there is a flashback of Gatsby with Daisy in 1917, when she becomes the embodiment of his dream: "At his lips' touch," Carraway says, "she blossomed for him like a flower" (p. 86). The novel ends at Gatsby's mansion in the autumn, during the yearly dying of the trees, and the flower idea is evoked again, achieving its final statement as vision in Carraway's sense of the island here "that flowered once for Dutch sailors' eyes" (p. 137); and all of the imagery of blooms scattered throughout the work comes together at once as an expression of imagination and its cancellation in the world Fitzgerald has envisioned.

Fitzgerald's intricate patterns of imagery also involve an extensive use of color imagery, which accents motifs within the work. Although his use of color imagery does not need to be outlined fully,[5] its general nature might be indicated. The color green, in literary tradition associated with hope (Whitman's grass that is "hopeful green stuff," the doorway to the silver mine in Nostromo that is painted green, "the color of hope"), has a suggestive relation to the novel's theme. The green dock light toward which he gazes yearningly is identified with Gatsby on his initial appearance, and the implication of the green dock light expands at the end when the lawns of Gatsby's estate are envisioned as "the green breast of the new world" (p. 137). The connotation of green in the novel remains constant, like that of two other colors, red and gray, the latter appearing more dominantly. It is dominant certainly in the chapter devoted to the valley of ashes, where everything is described in grays, implying spiritual death. As the living room of the Washington Heights apartment turns gray in a haze of cigarette smoke, Fitzgerald's characters are shown at the climax of their empty party. Less conspicuously, the color comments on the guests at Gatsby's parties, "gray names" (p. 47) on a faded timetable. And the reference to Dan Cody as a "gray, florid man" (p. 76) is also relevant as characterization, since it combines the flower idea with the gray association of spiritual failure. The color red appears less frequently, but when Fitzgerald uses it, he does so in a way the literary naturalists had before him, associating it with violence. It occurs early in the allusion to Carraway's books on economics, bound in "red and gold" (p. 5); in the complexion of the Buchanan living room as it turns by late afternoon from rose to "crimson"; and again, after Carraway leaves, in the spotlighted impression of "new red gasoline pumps [sitting out] in pools of light" (p. 17), an image that points toward the violence that will be enacted by the filling station in the valley of ashes and of the further violence culminating in the trail of Gatsby's blood in the swimming pool.

Blues are used to accent vision and dream, particularly with respect to Daisy and Gatsby. Almost the first reference to Gatsby in the third chapter, which he dominates, is to his "blue gardens" (p. 31), and when Daisy appears at Carraway's cottage to meet Gatsby, she is framed by blue lilic trees, and her hair is like "blue paint" (p. 65). Later, at the Buchanan estate, Gatsby feels that he is about to claim Daisy, and he looks out across the bay at a sailboat as it moves "against the blue cool limit of the sky. Ahead lay the abounding blessed isles" (p. 90). But what lies ahead is the reverse of blessedness, and with the death of Gatsby, Carraway hears "ghostly birds singing among the blue leaves" (p. 115), and is aware of "the blue smoke of brittle leaves" (p. 115).

Another set of accentuating colors—rose, gold, and silver—

are first associated with Daisy, and then with Gatsby. In the opening view of the Buchanan estate, a line of French windows are "glowing now with reflected gold" (p. 7), and nearby are not merely a few beds but a "half acre of deep pungent roses" (p. 8). Daisy is first seen in the living-room, "a rosy-colored space bound fragilely into the house" (p. 8), and then on her "rosy-colored porch, open toward the sunset" (p. 10). Like the Keatsian nightingale, singing on the lawn, these colors insinuate Gatsby's presence even before he appears, and his love for Daisy. For these colors are most truly Gatsby's own. Gatsby is remembered by the "gorgeous pink rag of a suit" (p. 177) he wears, and when he shows Daisy his collection of shirts, she says that she would like "to just get one of those pink clouds and put you in it and push you around" (p. 71). Gatsby is also associated, so strongly that it seems part of his identity, with gold, and with golden light, and it is with golden sunlight that Gatsby endows Daisy in his imagining. In a late flashback, he remembers the cotillion balls with Daisy in Louisville during World War I, where "fresh faces drifted here and there like rose petals blown by the sad horns around the floor," and where "a hundred pairs of golden and silver slippers shuffled the shining dust" (p. 118). But most of all, Gatsby knows that Daisy is golden in the wealth gold represents; she is "the king's daughter, the golden girl" (p. 91). "Gatsby was overwhelmingly aware of the youth and mystery that wealth imprisons and preserves, of the freshness of many clothes, and of Daisy, gleaming like silver, safe, and proud above the hot struggling of the poor" (p. 114). Rose, silver, and golden light are the colors of Gatsby's imagination, and the hues of morning, of the expansion of hope, of nearly infinite promise the novel in time will firmly deny.

As important as these colors—more important even—are the recurrences of white and black imagery, played off against each other throughout the work. Carraway remarks early that "the white palaces of fashionable East Egg glittered along the water"

(p. 6), and in the scene that follows, Daisy and Jordan Baker
are seen wearing white dresses in the Buchanan living room,
where Daisy speaks of her "beautiful white" (p. 16) girlhood
in Louisville. Later, Daisy is alluded to as the inaccessible girl,
"high in a white palace" (p. 91). But the imagery of whiteness
is scattered throughout the novel and can be seen variously in
the white suit Gatsby wears appropriately when he is reunited
with Daisy; the white marble steps that front Gatsby's mansion;
and the "white chasms" (p. 43) of Wall Street where Carraway works in investment securities. In these allusions whiteness
is made to seem synonymous with purity and wonder; yet in its
association at the same time with wealth this connotation has a
troublingly ambiguous quality.

The ambiguous imagery of whiteness occurs pointedly at least
twice in connection with New York City. "We drove to Fifth
Avenue," Carraway remarks in chapter 2, "so warm and soft,
almost pastoral, on the summer Sunday afternoon that I
wouldn't have been surprised to see a great flock of white sheep
turn the corner" (p. 22). But he is then on his way, with Tom
and Myrtle, to the Washington Heights apartment, whose implications are the reverse of a pastoral innocence. Later, from the
Queensboro Bridge, New York rises up like a white city, with
the "promise of all the mystery and beauty in the world" (p.
52). But the whiteness of the city is literally an optical illusion.
Moreover, this glimpse of the city is followed immediately by
the sight of death. A funeral cortege passes, and the "tragic
eyes" (p. 52) of Southern European immigrants cast mournful
glances at Carraway. The cortege is followed by a limousine in
which haughty black men are driven by a white chauffeur, a
sudden reversal of usual expectations that implies that the whiteness of purity, in the glimpse of the city from the bridge, will
be subjected to a reversal by the city as it is in its reality. Finally,
Carraway arrives at the Times Square café, in the darkness of
which he is to meet Meyer Wolfsheim, the underworld figure
with the rapacious name who is in his way, too, a comment on

the "white city." In the end neither Daisy nor the white city fulfills the promise of wonder; instead, Gatsby is fated for "a motor hearse, *horribly black and wet*" (p. 132). White imagery accrues in the novel, evoking illusion, and the work concludes in an engulfing darkness.

Fitzgerald's concern with imagery as motif is so pervasive that *The Great Gatsby* develops to a large extent like a poem, through a complicated deployment of images, which all come together at the end to multiply an impression of finality, of a tremendous foreclosure on Gatsby's dream. But Fitzgerald's aesthetic strategies involve more than a complicated elaboration of imagery. Another aspect of the novel's art may be seen in Fitzgerald's distinctive handling of time. One might say that there is no time in *The Great Gatsby* when one is not conscious of time. The novel is filled with clocks and schedules and time-tables, and allusions to the time of day and night, and progresses seasonally, from spring to autumn, in the course of the work. It is also informed by the recall of other time and other seasons, particularly the autumns of the past where the novel's meanings are concentrated. A sense of the past suffuses the work. There are conversations overheard at his parties of Gatsby's mysterious past; it is whispered that he is Kaiser Wilhelm's cousin, and Von Hindenburg's nephew. But his actual past is more improbable than anything that is conjectured. The past is continually evoked—the past of Daisy Fay's Louisville house, its porch "bright with the bought luxury of star-shine" (p. 114), its rooms romantic and mysterious and "redolent of this year's shining motor-cars and of dances whose flowers were scarcely withered" (p. 113); the past of a North Dakota farm boy who cannot recognize himself as the son of his parents; the past of James Gatz along the mudflats of Lake Superior, where Jay Gatsby is conceived from the fervid brain of young Gatz; the past of two autumns in Louisville, one in which Gatsby is "a penniless young man without a past" (p. 113) and a second in which he revisits "the past" he has lost and is to lose again in his strange house at West Egg, which at the end is ghostly with the past.

The consciousness of time is also heightened, in another way, by Fitzgerald's fragmented arrangement of it in his narrative. Carraway comes East in the spring of 1922 to find "great bursts of leaves growing on the trees, just as things grow in fast movies" (p. 5), and already time seems accelerated and dreamlike, like Gatsby's own time sense. By the first scene at the Plaza Hotel, the forward movement of time is interrupted by a brief change of narrators, and a dropping back in time, as Jordan Baker relates the events of October 1917, when she witnessed a fragment of the affair between Daisy and Gatsby. After this first, sudden revelation of the past, the novel proceeds forward again through the reunion of Gatsby and Daisy; but immediately after this emotional climax is reached, the narrative loops back in time to the youth who was James Gatz, and his joining Cody aboard the *Tuolomee*, a flashback that reveals the first glimpse of Gatsby's past before meeting Daisy and adds a new dimension to the reunion scene just witnessed. The narrative then moves forward to the party at Gatsby's that Tom and Daisy attend and that Daisy does not enjoy. In its aftermath, late that evening, there is another flashback, this time to Louisville on an autumn night when Daisy becomes the embodiment of Gatsby's naive dream, a revelation of the intensity of Gatsby's original affair that comes poignantly at the moment when Daisy is beginning to slip away from Gatsby again.[6]

After this, the novel continues forward to the death of Myrtle, but late the same night at Gatsby's now "ghostly" mansion, the narrative fades back once more, into the past of Gatsby's first meeting with Daisy, and of her house, with its romantic intimations; by dawn the flashback moves forward to Gatsby's revisiting Louisville an autumn later, after Daisy's marriage to Tom Buchanan, its sense of aftermath complementing the mood of aftermath of chapter 8 itself. In the final chapter, there are no further flashbacks, but Fitzgerald uses the device of recall in a different way, by bringing forward figures who are like ghosts of Gatsby's past—Wolfsheim, Owl Eyes, and most of all Henry Gatz of North Dakota, whose resurrected list of Gatsby's boyhood resolves leads further back into Gatsby's past than anything yet has, to focus attention on the American-dream origins of Gatsby and his illusion. Fitzgerald's handling of time may deservedly be called masterful; time broken up and scattered through the work has been used in *every* instance with maximum aesthetic effect, so that a richer texture is achieved than might have been thought possible in a work so brief. At the same time, Fitzgerald uses time to dramatize and comple-- ment his theme, by having the novel proceed forward by simul-taneously moving further and further back into the past, to the ultimate sources of illusion.

Complementing the strategic importance of time in the novel is the sense of movement, of continual agitated motion, that comes ultimately to characterize the world Fitzgerald has imagined. There are many incidents occurring in the later part of the work, but they alone do not account for the sense of continual movement that is felt. That impression is reinforced partly through Fitzgerald's use of the miniaturized effect. This effect may be seen in Gatsby's first party, where a large orchestra plays Tostoff's "Jazz History of the World," an improvisational or "tossed-off" scrambling of time and experience in which the medium of existence is motion. Although a small detail, it suggests a vastness of experience, and in this way is like the guest list at the beginning of chapter 4.[7] The guest list is not quite two pages long, and yet it creates the illusion of a large canvas, of many characters, of a large excitement and mingling.

The nature of the guests' heterogeneous lives, called a "short cut from nothing to nothing" (p. 82), has been evoked partly through their names. Some, strangely, have the names of ani-mals—the Leeches, Francis Bull, Edgar Beaver, Webster Civet, James B. Ferret, Cecil Roebuck. Some have the names of fish—Beluga, and the Hammerheads; or have names with fishy associations—the Fishguards, and S. B. Whitebait. One has the name of a water plant—George Duckweed; two the names of flowers —Ernest Lilly and Newton Orchid; one that of an herb used in salads—Clarence Endive. Two others have the names of trees— the Hornbeams and Henry L. Palmetto; and one couple the name of a metal—the Chromes. Animal, vegetable, and mineral, fish and flesh, the guests, in their names, take in the world. With a strange foreshortened effect that their names produce, they also suggest the bizarre nature of the "real."

In a miniaturized way, Fitzgerald has been able to suggest cacophony, oddity, and personal indistinctness in his guests. Some have names that indicate waste—Eckhaust and Swett; or denote rude sounds and facial expressions—S. W. Belcher and the Smirks. There are harshly blunt names like Maurice A. Flink; and mellifluous, epicene names like Russell Betty. There is frequently an element of incongruity in their names—as in the name of Faustina O'Brien, which combines, unexpectedly, the romantic and remote with the near at hand and mundane. The Catlips have a name evoking an image so impossible to imagine that its effect is almost surreal. The name of Claudia Hip indicates a part of the anatomy, and suggests an exaggerated importance of this part rather than the whole. The Blackbucks have a name suggesting social outcasts, and yet, disconcertingly, are actually the most blatant snobs present, people who "flipped up their noses like goats at whosoever came near" (p. 47). The Blackbucks are pictured with a kind of blurring effect, since they are all indistinguishable from one another; and this idea—the diminishment of individual identity—is noticed also in Benny McClenahan, who comes to Gatsby's parties with four different girls, with each separately, but all looking alike, and all named after either flowers or months. "Claudia Hip . . . came with a man reputed to be her chauffeur and a prince of something, whom we called Duke" (p. 49). Duke only in name, possibly a prince, but reputedly a chauffeur—his identity is incredibly unclear.

If some of the guests have been mocked by their animal names or their resemblance to animals (implying their lack of fully human dimension), the names of others involve a diminishment of stature through association with greater, more strongly directed, or heroic, lives of the past—the Willie Voltaires, Newton Orchid, the Stonewall Jackson Abrams, and Mrs. Ulysses Swett. A lack of stature in the guests has also been evoked in their personal histories, their pasts or futures, which seem to be out of control, or to be subject to violent dislocations. There is "Edgar Beaver, whose hair, they say, turned cotton-white one winter afternoon for no good reason at all" (p. 47); Doctor Webster Civet, "who was drowned last summer up in Maine" (p. 47); and "young Brewer, who had his nose shot off in the war" (p. 48). Ripley Snell was at Gatsby's "three days before he went to the penitentiary so drunk out on the gravel drive that Mrs. Ulysses Swett's automobile ran over his right hand" (p. 47).

A loss of outline is emphasized further by the guests' diverse backgrounds; by the effect with which they seem scrambled together incongruously. There is a large proportion of new immigrant groups—Irish and Jews and Italians ("The Bembergs and G. Earl Muldoon, brother to that Muldoon who afterwards strangled his wife. Da Fontano the promoter came there" [p. 48]); and they mingle with others who appear to have social register names—the Chrysties, and the De Jongs. The Backhyssons and the Dennickers of New York associate with the Corrigans and the Kellehers and the Scullys. "Rot-Gut" Ferret is probably a bootlegger, but he mixes with Gulick, the state senator. Gulick mingles, too, with Beluga, the tobacco importer, and "Beluga's girls," and they with people from the New York theater—Gus Waize and Horace O'Donavan and Lester Myer. There are also some film people—Arthur McCarty and Don S. Schwartze (the son), and Newton Orchid, who controls Films Par Excellence, which in *The Beautiful and Damned* had been the company served by Joseph Bloeckman.

This coincidence is in itself revealing, for it is a reminder of the preoccupation in that novel with social mobility. The names of those who came to Gatsby's are recorded by Carraway on an old timetable, on which is noted: "This schedule in effect July 5th, 1922" (p. 47), and the date is undoubtedly significant, coming as it does on the day following Independence Day, when the American democracy was born. For this guest list is nothing if not a satire of democracy—of a preposterous mingling, and with it a blurring and loss of identity.

The "Jazz History of the World" and the guest list evoke a social background where movement, mingling, and commotion are a norm, but Fitzgerald has affected the reader's reaction to the society he depicts in another suggestive way also, through the mobile backgrounds of his chief characters. The Buchanans, for example, are married in Louisville, honeymoon for several months in the South Seas, and then in California, move on to France, and then to Chicago, before coming East. Carraway grows up in the Midwest, attends college in the East, returns to the Midwest, and later migrates east, to settle on the Island, before returning west again. Gatsby was once James Gatz, his boyhood spent on a midwestern farm, before he becomes a drifter in Michigan, meets Dan Cody, and circles the continent aboard Cody's yacht. During the war, he is stationed near Louisville, is then in combat overseas, and later still attends Oxford for a time, before coming to New York, where he meets Meyer Wolfsheim and acquires a mansion on the Island. The continual changes of address, and shiftings about, of the Buchanans and Gatsby and the others are indicative of their restless, mobile society, which their personal backgrounds help to characterize.

The unsettled and restless nature of their society has been emphasized further by the attention that is called to vehicles throughout the novel—hydroplanes, sailboats, yachts, ocean liners, commuter and continental trains, but particularly automobiles. Many of the characters, in fact, are closely identified with their cars—like Gatsby, associated with flight, who has a car with fenders spread like wings. Carraway, in character, has merely an unassuming old model Dodge, and he is less often a driver himself than a passenger in the cars of others, riding with Gatsby, Buchanan, and Jordan Baker. In chapter 7 there is an exchange of cars resulting in mistaken identities, as the main characters pass through the valley of ashes to reach New York, and then cross it again on their way back to East Egg. Ironically, it is in the valley of ashes, the nadir of hope, that the fatal accident occurs, leaving Myrtle on the highway, in the grotesque imagery of a martyr, *kneeling in her own blood*, and setting in motion the fatalities that follow.

The circumstances leading to Myrtle's death involve a complicated set of coincidences, but the accident escapes seeming too grossly coincidental by the many previous references to injury and accident in the work. The list of guests at Gatsby's party reads like a catalogue of mishap and disfigurement and includes at least two instances of people maimed or killed by vehicles. More particularly, the principal characters themselves are implicated in accidents or near accidents. When Tom and Carraway, at the beginning, visit Wilson's garage, they notice inside "the dust-covered wreck of a Ford" (p. 20), and later it comes out that Buchanan had been in an accident (revealing his infidelity with a chambermaid while he was on his honeymoon), in which the front wheel had been ripped off his car. Through a duplication of detail, the figure of Buchanan (who disseminates confusion) is implied, in a very muted way, in the collision that takes place on Gatsby's drive, where a long line of vehicles are backed up behind a car that has struck an abutment and lost its front wheel. Jordan Baker is a bad driver, and later she accuses Carraway of being one; and Tom and Daisy are characterized generally as people who "smashed up things and creatures and then retreated back into their money or their vast carelessness . . . and let other people clean up the mess they had made" (p. 136).

There is an unusual concern in the novel with houses, but the houses belong to a vanished past, or are inaccessible, or, as in the case of Gatsby's house, represent illusion. It is with automobiles that Fitzgerald has suggested an essential relevance to the society he treats. His use of cars contributes to an impression of externalization, of lives without internal direction, of casual accidents and wrecks as representing almost a norm. There is a logic, therefore, that the tragedies of the novel should be precipitated by the auto accident in the valley of ashes and that Myrtle Wilson should die as brutally and impersonally as she does, struck down and left to die on the highway, like a dog.

The impression of restless movement and casual wrecks comments on the society in the novel, but that society is revealed most deeply in Fitzgerald's depiction of his characters. His characterizations are an important dimension of the novel's art. It is through the eyes of Nick Carraway, the narrator, that the other characters are observed, and as a marginal participant they are also measured by him. He is, in particular, a character double of Gatsby,[8] having in his own life many parallels with Gatsby's experience. Both grew up in the Midwest, where they have their "winter dreams," before coming East to settle on Long Island, and deal—in different ways—in "bonds." They are neighbors who live in adjoining houses, one vast and overshadowing, the other small and sensible; and they both come into contact with the Buchanans' set at East Egg and have an affair with a young woman of that set during the same summer. By the end of the summer Carraway's illusions are shattered, along with Gatsby's greater ones. Sane and moderate, Carraway is a continuing reminder of Gatsby's aberrancy, but in his modest stature—his inhibitions and lack of boldness—he is also a reminder of Gatsby's heroic size.

At the same time, in his normative voice, he acts as a critic of the Buchanans—from the moment they appear, until he repudiates them formally at the end. At the opening, Carraway remembers the words of his father: "Whenever you feel like criticizing any one . . . just remember that all people in this world haven't had the advantages you've had" (p. 3). The question of advantages and "fundamental decencies," of background and class, is relevant to the novel, but as East Egg reveals, social advantages and fundamental decencies do not mean the same thing. The Buchanans express, in a refracted and concentrated way, at least one aspect of the very rich; and they are in particular closely identified with the leisured, poloplaying rich class of Long Island, a class that held a peculiar fascination for Fitzgerald, in its special attitudes and reactions to life, and upon which he has commented astringently in *The Great Gatsby*.

In the opening chapter Fitzgerald indicates not only that the Buchanans and Jordan Baker are wealthy, but also that they have been molded by the social and economic class to which they belong. Buchanan is not complicated; he is seen in the clear outline of a few characteristics—his arrogance and intimidating physical strength. The relation of his arrogance to his social background is implied in the opening scene when Carraway remarks: "Wedging his tense arm imperatively under mine, Tom Buchanan compelled me from the room as though he were moving a checker to another square" (p. 10). That Buchanan regards other people as counters to be moved about at his will (in the original manuscript, "checker" had read "chess pawn") is a comment upon his assumptions of class.

Buchanan represents money, and therefore power, but in his own case it is power that is not put to any reasoned use. Almost anyone who has read *The Great Gatsby* will remember Fitzgerald's physical description of Buchanan—of his "cruel body" (p. 7) and "the great pack of muscle shifting when his shoulder moved under his thin coat" (p. 7). He had been one of the most powerful ends who ever played football at Yale, and it seems as if he still longs wistfully for the "dramatic turbulence of some irrecoverable football game" (p. 7). That Buchanan has not developed beyond the stage of the collegiate gridiron is made clear in the account of his "defense" of civilization:

"Civilization's going to pieces," broke out Tom violently. "I've gotten to be a terrible pessimist about things. Have you read 'The Rise of the Colored Empires' by this man Goddard?"

"Why, no," I answered, rather surprised by his tone.

"Well, it's a fine book and everybody ought to read it. The idea is if we don't look out the white race will be utterly submerged. It's all scientific stuff; it's been proved." . . .

"The idea is that we're Nordics. I am, and you are, and you are, and—" After an infinitesimal hesitation he included Daisy with a slight nod, and she winked at me again. "—And we've produced all the things that go to make a civilization— oh, science and art, and all that. Do you see?"

There was something pathetic in his concentration. (Pp. 11–12)

Buchanan's conception of civilization as an aggressive act of putting down a rising but inferior people is a racial version of his sense of class.

What is striking about Buchanan, too, as a reflector of his set, is his restlessness. Others in the novel, including Carraway, share his restlessness to a degree, since they all belong to a restless postwar world, but it is pronounced in Buchanan and is related to his wealth. As Carraway arrives, Buchanan talks to him on his porch, "his eyes flashing about restlessly" (p. 7). Later they go into the living room, where he is described as "hovering restlessly about the room" (p. 9). His attitude, indeed, is characteristic of the social set to which the Buchanans belong. Before he goes to see them for the first time, Carraway comments: "Why they came East I don't know. They had spent a year in France for no particular reason, and then drifted here and there unrestfully wherever people played polo and were rich together" (p. 6). Jordan Baker, an intimate member of their circle, is also restless and nomadic. Carraway remembers that her "pleasing contemptuous expression" had looked out at him from "rotogravure pictures of the sporting life at Asheville and Hot Springs and Palm Beach" (p. 16). And it is not surprising to learn that while the Buchanans are in France they run into Jordan at Cannes and Deauville. One day she telephones Carraway to tell him that she is at Hampstead at that moment, but will be in Southamton in the afternoon, a schedule typical of her unsettled life, a life spent to a large degree on one golf course or another.

Jordan Baker is not characterized in great detail, but there are a few lines of description about her that are very suggestive. Fitzgerald remarks, for example, that she "wore her evening-dress, all her dresses, like sports clothes—there was a jauntiness about her movements as if she had first learned to walk upon golf courses on clean, crisp mornings" (p. 39). Elsewhere, she is described as a "slender, small-breasted girl, with an erect carriage, which was accentuated by throwing her body back at the shoulders like a young cadet" (p. 10). Her appearance and manner have, in fact, much to do with her money. In her apparently perpetual youth and "jauntiness," there is no suggestion that she has ever had to make commitments, or to shoulder any burdens. The closest she comes to a commitment is in her golf involvement; but her identification with this sport (compare Tom's identification with the leisure-class sport of polo, another instance of character doubling) implies more than anything else a privileged aloofness from life. Jordan can always look like a "young cadet" (training herself in aloofness) because her wealth acts as insulation, keeps life from touching her deeply; but at the same time it is because she is insulated from life that she has not achieved any large development as a human being. There is about her a quality of incompleteness, implied even in her sexually neutral name Jordan. With the great exemptions money gives her, she is denied moral growth, which comes out of shared experience and emotional commitment to things outside the self.

Another of Miss Baker's traits is that she is a cheat. She leaves a borrowed car with the top down out in the rain, and then lies about having done it; and she once barely avoided a scandal, in her first golf tournament, when she changed the lay of a golf ball for a better position. "She wasn't able to endure being at a disadvantage," Carraway observes at one point, "and given this unwillingness, I suppose she had begun dealing in subterfuge when she was very young in order to keep that cool, insolent smile turned toward the world and yet satisfy the demands of her hard, jaunty body" (p. 45). Jordan is so constitutionally a cheat that she avoids "clever men," who would find her out. The money that has given her social privileges also exempts her from submitting to the rules required of everyone else.

Identified closely by the white dresses they both wear at the beginning, Jordan and Daisy also share many of the same qualities. Jordan's dishonesty, for example, is apparent in Daisy. Daisy has been evoked with an aura of romance, or is at least perceived in this way by Gatsby, but Fitzgerald makes it clear that Gatsby is deceived about her, and has judged her severely. She is of the same kind as Ella Kaye, who fleeced Dan Cody, and it is not unintentional on Fitzgerald's part that Ella Kaye's name has been rhymed with Daisy Fay's. Like Cody to Ella Kaye, Gatsby is Daisy's dupe. She leads him on—up to the point at which the situation begins to become real. At this point, in the scene at the Plaza Hotel, Fitzgerald remarks that it was suddenly "as though she realized at last what she was doing— *and as though she had never, all along, intended doing anything at all*" (p. 100, emphasis added).

More intelligent, more graceful than Tom, Daisy is nevertheless no deeper as a person; they are perfectly matched and alike. Her lack of depth is shown in an early scene in which she tells Carraway how disillusioned she feels. "The instant her voice broke off," Carraway says, "ceasing to compel my attention, my belief, I felt the basic insincerity of what she had said. It made me uneasy, as though the whole evening had been a trick of some sort to exact a contributary emotion from me. I waited, and sure enough, in a moment she looked at me with an absolute smirk on her lovely face, as if she had asserted her membership in a rather distinguished secret society to which she and Tom belonged" (p. 15). In this passage, Daisy had just lamented to Carraway that she has become disillusioned and pessimistic since her marriage to Tom, but her discouragement is no more real than Tom's "pessimism" about civilization.

The "secret society" to which Tom and Daisy belong, the money that stands behind them, has conditioned them to regard other people unequally. In the opening scene where Carraway says that Buchanan "compelled" him from the room "as though he were moving a checker to another square" (p. 19), Fitzgerald implies not only that Tom is peremptory, but also that he regards other people as counters to be moved about by him as in a merely pastime game. His doing so is exactly the nature of his relationship with Myrtle, which costs Myrtle her life. At the end, Tom says that when he gave up the flat and "saw that dam box of dog biscuits there on the sideboard, I sat down and cried like a baby" (p. 136), a maudlin remark that is a pretention of a grief he does not feel. In this respect, Daisy is exactly like Tom, because her romance with Gatsby is at bottom, an amusement—for which Gatsby will pay dearly.

Fitzgerald has carefully demonstrated the psychological effect of money on the rich, has observed them as a distinct class. *The Great Gatsby*, however, is less a genre study of the very rich than an anatomy of a society. It is one of Fitzgerald's most important aesthetic strategies in the work that he has probed the special psychologies of *each* of the spheres he treats. The Buchanans' set reflects the corrupting effect of money on values (the Buchanans believe in nothing), but Fitzgerald has also studied its effect, manifested in a different way, on the manners of the upper-middle class at West Egg. Its effect can be noticed in Gatsby's guests, who have been conditioned by money values and live for momentary things. They provide a contrast with

Gatsby and his cool vision; for if vision implies a transcendence of the self, money is identified in the work with the self merely, and thus with the volatile, impermanent world of time.

The period of Gatsby's parties has been strongly evoked, and in their opulent style, and accompanying allusions, like that of the girl mistaken for Gilda Gray's understudy, they suggest Ziegfeld, and the *Follies*. Gatsby's parties shimmer with the presence of beautiful girls, and thus have a natural affinity with Ziegfeld,[9] who boasted that he had "glorified the American girl," making her the expensive and glamorous object of man's desire. But Ziegfeld girls were creations of fantasy, "dream girls" fashioned out of money, and offering no more substantial fulfillment of the dreams Ziegfeld sold to the public than Daisy Fay is to provide Gatsby.

What one finds at Gatsby's parties, and having the closest possible relation and meaning, are money, girls, and dreams. At the scene of the first party, Carraway remarks: "I was immediately struck by the number of young Englishmen dotted about; all well dressed, all looking a little hungry, and all talking in low, earnest voices to solid and prosperous Americans. I was sure that they were selling something: bonds or insurance or automobiles. They were at least agonizingly aware of the easy money in the vicinity and convinced that it was theirs for a few words in the right key" (p. 33). Without a doubt, the hungry Englishmen are right; money is everywhere around them. Da Fontano, "the promoter," Ed Legros, and Ferret go ot Gatsby's to gamble, and when Ferret is "cleaned out" he wanders out into the garden, hoping for a favorable turn on the next day's stock market, another version of gambling, and part of the sense of money-flux at Gatsby's parties. Among others, there are many new-money people present from silent films and the theater, politicians, and businessmen like the "big fish" Beluga, whose importing business enables him to buy his "girls." Fitzgerald refers to a "many-colored, many-keyed commotion" (p. 79), and at the center of this commotion are girls and money:

> Laughter is easier minute by minute, spilled with prodigality, tipped out at a cheerful word. The groups change more swiftly, swell with new arrivals, dissolve and form in the same breath; already there are wanderers, confident girls who weave here and there among the stouter and more stable, become for a sharp, joyous moment the center of a group, and then, excited with triumph, glide on through the sea-change of faces and voices and colors under the continually changing light. (p. 32)

This spectacle of ephemeral glamor, highlighted by girls who have a momentary dazzle, is a comment upon Gatsby's own folly. Quickly enough this glamor dissolves into anticlimax, as in the case of the girl whose vivacity dissipates and, with tears dripping marks of mascara on her cheeks, would be able to sing "the notes on her face" (p. 40), and of the men who are forced to return their wives "lifted, kicking" (p. 41) to their automobiles. But if the parties comment on Gatsby's illusion, they also reveal his guests, the "moths" for whom the parties are a cul-de-sac. Gatsby's parties reek of money, but in Gatsby's case, it is money given away, important not in itself but for the romance that beckons beyond it. It is otherwise with his guests, who are trapped in themselves, in the momentary, and do not give but take. Klipspringer might be called the guest of guests, since he takes as much as possible and gives as little. He is a reminder of the cannibalism motif in the work; described in a way that is reminiscent of the "hungry Englishmen" who roam Gatsby's grounds on the scent of money, he is seen "wandering hungrily about the beach" (p. 69). The sense of a selfish use of others is felt as a dark shadow at Gatsby's parties, and elsewhere it is suggested in the carnivorous image of Wolfsheim's cuff buttons that are made of human molars.

At one party, after six cocktails, Miss Baedecker (who has the name, although not the nature, of a guidebook) begins screaming, and Doc Civet has to plunge her head in a pool to calm her, after which she accuses him of being no more sober than she is herself: "Your hand shakes. I wouldn't let you operate on me!" (p. 81). In a sense, they are merely two guests who have had too much to drink, and yet they are also part of a pattern in which all the guests figure and are alike, one of lost directions. Loss of direction is implied in the guest list, at first as unobtrusively as the allusion to "the young Quinns, divorced now" (p. 84), but then building through the reference to Ripley Snell, whose right hand was crushed by a car on the drive, where he had apparently crawled drunkenly, and only a few days before being sent to the penitentiary; his unspecified crime leads to one that is, in the reference to Muldoon's brother, the wife strangler, and finally to the fate of Henry Palmetto (his name denoting a mere reed), who is broken under the wheels of a Times Square subway train in the course of ending his life in the most public kind of way. The casualties of the guest list reflect the relation Fitzgerald has established between money, and the propensity to restless and aimless impulse and violence, an aspect of *The Great Gatsby* that fascinated John O'Hara and was reproduced by him in his own novels.

At a social level below the partying world of West Egg, in the lower-middle class valley of ashes, the central importance of money can also be noticed. Indeed, the presence that "broods" over it is an advertising billboard taking the form of the faded eyes of Doctor T. J. Eckleburg. "Evidently," Fitzgerald comments, "some wild wag of an oculist set them there to fatten his practice in the borough of Queens, and then sank himself down into eternal blindness" (p. 19). It is appropriate that the blind, commercial Eckleburg should loom above their garage, since all of their small dreams have been conditioned by money. In the opening chapters set in East and West Egg, there are important references to gardens, but in the valley of ashes, there are only "grotesque gardens" (p. 19) of ashes, expressing its dearth of imagination, energy, and joy.

In the Washington Heights apartment, Myrtle Wilson has lying about a book entitled *Simon Called Peter*, which was, in actual fact, a best-selling book in 1922. Written by Robert Keable, it concerned a young clergyman who went through World War I as a chaplain, and in doing so lost his faith in the church. *Simon Called Peter* is a reminder of a spiritual breakdown that has overtaken a whole world, in which Myrtle Wilson appears as a small but exemplary figure, arrayed in a spotted dress of crepe de chine by the dumping ground that is the metaphor of her life. Capable of dreaming only of dresses and gimcracks, her imagination conditioned by movie-magazine romance that leads merely to a miserable roadside death, she is the waste product of a commercial culture.

Thus, on all three social levels—represented by East Egg, West Egg, and the valley of ashes—money is the determining metaphor of existence. Fitzgerald has carefully demonstrated its peculiar effect on each of the different social spheres with which he is concerned and controlled the reader's response to the society he treats far more persuasively than he could ever have done through generalization. Even by the end of the first three chapters, in fact, Fitzgerald has already drawn attention to the destructive effect of money on each level of society, has shown its effect to be corrosive of idealism, and to operate from the highest level down to the lowest. Fitzgerald's anatomy of this society, moreover, is closely related to his mode of characterization in the novel, since his characters are rigidly defined by the social spheres to which they belong. The lower-middle class characters who gather at the Washington Heights apartment— Myrtle, Catherine, and the McKees—are all different from one another, and yet are all alike, in their dim aspirations and baseless pretensions. The East Egg set—the Buchanans and Jordan Baker—are also different from one another and yet the same, their psychologies having been molded by the same environment. In neither case is there any possibility of their developing beyond the limits of the environments that brought them into being; and in their intrinsic limitation they enhance tremendously the stature of Gatsby, who alone in the novel has been given the capacity for transcendence.

Sharp definition and contrast are part of Fitzgerald's complicated aesthetic strategies in the novel. But the art and vision of the work are also revealed by the qualities of imagination that went into shaping it. It is an imagination most particularly of poise and balance, an imagination that manages to reconcile opposing creative energies. The reconciliation of opposing energies can be noticed in the intellectual precision of the novel's outline and formal movement, which has a quality of detachment, and in the emotional warmth that suffuses the work with a romantic poignancy. It is seen in its convincingly realistic depiction of society, and yet in its dreamlike and expressionistic atmosphere. It is present in its deeply engaged and almost loving response to the aesthetic textures of the twenties, and in its powerful, overriding mood of a melancholic disenchantment. In *The Great Gatsby*, Fitzgerald accomplishes what he could not in *This Side of Paradise* and *The Beautiful and Damned*, in which his realism and his romanticism were not fully integrated. His early heroes fail, and Fitzgerald attempts to cast their failure in current literary modes—the novel of youth's initiation, the naturalistic study in which aspiration is mocked by an anti-rational world—but he is unable to give a tragic validation to their experience. Such fullness of understanding does not occur until *The Great Gatsby*, when Fitzgerald's romanticism is allowed a large expression while at the same time being disciplined by his realism. The sense of a romantic alienation from life (the 1890s theme with which Fitzgerald's early career begins) that appears in *The Great Gatsby* seems convincing, partly because Gatsby evokes a deeply felt and lyric response to life that is checked and contained by Fitzgerald's irony, and partly because his grasp upon the spiritual failure of the society he treats is so firm, is the result of a really searching observation.

The successful fusion of romance and realism in *The Great*

Gatsby is one aspect of the novel's reconciliative imagination; in another way, this imagination is revealed in the incorporation in the work of such apparently dissimilar modes of tragic myth and social satire. Social satire is a striking feature of the novel and is seen frequently in Fitzgerald's mordantly comic depiction of many of his characters. There is an acerbic wittiness in his drawing of Myrtle Wilson, who has been created so that she is both a particularized individual and yet so much an embodiment of the mass mind that she has no individuality at all. It is part of her pitifulness that she should always be striving to rise above the common, and yet even while doing so should exemplify what commonness is. In the apartment scene, her conversation has a quality of banality that is almost unpredictable in its preposterousness, as when she refers to the earth-bound Mrs. Eberhardt, who "goes around looking at people's feet in their own homes" (p. 25). No one could have foretold such a social being as Mrs. Eberhardt, and yet once brought forward she has a tremendous plausibility.

Although her social better, Tom Buchanan has a natural affinity with Myrtle because his instincts are as rudimentary as hers. At one point Tom is described as he appears in a doorway and "blocked out its space with his thick body" (p. 88), an image that is identical to the one of Myrtle as she first appears in the novel. And he, too, is always verging on the preposterous, as when, in the Plaza Hotel scene, he condemns Gatsby as an adulterer, tapping "his thick fingers together like a clergyman" (p. 73), or when he attempts to think ("I read somewhere that the sun's getting hotter every year . . . pretty soon the earth's going to fall into the sun—or wait a minute . . . the sun's getting colder every year" [p. 89]). Something of the cartoon quality he has been given is conveyed in a brief impression of him at the end, as he appears in the imagery of a football player. "He was walking ahead of me along Fifth Avenue," Carraway remarks, "in his alert, aggressive way, his hands out a little from his body as if to fight off interference, his head moving sharply here and there, adapting itself to his restless eyes" (p. 135).

A similar comic virtuosity can be seen in Fitzgerald's sketching of Meyer Wolfsheim, who is first seen in the Times Square café, his "tiny eyes" (p. 53) straining to see in the dim light. His initial associations—and they are of a humorous kind—are with dim light and confusion, since his conversation with Nick and Gatsby is made up of lines of thought as between one character and another that do not connect, with mistaken impressions ("I see you're looking at my cuff buttons"—when he is not), and mistaken identities, as in Wolfsheim's confusion as to who Carraway is:

> "Four of them were electrocuted," I said, remembering.
> "Five, with Becker." His nostrils turned to me in an interested way. "I understand you're looking for a business gonnegtion."
> The juxtaposition of these two remarks was startling. Gatsby answered for me.
> "Oh, no," he exclaimed, "this isn't the man." . . .
>
> "I beg your pardon," said Mr. Wolfsheim, "I had a wrong man." (P. 54)

Wolfsheim appears only briefly in two passages of the novel, and it is thus all the more surprising that he should be so unforgettable. It is difficult to forget Wolfsheim's "tragic nose" from which fine hairs "luxuriate," his cuff buttons of human molars, the idiosyncracies of his pronunciation, and the way he fractures the English language—"when he told me he was an Oggsford I knew I could use him good" (p. 130) In the hands of a less resourceful writer, Wolfsheim might merely have been a predictable underworld stereotype; yet Fitzgerald, without forgetting the perversion of values he represents, has envisioned Wolfsheim as being profoundly comic; everything about him is surprising, and human. Most unexpectedly of all, Wolfsheim

deplores "the modern world," of which he is himself an ex-
emplar, and has the mellow sentiments of the "old school." He
has an old-fashioned regard for fellow racketeers who have
fallen under gunfire, for mothers and sisters, for young men like
Gatsby who have "fine breeding," and even, one suspects, for
Oggsford.

> "You're very polite, but I belong to another generation,"
> [Wolfsheim] announced solemnly. "You sit here and discuss
> your sports and your ladies and your—" He supplied an imag-
> inary noun with another wave of his hand. "As for me, I am
> fifty years old, and I won't impose myself on you any longer."
> As he shook hands and turned away his tragic nose was
> trembling. I wondered if I had said anything to offend him.
> "He becomes very sentimental sometimes," explained
> Gatsby. (P. 56)

The Great Gatsby alternates from light to dark like an over-
cast and then brightening autumn sky, even as it is charged
with a sense of continual movement and change. Its tone modu-
lates with surprising ease from comic lightness to a tender
sadness, and although The Great Gatsby does not have the
weight of tragedy, it does by the end face in a tragic direction.
Arthur Mizener has called The Great Gatsby a "tragic pastoral,"
and it is true that its events take place during the course of a
single summer, and that like certain Greek pastorals, it has the
nature of a lament or elegy for a dead friend. It has the nature,
too, of mythic literature, or makes sophisticated use of the
mythic mode, which exemplifies profound truths of man's universal experience. Gatsby is sometimes evoked mythopoeically,
and at the end has been evoked as a slain god, a youthful deity
of spring, or of morning light, sacrificed to the progression of
time. There is a heightened sense of Gatsby in the final view of
him, particularly in the contrast implied between Gatsby's death
and the squalid death on the highway of his fellow martyr
Myrtle Wilson. Gatsby has been shown most characteristically

at night, as in the opening chapter in which he seems mysteriously to invoke the green dock light across the night-dark water; but at the end there is an ironic reversal. Gatsby's career ends during a "cool, lovely day" (p. 115), in which he awakens to the daylight of reality, and death. In this final impression, he is adrift on the air mattress in the great marble pool. "With little ripples that were hardly the shadows of waves," Carraway remarks, "the laden mattress moved irregularly down the pool. A small gust of wind that scarcely corrugated its surface was enough to disturb its accidental course with its accidental burden. The touch of a cluster of leaves revolved it slowly, tracing, like the leg of transit, a thin red circle in the water" (p. 23). The stillness of the setting, the solitariness of Gatsby beneath the broad, azure sky, his body adrift on the water on which the trail of his blood inscribes a circle,[10] all suggest a ritualistic sacrifice. Moreover, the few leaves whose touch can now deflect Gatsby's course are a reminder not only that he is now absent of purpose and will, but also of how great his purpose and will had once been.

Gatsby's mythic stature puzzled some of Fitzgerald's contemporaries, who felt that he had not drawn Gatsby realistically enough. When *The Great Gatsby* was first published, for example, Mrs. Wharton wrote to Fitzgerald that she had been impressed by the novel, but that she thought Gatsby's background should have been specified more fully. Fitzgerald was right, however, in not doing so, for to have explained Gatsby's circumstances in detail would have robbed him of his mystery and stature. The nature of his connection with Wolfsheim is established in such a way (sometimes so humorously that it is, in effect, almost "laughed away") that it seems to touch him only lightly and does not stain Gatsby's imaginative identity. More recently, a critic has remarked that Fitzgerald should have specified Gatsby's emotional relationship with Daisy more fully; there is behind it, he claims, only an "emotional vacuum." But if Fitzgerald dealt with the love relationship more fully, he would have destroyed Gatsby's uniqueness, would have reduced him to being no more or less than all other men in love, whereas one is made to feel in Fitzgerald's handling of it that Gatsby's love for Daisy somehow transcends Daisy herself. It is Gatsby's Platonic conception that is always stressed, with the result that one feels that Gatsby's love for Daisy is, in an important respect, not *personal*. The reader is continually conscious of the way Gatsby overdreams reality, and in the extraordinary largeness that he has, in the way his imagination is uncorrupted by its contact with reality, Gatsby's mythic stature is confirmed.

Gatsby's mythic associations, moreover, are quite specific. The clue Fitzgerald gives to Gatsby's mythic identification is found in the name of Wolfsheim's firm, the Swastika Holding Company. The swastika is the symbol of the sun (compare Fitzgerald's use of the swastika as a sun symbol in "Absolution") in the nature religions of Aryan races, and is invariably associated with the Aryan sun-gods, Apollo and Odin. In the 1930s, the Nazis adopted the swastika as a national symbol, but it was with Odin, and his warrior entourage of Valkyries, of whom they were thinking, not Apollo. In the swastika allusion, Fitzgerald clearly has in mind the Greek god Apollo, many of whose attributes have been given to Gatsby. Apollo presided at the festivals of the gods and those of men in which the gods took part; he played the lyre (which, according to some sources, he also invented), while the muses danced around him. In a 1920s context, Gatsby has a rather comparable role, is seen against a background of festival and music, and is associated with creative energy.

Quite as importantly, Apollo was the god of eternal youth and sunlight (his epithet Phoebus indicating brilliance or radiance), attributes shared by Gatsby, called the "ecstatic patron of recurrent light" (p. 68) that the sun brings at dawn. His gardens are described as "glowing," and his imagining of Daisy is frequently gilded richly by sunlight; he is present without yet having appeared by the great flood of sunlight that pours over

Daisy's porch, as she looks out at "the fervent sun" (p. 12).
Gatsby's winged sun-car (in the manuscript, a "compact sun"),
entering the city, appears to scatter a brilliant sunburst through
half a suburb. His house is "splendid" as its windows shimmer
with sunlight, and sunlight is, again, suggested even in small
details of his appearance, such as his smile, which is characterized as being "radiant." The impression of Gatsby's heroic size
has been achieved in a number of different ways at once, has
been achieved through multiplication of effect. He is associated
closely with the moon, with night and dreams, with imagination
as it comes fully into play. At the same time, he is evoked in his
association with Apollo, the god of youth, sunlight, and spiritual
energy; and the poignancy of his death is heightened by the
subtle intimation that this Apollo figure has been defeated and
destroyed by the gathered forces of darkness.

But in addition to this enriching use of Greek myth, Fitzgerald has also drawn upon Christian myth. At the end of *The
American Adam*, R. W. B. Lewis has placed Gatsby in an
Adamic tradition in American literature, describing him as "a
self-created innocent." But Gatsby is also an Adam beguiled
and by the end fallen from his paradise into the world; his
garden becomes an Eden in ruins, and at this point Fitzgerald's
phrasing indicates unmistakably a fall into a lower and hitherto
unfamiliar world. Fitzgerald comments that on his last day of
life Gatsby "must have looked up at an unfamiliar sky through
frightening leaves and shivered as he found what a grotesque
thing a rose is and how raw the sunlight was upon the scarcely
created grass" (p. 123).

And if there is a paradise lost, and a lower order of mortal
existence, there is also an underworld, or hell, that is the valley
of ashes. The valley of ashes is associated with death (even more
strongly in the manuscript than in the book) and in the manuscript is described as "the back alleyway of Hell." In a discreet
way, the valley of ashes has been pictured in the imagery of
Dante's Inferno. Called "dismal" and "desolate," it is "bounded

on one side by a small foul river" (p. 19), a version of the river Styx. Carraway's ferryman into this underworld, where all hope must be left behind, is Tom Buchanan, who is allied in the work with darkness and confusion. When Wilson first sees Buchanan and Carraway "a damp gleam of hope sprang into his light blue eyes" (p. 20), but that hope is only momentary, for there is no hope here. More than once Wilson is described as a gray phantom or ghost, rather than as a living being. When Myrtle says that "he doesn't know he's alive" (p. 21), she could not be more correct, for he, like Myrtle herself, does not possess the substance of life, is inwardly dead. At one point he is shown "straining" at the gas pumps, later as looking sick and pale, and finally as writhing with pain and calling out in a "hollow" wail.

Myrtle is hollow, too, or rather is "metallic," like the ring of the telephone with which she is first identified, and the automobile wreckage she comes to resemble in the weird, final image of her in the Wilson garage, when Fitzgerald remarks that "Myrtle Wilson's body, wrapped in a blanket, and then in another blanket, as though she suffered from a chill in the hot night, lay on a work-table by the wall" (p. 105). Wilson, her fellow sufferer in torment, provides the chorus of wailing and lamentation of the damned:

And he gave out incessantly his high, horrible call:
"Oh, my Ga-od! Oh, my Ga-od, Oh, Ga-od! Oh, my Ga-od!"
(P. 106)

But the God he cries out to is absent from the world, or rather is present as Doctor Eckleburg, whose blindness, like Wilson's torment, is called "eternal." Wilson's only companion in this scene is his neighbor Michaelis, whose name comes from Michael, the archangel who was man's "heavenly protector." But this version of St. Michael is merely a Greek immigrant who owns "a coffee-joint" in a dark world, "an all-night restaurant approached by a trail of ashes" (p. 20). And as a heavenly protector, he is singularly ineffectual. He can only say: "Have you got a church . . . George? . . . You ought to have a church, George" (p. 120), as Wilson continues to call out, strangely, toward the billboard eyes of Doctor Eckleburg.

But in addition to this use of Christian myth, which deepens the suggestion of the Wilsons as belonging to a dark and fallen world, Fitzgerald has also anchored *The Great Gatsby* in national myth. Lionel Trilling, among others, has commented on Gatsby as an embodiment of the American dream. "For Gatsby," he observes, "divided between power and dream, comes inevitably to stand for American itself. Ours is the only nation that prides itself upon a dream, and gives its name to one, 'the American dream.' We are told that 'the truth was that Jay Gatsby of West Egg, Long Island sprang from his Platonic conception of himself,' . . . Clearly it is Fitzgerald's intention that our mind should turn to the thought of the nation that has sprung from its 'Platonic conception' of itself. To the world it is anomalous in America, just as in the novel it is anomalous in Gatsby, that so much raw power should be haunted by envisioned romance. Yet in that anomaly lies, for good and bad, much of the truth of our national life, as, at the present moment we think about it."[11]

As mythic analogue of America, however, Gatsby is a disturbing figure, since the dream he serves is so impotent before the America of present fact. Gatsby is the only character who still believes in the American dream, and he is first alienated radically and then destroyed. The America Fitzgerald envisions has so little cultural coherence that money only is of any matter. In this respect, Fitzgerald moves far beyond Mrs. Wharton's drawing-room novels, in which New York society is in transition, to a vision of disorder that prepares for the contemporary novel of an existentially senseless world. This vision is the "modern" note of *The Great Gatsby*, the idea beneath the lightness and delicacy of the work that Fitzgerald has grasped with such assurance and force.

The society depicted in *The Great Gatsby* has been shown in the separate social spheres of East and West Egg, and the valley of ashes; but there is another world coexisting in the work that also has an interest and relevance, New York City. New York has not been pictured as fully as its suburbs, but it is always a looming presence in the background, and several scenes are set there. In an essay entitled "My Lost City" (1932),[12] Fitzgerald was later to write of New York and of what it had once meant to him on his first discovery of it. He describes it in the essay as "the tall white city," and even calls to it: "O glittering and white." He speaks of it as "wrapped cool in its mystery and promise" and of its having "all the irridescence of the beginning of the world." *It is when he is driving with Gatsby* that Carraway perceives New York as being "wondrous" and "white." Yet note, also, the line that immediately follows: "A dead man passed us in a hearse heaped with blooms," which repudiates this "vision" of the city and looks ahead to Gatsby's being borne to his grave in a "motor hearse, horribly black and wet."

Fitzgerald has very clearly not depicted a New York whose glamour offers fulfillment in fact; indeed, he has evoked its promise as being purely illusory. When Carraway, Buchanan, and Myrtle Wilson enter the city together, almost the first person they encounter, selling dogs from a basket, is "a gray old man who bore an absurd resemblance to John D. Rockefeller" (p. 22). A swindler on a small scale and characterized by the ominous color "gray," he comments on the city. The dogs he sells are vastly overpriced and do not have the pedigree he claims, and in a sense he is a microbic version of the greater (moral) swindlers, the Rockefellers and Morgans. For the gleaming metropolis (in the manuscript, "the tall, incandescent city") is, above all else, identified with money. It is in New York that Tom Buchanan's upper-class friend Walter Chase becomes involved with "Wolfsheim's crowd"; that Gatsby, just out of the army, meets Wolfsheim in Winebrinner's poolroom at Forty-third Street, and is soon buying a palace on Long Island,

and doing a "favor" for the police commissioner; that even the World Series is rigged; that Rosy Rosenthal, at the entrance of the old Metropole, is shot "three times in the full belly" (p. 54); that Tom Buchanan makes purchases in six figures at jewelry establishments on Fifth Avenue, while Mrs. Eberhardt looks at people's feet; that Wolfsheim raises his hand "in a sort of benediction" (p. 55) over Times Square, the crossroads of democracy; that ghetto immigrants stare forsakenly from funeral processions at the "new world," the second chance, of which they have dreamed. It is money, in its raw power and destructive potential, for which New York stands. At the beginning, Fitzgerald compares Gatsby to "one of those intricate machines that register earthquakes ten thousand miles away" (p. 4), and it can be said, too, that Fitzgerald's imagining of New York City is an act of prophecy, registering the "earthquake" of an emerging age of confusion. It is a prophecy, moreover, that has been borne out in scores of contemporary novels (such as Saul Bellow's *Seize the Day* and Edward Lewis Wallant's *The Pawnbroker*), in which New York is the setting of experience whose theme is life's horror. It might be said, almost as a point of summation, that New York focuses the novel's reconciliative imagination, its balancing of opposing energies—its lyric vision and the nightmare that erupts from it. In *The Great Gatsby*, as Gertrude Stein once admiringly said, Fitzgerald creates the "contemporary world."[13]

4

Conclusion: *The Great Gatsby* and the Twenties

With its large assimilation of the twenties era, *The Great Gatsby* also gives that era historical definition. Near the end of the novel, Carraway searches in Gatsby's desk for the names of relatives, or other information revealing his origins; he finds nothing, notices only, above the desk, the picture of Dan Cody, "a token of forgotten violence, staring down from the wall" (p. 125). When James Gatz comes across Cody's yacht in a Michigan bay, Fitzgerald remarks that it represented all the beauty and glamour in the world" (p. 76); and it is exactly at this moment that Gatz becomes Jay Gatsby. In the same passage, however, and more ominously, Fitzgerald refers to Cody's "hard, empty face" (p. 76) and his life as a "pioneer debauchee" (p. 76). Cody acquired his wealth at the end of a long trail that led through the gold country of the Yukon and the Nevada silver fields. He is a token of forgotten violence not only in the brothels and saloons he knew, but in the money-oriented dream he followed. More specifically, he is associated with the frontier experience itself, an association reinforced by his name, which links him with William Cody, "Buffalo Bill," the famous scout and Indian fighter, who toured the East and Europe for twenty years with his exhibition of frontier life. When Gatsby's father appears at West Egg, he produces a keepsake of Gatsby's youth, a ragged copy of *Hopalong Cassidy* on which young Gatsby had inscribed his resolves connected with boyhood ambition; and the keepsake, too, has a frontier or Western connotation. In this same Western tradition, moreover, is James J. Hill, with whom Henry C. Gatz (the unsuccessful farm person with the beautifully built-up name) compares his son "if he'd of lived"; for Hill's career was a real-life fulfillment of American folklore, of the young man who goes west and makes his fortune. A poor boy, employed in a country store, Hill traveled out West, working at times as a clerk, until he began to become successful. Based in St. Paul–Minneapolis, he gained controlling interest in the Great Northern Railway Company and became a financier of national prominence. The Cody-Hill associations in the novel illustrate how the social cult of success, which gripped the American popular mind,[1] had its source in the frontier vision; a vision that, expansive and optimistic, was contradicted by the frontier experience itself, with its harsh brutalization of values.

In associating Gatsby's experience with the frontier experience, Fitzgerald identifies the source of American social values in the twenties, which Gatsby's career illustrates. In this respect, *The Great Gatsby* has a very close affinity with other writing of the early twenties period, particularly with Van Wyck Brooks's critical study *The Ordeal of Mark Twain* (1920), which Fitzgerald had read with considerable interest, having underlined and annotated his copy of the book extensively.[2] *The Ordeal of Mark Twain*, which analyzes the frontier as perhaps the most formative stage of American cultural values, is not disinterested as a work of criticism; its argument is biased, its tone frequently rhetorical. Yet it is an arresting study, which mounts a sweeping indictment of the "puritanic catchpenny opportunism of American civilization" that Brooks feels has worked against American writers of promise. Twain is Brooks's great case in point, the case of literary genius arrested and thwarted by the frontier culture out of which he came and by the Gilded Age in which he wrote. Brooks's depiction of the frontier has such relevance that I would like to quote from it at some length:

> What a world it was, that little world into which Mark Twain was born! It was drab, it was tragic. In *Huckleberry Finn* and *Tom Sawyer*, we see it in the color of rose; and besides, we see there only a later phase of it, after Mark Twain's family had settled in Hannibal, on the Mississippi. He was five at that time: his eyes had opened on such a scene as we find in the early pages of *The Gilded Age*. That weary, discouraged father, struggling against conditions amid which as he says, a man can do nothing but rot away, the kind, worn, wan, desperately optimistic, fanatically energetic mother, those ragged, wretched little children, sprawling on the floor, "sopping corn-bread in some gravy left in the bottom of a frying pan"—it is the epic not only of Mark Twain's infancy but of a whole phase of American civilization. How many books have been published of late years letting us behind the scenes of the glamorous myth of pioneering! There is E. W. Howe's *Story of a Country Town.* . . . Howe, who is almost painfully honest, tells us in so many words that in all his early days he never saw a woman who was not stunted from hard labor or undernourishment. . . . Think of those villages Mark Twain himself has pictured for us, with their shabby, unpainted shacks, dropping with decay, the broken fences, the litter of rusty cans, the mud, the weeds, the dirt! Human nature was scarcely responsible for this debris of a too unequal combat with circumstances, nor could human nature rise very far above it. . . . The gods of Greece would have gone unwashed and turned gray at forty and lost their digestion and neglected their children if they had been pioneers; Apollo himself would have lapsed into an irritable silence.[3]

Brooks's point, however, is not merely that conditions on the frontier were straitened and that it offered little encouragement for culture. His argument is that it opposed culture in its essence—the critical spirit and defined individuality that support the creative life. It demanded a uniformity of manners and opinion, an adherence to the single ideal of material success. Brooks, furthermore, explains the Gilded Age, which he calls an era of "industrial pioneering," as the direct outgrowth of the western pioneering experience:

> We cannot understand this mood, this creed, this morality unless we realize that the business men of the generation after the Civil War were, essentially, still pioneers and that all their habits of thought were the fruits of the experience of pioneering. The whole country was, in fact, engaged in a vast crusade that required an absolute homogeneity of feeling, almost every American family had some sort of stake in the West and acquiesced naturally, therefore, in that worship of success, that instinctive belief that there was something sacred in the pursuit of wealth without which the pioneers themselves could hardly have survived. . . . What kept them up if it was not the hope, hardly in a competence, but of great wealth? Faith in the possibility of a lucky strike, the fact that immeasurable riches lay before some of them at least, that the mountains were full of gold and the lands of oil, that great cities were certainly destined to rise up some day in the wilderness, that these fertile territories, these great rivers, these rich forests lay there brimming over with fortune for a race to come—that vision was ever in their minds. . . . Private enterprise became for the pioneer a sort of obligation to the society of the future. . . . To the pioneer, in short, private and public interest were identical and the worship of success was a social cult.[4]

The pioneers submitted to and at the same time propagated the "myth" of pioneering. They stood as a collective block against anything that "attacked the idea of success, that made the country seem unattractive or the future uncertain." But if individually, and in their collective experience, they threw a veil of romance over their pioneering, what was its essential reality?

Brooks answers by quoting from Twain's own factual account, in *Roughing It*, of Virginia City:

> Money was plenty as dust. . . . There were military companies, fire companies, brass bands, banks, hotels, theatres, "hurdy-gurdy houses," wide-open gambling palaces, political pow-wows, civic processions, street fights, murders, inquests, riots, a whiskey mill every fifteen steps, a dozen breweries, and half a dozen jails and station houses in full operation, and some talk of building a church! . . . The great "Comstock Lode" stretched its opulent length straight through the town from North to South, and every mine on it was in diligent process of development.[5]

Of Twain's description, Brooks comments:

> In becoming pioneers they had, as Mr. Paine says, to accept a common mould; they were obliged to surrender their individuality, to conceal their differences and their personal pretensions under the rough good fellowship that found expression mainly in the nervously and emotionally devastating terms of the saloon, the brothel, and the gambling-hell. Mark Twain has described for us the "gallant host" which peopled this hectic scene; that array of "erect, bright-eyed, quick-moving, strong-handed young giants—the very pick and choice of the world's glorious ones." Where are they now? he asks in *Roughing It.* "Scattered to the ends of the earth, or prematurely aged or decrepit—or shot or stabbed in street affrays— or dead of disappointed hopes and broken hearts—all gone, or nearly all, victims devoted upon the altar of the golden calf." We could not have a more conclusive proof of the atrophying effects upon human nature which this old Nevada life entailed.[6]

In locating the source of the American worship of success and riches in the frontier experience, Fitzgerald has, and probably not by coincidence, reproduced Brooks's thesis. Gatsby is made the heir to Dan Cody, the "pioneer debauchee," and veteran of "the Nevada silver fields." Cody, indeed, comes out of the very world of Virginia City, with its brothels, saloons, and violence described by Twain in *Roughing It* and quoted by Brooks as evidence of the warping effect of money on ideals. Although different personally from Cody, Gatsby is like him in the important respect that he, too, is a dupe of this optimistic frontier vision, which involved a brutalization of values in fact.

The similar criticism of America in Brooks and Fitzgerald falls within the same five-year period, between 1920 and 1925; but it is not surprising to find Brooks's study and Fitzgerald's novel appearing in the same period if *The Great Gatsby* is seen in the context of the intellectual and literary movements in America during the early twenties. An extraordinary consciousness of America and its failing as a society permeated the post–World War I literary milieu. This preoccupation is apparent in a very pronounced form in the literary and social criticism of Mencken, and it is implicit in the mordant satire of Sinclair Lewis and Ring Lardner and in the criticism of Brooks. It was visible in a great many ways. *Civilization in the United States* (1922), a symposium of over thirty writers, each surveying a different aspect of society, reached notably pessimistic conclusions about the state of postwar America. Brooks contributed perhaps the best of the essays, "The Literary Life," in which he writes that "what immediately strikes one as one surveys the history of our literature during the last half century, is the singular impotence of its creative spirit."[7] Yet his is only one of many negative readings of the nation's life; in a similar spirit, Lewis Mumford writes on the lack of planning in American cities, George Jean Nathan on the parochialism of the New York theater, Mencken on the low caliber of men in public office. In a similar spirit, too, in his posthumous *History of a Literary Radical* (1920), Randolph Bourne writes of "the flotsam and jetsam of American life, the downward undertow of our civilization with its leering cheapness and falseness of taste, and spiritual outlook, the absence of mind and sincere feeling which we see in our slovenly towns, our vapid moving pictures, our popular novels, and in the vacuous faces of the crowds on the city street. . . . This is the cultural wreckage of our time."[8]

Writers like Brooks who were active after World War I reacted upon one another, and upon younger writers. In his office at the *Freeman*, Brooks met many of the young intellectuals who were in some degree affected by him—men like Lewis Mumford, Newton Arvin, Walter Lippmann, and Edmund Wilson; and they all, in their different ways, were critical of the money-oriented culture the 1890s gave to the 1920s. It was in this environment of attack upon American materialism that Fitzgerald came of age as a novelist, and it is not surprising that his criticism of American values in *The Great Gatsby* should reflect as much as it does the intellectual life of the twenties. In 1924 Edmund Wilson published a satire entitled "the Delegate from Great Neck,"[9] in which Brooks and Fitzgerald, sketched as diametrical opposites, hold an imaginary conversation in which each exposes the other's weakness. Scholarly, serious, preoccupied by the threat to the artist of a commercial society, Brooks is perhaps too aloof from the spectacle of contemporary life to appreciate the material it offers the creative writer. Wilson's Fitzgerald, on the other hand, is too involved personally in the spectacle to realize fully its threat to him as a serious writer. "I must confess," Wilson's version of Fitzgerald says, "that I get a big kick out of all the glittering expensive things." Yet even as this satire was being written, Fitzgerald was at work on *The Great Gatsby*, in which his criticism of American worship of success carried the thrust of Brooks's own thought. It did so with the difference that Fitzgerald went further than Brooks who, after all, hoped for a cultural reconstruction, while Fitzgerald's imagining of America left no room for amelioration or hope.

The Great Gatsby emerges out of a quite definite intellectual-literary milieu, and expresses its concerns. But the novel is relevant to that time, too, in ways Fitzgerald could not have fore-seen, since it appeared in the same year as Dreiser's *An American Tragedy* and Dos Passos's *Manhattan Transfer*, which are, like *The Great Gatsby*, about the end of the American dream. Fitz-gerald did not know of the other works until they were pub-lished, and there is no question of influence on any side; but the appearance of them all at once, in 1925, is a reminder of the prescience of Fitzgerald's conception and theme. Dreiser's huge work is unlike Fitzgerald's in terms of volume, but their data are in many ways similar. Their heroes are young men of humble origins who make their way upward in the world, in different degrees, and come into contact with the rich, most particularly with a rich girl. They feel that these rich girls are "above" them, but aspire to possess them, and in the course of their attempting to do so both are destroyed. The conception of both heroes has been conditioned by the Horatio Alger folklore of "making good," of succeeding in America, and both novels end with a death, and a denial of the success dream the youthful heroes had believed to be realizable. There are further similarities also. The heroes have illusions about the rich girls and their worlds; neither Daisy Fay nor Sondra Finchley has very much depth and neither offers any fulfillment for the aspiring heroes, were they attainable. In both novels, in which money plays a very large and influential part, murders are committed, and the novels end with a sense of profound estrangement.

In *An American Tragedy*, Dreiser has laid out the circum-stances of his heroe's "tragedy" in massive detail, has created the upstate New York town of Lycurgus with minute authenticity, its mills and its social stratifications, its small upper-class elite and its local proletariat, its rigidities and moralistic attitudes. Griffiths' trial for murder is accounted for in a large documentary way; and all of this builds an impression of inevitability in Griffiths' fate, creates the sense that, given his inner impulses and vulnerabilities, and the conditions in which he finds him-self, he has, whatever his illusions of free will, been a pawn in a chain of occurrences over which he has little or no control. He is an "outsider" at the end, as he was at the beginning. But it is in the superb early section of the novel that Clyde Griffiths is most archetypally presented in his role as the rootless American youth, a naive searcher for a better, more fulfilling life. It is here that one sees his pathetic background, his mission-house parents, with their illusions of a guiding providence, their grinding poverty, a world from which the youth must escape, as James Gatz must escape at all costs from the bleakness of his farm community, his failed, spectral parents. Both James Gatz and Clyde Griffiths are impressionable (Gatz, of course, much more so than Griffiths) and susceptible to the attraction of girls, particularly rich girls, and their journey is outward, toward the rich girls' world. The Green-Davidson Hotel in Kansas City, where he works as a bellhop is a luxurious, alluring setting to Clyde Griffiths; it is his first real contact with money—and it is in this section that he meets with his first disaster, before his odyssey brings him east, to his final one. The course of his experience, from the Midwest to the East, is surprisingly similar to that of Gatsby, who also learns that there is no escape into fulfillment, only a brutal death awaiting him, a death that has, like Clyde Griffiths', a sacrificial quality.

The foreclosure on the American dream in *The Great Gatsby* and *An American Tragedy* and the heroes' accession to "success" that is repudiated and denied bring Fitzgerald and Dreiser into extremely close relation at this point in their careers. Both tap the same archetype of the poor boy as "outsider" that is so deeply embedded in the American imagination. John Berryman, indeed, has commented quite tellingly on the poor boy as "outsider" in *An American Tragedy*, and the kind of emotion that stands behind him, that "bright, vague longing or aspiration or *yearning* that every reader will probably recognize as Dreiser's central and characteristic emotion. This emotion is American. We remember it less broodingly, in sharper, more polished works . . . in *The Great Gatsby*. The objects vary—money and fame and love—but the clustered, helpless emotions persist without change even through their gratification—because it was the emotions and not their objects that mattered."[10] It is this kind of emotion that informs *The Great Gatsby*, that reveals Fitzgerald's immersion in an archetypal pattern of American consciousness.

Dos Passos did not possess the empathetic imagination of Dreiser or Fitzgerald, but his *Manhattan Transfer* is also concerned with the American dream turned sour; and like *The Great Gatsby*, it is focused by the New York metropolis, a culture symbol, a society in microcosm that is both intensely dynamic and extraordinarily destructive. At the opening, at the ferry station, gates "fold upwards, feet step out across the crack, men and women press through the manuresmelling wooden tunnel of the ferryhouse, crushed and jostling like apples fed down a chute into a press." Dos Passos's opening image introduces a city under great pressure, individuals who are "crushed and jostling" and by the end almost wholly dehumanized. Some of Dos Passos's early images evoke a grotesqueness of the actual —"the newborn baby squirmed in the cottonwool feebly like a knot of earthworms"; but the strangeness of the real soon expands to include what seem like hundreds of lives, which intersect without establishing a human connection. At the end, his protagonist, Jimmy Herf, leaves the city, is practically spewed out by it; sunrise finds him in the New Jersey industrial flats, walking along a cement road between dumping grounds full of smoking rubbish heaps, a wasteland image that is familiar from *The Great Gatsby.*

Dos Passos has evoked New York in the twenties with a hundred lives, while Fitzgerald has captured it with half a dozen, but in many respects it is the same city. It is a money city, and Dos Passos's characters are all depicted in one way or another in their relation to money. King Gillette has "dollarproud eyes"; James Merivale returns from the war to make his way upward, becoming president of the Bank & Trust Company; Phineas Blackhead, who owns a large house in Great Neck, has acquired a substantial amount of money, only to lose it. His case is typical, since nothing in the novel is stable. Careers are disjointed, fragmented at odd places. Joe Harland at forty-five finds himself without a job or money, and a "loser" like Bud Korpenning jumps to his death from the Brooklyn Bridge. The city forms a setting of callous indifference of human beings toward one another, seethes with frustration. Dos Passos's scenes of human encounter are all terse, compressed, jagged, unfinished; the pace of the novel is very rapid, like the velocity of Dos Passos's images, and suggests a world of time and pressure and change; but what meaningful purpose this obsessed city, this civilization, is hurrying toward is unclear. Perhaps, as some of Dos Passos's images seem to suggest, it hurries toward some final conflagration and extinction.

Manhattan Transfer begins before World War I, moves on through the war and into the twenties, but it is the postwar society that interests Dos Passos particularly and that he treats most fully. In their evocation of New York in the twenties, Dos Passos and Fitzgerald are at times on common ground. There are signs of the times in *Manhattan Transfer* that are similar to those in *The Great Gatsby*—prohibition alcohol, bootleggers (Congo Jake, who keeps reappearing, finally "succeeds" in a large way as a bootlegger, changing his name to Armand Duvall), new-money people in the theater, *Follies* girls, gossip sheets like "Town Topics" (Fitzgerald's "Town Tattle"), new cars, the craze among the rich for hydroplanes, wisps of popular tunes, thin, insubstantial as poor dreams, forgotten. It is also the era of large-scale crime, of corrupt public officials, many kinds of racketeering and swindles, violence and murder. Many of Dos Passos's characters could have attended Gatsby's parties, since their lives, too, are shortcuts from nothing to nothing. One and all, they are disfigured in some way as human beings, seem incapable of wholeness, or deeply spiritual or religious experience. Through the novel a motif keeps reappearing: "The Ten Million Dollar Success"; "Oh success . . . success . . .

what does it mean?"; "Failure, Success"; "In the empty chamber of his brain, a double word clinked like a coin: Success, Failure, Success, Failure." Success in *Manhattan Transfer* has the quality of a nightmare, and when Herf is ejected from the city at the end one feels that he is leaving behind a world of the anguished, the half-formed, the disfigured, and that the national success worship it represents has been revealed as a malignant delusion.

Dos Passos, Dreiser, and Fitzgerald approach their common subject from different sides, in works different in kind; but the shared theme itself, occurring in significant novels of the same year, is a reminder of how deeply *The Great Gatsby* is part of its moment, rather than being, as it might seem on a casual reading, the expression of a purely special sensibility. Fitzgerald is so central to the American twenties that it would be difficult to picture that time fully had he not existed. Part of his central role has to do with the style with which he responded to his immediate experience, that made him see certain aspects of the life of the twenties as having a stronger actuality than they had for his contemporaries. He named the Jazz Age and was in part a historian of its social surfaces. But *The Great Gatsby* is central to the literature of the twenties in more than surfaces; in its articulation of modern estrangement, it is in the mainstream of American realism as it emerged after World War I.

The central character in many of the postwar realistic novels is often a young man, who has been in, or has been exposed to, the war. Martin Howe in Dos Passos's *1917* enters the war to lose such belief as he had had in the purpose of the war, and all of his belief in the assumptions of patriots at home. At the end, spiritually alone, he is shown amid a scene of the dead, the dying, and the soon to die. In *Three Soldiers*, Dos Passos is less concerned with the carnage of the battlefield than with the effect of military regimentation on the individual, particularly on his hero, John Andrews, who, by the end, is headed for a long term in a military prison. But the military machine, characterized persistently in terms of inert metal, is merely a symptom of the contemporary society that stands behind it, and in later works—in *Manhattan Transfer* and the *U.S.A.* trilogy—Dos Passos depicts that society in a way that evokes its spiritual deadness. Jimmy Herf appears at various points in *Manhattan Transfer* and is present at the end, but although a focal figure he cannot really be called a hero, since he seems to have hardly more stature than the others, characters without full human dimension in a society formed wholly by money values. Dos Passos's characters are sketched more fully later in the *U.S.A.* trilogy, but they remain grotesques, figures like Margot Dowling, the film star, who is admired by millions, epitomizing their aspirations and fantasies, and is as soulless as celluloid. As Sartre has written, Dos Passos's world has a strongly existential quality, is a world in which the individual is unable to locate any meaning from without, or at the center of his society.

The sense of estrangement in John Andrews is multiplied a hundred times in Faulkner's Donald Mahon, the returning veteran in *Soldiers' Pay*. Mahon is, in fact, practically a ghoul; going blind, and all but a vegetable, his identity is formed by the war wound that scars his face. He comes back to America, to his home in the Southland, where his fellow townspeople are either unable to look at him, or peep not at him but at the "war freak" he has become to them. Grouped about him are the others, who all live in their own inner space. His clergyman father, with his mild, received, faltering belief in providence, cannot accept the fact of his son's brutal maiming and dying; the Mahon's neighbor Mrs. Burney lives with solacing illusions of her son, killed in the war, as a hero, which he was the reverse of being; Mahon's fiancée, Cecily Saunders, is a "town tease" involved with many other young men of the locality, is immersed in her own epicene body and selfish emotions; Januarius Jones hovers about like an obscene satyr, a figure of cynical lust. By the end one sees that Mahon's gruesome return home to die brings into perspective the inner despair and emptiness of all the others, who seem to search for what they cannot find.

This is the postwar world Faulkner outlines, in its lost connection with meaning. In *Sartoris*, he envisions such a world again, with a stronger regional definition, notes the return from the war of another aviator, John Sartoris, who prefers to die rather than to live. Like *Soldiers' Pay*, *Sartoris* reeks of estrangement; its characters are mindless primitives, or genteel women who bear their fragmented lives stoically, or men cut off from a meaningful tradition who suffer inner anguish.

Hemingway's early protagonists are also young men who have been exposed to the war. Later in the twenties, in *A Farewell to Arms*, Hemingway describes the war experience in graphic detail, particularly in his famous scene of the retreat from Caporetto. But in his earliest stories, the war serves largely as a background against which the inner life of the postwar world can be gauged. In his early collection of stories, *In Our Time*, short sketches of the war (and other scenes of violence and maiming) are interspersed between the stories and have the effect of photographic slides flashed onto a screen as a reminder of the nature of the world in essence. There is, for example, a paragraph-length vignette that describes the execution of six cabinet ministers in the courtyard of a hospital. They are all sick as they are brought out into the courtyard where "it rained hard" and lined up against a wall, but one is so ill with typhoid that he cannot even stand upright to be shot. "When they fired the first volley he was sitting down in the water with his head on his knees." The sketch is the more effective because there is no explanation of why they are being killed; the victims have no names, like the soldiers who fire on them; they belong to a theater of violence that is impersonal.

This miniaturized sketch appears immediately before a story called "The Battler," in which brutalization is shown at home. In "The Battler," freight hopping and tramping about, Nick Adams encounters the ex-prizefighter, Ad Francis, and his black companion Bugs, below a railway embankment. It is night, and by the light of their campfire Ad's face appears queerly formed and mutilated, putty colored, dead looking. Before long, it comes out that he has been hurt too much in the ring, has sudden personality changes in which he becomes hostile and threatening, has to be blackjacked unconscious by Bugs. The sudden change that comes over Ad Francis has a nightmarish quality, gives a frightening impression of what life has done to him. The weird change seems almost unreal, and yet is only too real, is in fact a regular occurrence accepted by Bugs as "normal." Bugs' casual acceptance of Ad's state reinforces the sense of cruelty latent in life, and the helplessness of people, including the apparently strong, to save themselves. The shock of the incident is the same one that is felt in the other stories in the collection. The themes of the stories in *In Our Time* come together later in *The Sun Also Rises*, where World War I is also a dividing line between the old and the new, chastened consciousness. Jake Barnes has been maimed, symbolically as it were, in the war; he cannot *act*, cannot dominate life, can at best endure stoically, achieve some degree of personal integrity, or have the courage and honesty to live without illusions.

In Fitzgerald's early fiction, like that of his contemporaries, a young man figures prominently. Amory Blaine and Anthony Patch both serve in the army during World War I, and Amory, supposedly, is in combat overseas; but the war itself seems remote in Fitzgerald's work. It is the postwar world that he knows, and its upper-middle-class life that he records. The novels in which Amory and Anthony appear are "apprenticeship" works in the deepest sense, since in them Fitzgerald searches for a major theme without being able to give it full expression. It is in *The Great Gatsby* that everything comes together for him, that he finds his vision. It is a vision that, like that of Hemingway, Dos Passos, and Faulkner, repudiates the old assumptions of order firmly, makes the emptiness and estrangement of the present convincing and dramatic.

In one specific respect, Fitzgerald's vision in *The Great Gatsby* is the most central to the twenties, since its darkness erupts from the exact middle of American society. Dos Passos's *Manhattan Transfer* has a leftist or Marxist orientation, and Faulkner's *Sartoris* is a study in regional or rural Southern realism. Hemingway's characters are characteristically somewhat at the edge of society, are suspicious of society, or are not fully committed to it, or are depicted at critical moments when they recognize their isolation, or must, like his bullfighters, prove their courage alone and under stress. But the darkness of the postwar world for Fitzgerald is felt at the exact social middle—and within a context of "manners." Unlike Hemingway's isolates, Fitzgerald's characters always belong to a social unit, function in a context of social differences, are socially defined. The difference of class in *The Great Gatsby* is essential to Fitzgerald's vision, a curiously dual vision, which delights in social discrimination and yet makes social order seem light-years in the past, is both classical and darkly apocalyptic.

It is the middle-class dream, the dream at the center, with which Fitzgerald deals in *The Great Gatsby*. Nick Carraway's voice is a "normal" one, suggesting a norm; it is solidly middle-class, sensitive within limits, a little complacent, even somewhat priggish. Gatsby himself comes out of the middle-class imagination. One of the great facts about him is his lack of familiarity with real wealth; when he acquires money he cannot quite believe in its reality, does not know what to do with it, converts it immediately into the material of romance, which had furnished his imagination earlier. He is nowhere with his dream, because he understands wealth only mythically; there is no fate he can embrace except estrangement and death. Gatsby's loneliness is emphasized even in the flaw of the novel's ending, the way in which Fitzgerald becomes entangled in the East versus West distinction, which he derived, apparently, from Willa Cather. At the end, Carraway returns to the West, where he can keep his moral distinctions straight. Or so he says. But there is a contradiction in terms in his return, since he has already envisioned a darkness spreading across the entire continent, including the West he returns to as sanctuary. Moreover, it is in the West, in the environs of Chicago, that the Buchanan money was made, that Gatsby was closed out of Daisy's life originally, that Daisy chose Tom. Further still, the frontier vision served first by Cody and then by Gatsby, and exploded as a cruel illusion, was a dream of the West. Carraway returns to the West not, it seems, as fact so much as admitted illusion of adolescence, which means that he, like Gatsby, has no place to go, can envision no alternatives to the nightmare he has lived through.

Hemingway's heroes may at least gird themselves for some testing moment of courage or endurance, but Fitzgerald's have no consolations, and in this respect Fitzgerald's pessimism is even more sweeping. The vision of *The Great Gatsby*, as Fitzgerald's later novel *Tender Is the Night* bears out, suggests a fiction of limited scope. Dick Diver is also undone by coming too close to the reality of money, at the end leaves his Mediterranean beach for the small factory towns of upstate New York, captured in their meanness and rigidity by Dreiser in *An American Tragedy* and by Harold Frederick in novels like *The Damnation of Theron Ware*, a return that is a virtual death. Fitzgerald's mature novels are variations of a single theme, and in this respect show the limited range of Fitzgerald's art, which lacks the possibilities of thematic expansion that can be seen in James and Faulkner.

There are impressive things, nevertheless, that Fitzgerald can do in these novels. *Tender Is the Night* has a richer social texture than *The Sun Also Rises*, which also deals with the American expatriate experience in the twenties. Hemingway's novel is more nearly perfect, but there are qualities of experience in *Tender Is the Night*, nuances of manners and of characters' psychology, that Hemingway leaves out, does not attempt even to treat, enclosed, as he is, within his own moral isolation. Most of all, *The Great Gatsby* is a work of permanence and greatness; at their best in the twenties, in *The Sun Also Rises* and in *The Sound and the Fury,* Hemingway and Faulkner produced no greater work.

In its vision of modern emptiness, *The Great Gatsby* is a key document of the twenties, so much so that had it not been written the twenties would actually seem diminished. It is as vivid today (and as "surprising") as when it was written, and has an intense life. Gatsby's vividness has been reinforced on so many different levels of myth and folklore that it is difficult to say which most controls his conception. The woodchopper's son, the young man from the provinces come to the great city, Dick Whittington, Horatio Alger—all stand in the background of his conception. But perhaps as importantly as from any other source, Gatsby comes from the fairy tale; for if the novel has, in Henry James's phrase "the imagination of disaster," it also has the imagination of enchantment. There is a sentence in the manuscript, but not included in the book, that reveals Gatsby. It occurs when he is among Daisy's circle at Louisville. "He was a nobody with an irrevealable past," Fitzgerald comments, "and under the invisible cloak of a uniform he had wandered into a palace." With its palaces and invisible cloaks, Gatsby's imagination has a fairy-tale quality. Almost instinctively, he regards Daisy Fay as a princess, a girl in a white palace, and the spell of the fairy tale, too, marks his ascendency from his mid-western farm to his own palace of a kind at West Egg. Gatsby becomes a kind of fairy-tale prince in disguise, is deprived of his princehood while retaining his princehood in essence, the consciousness of a noble inheritance, of an inner sovereignty belonging to a prince, even though he wears a shepherd's garments.

Fitzgerald refers to Long Island by name very rarely in the novel; it seems disembodied as well as real and is a region of wonder. Carraway's recall of his adolescence at the end is, too, part of the child's perception of life as wonder, as in the fairy tale. And there is a strong demarcation in the novel between good and evil; the Buchanans' world, and the Wilsons', seem somehow bewitched by evil forces, which are beyond containment or control. The evocative energies of the fairy tale help to account, I think, for the helplessness one feels before the enchanted horror of the world Fitzgerald creates in the novel, a world in which the good prince is put to death, and the dark prince reigns. Other American novelists before Fitzgerald drew from the fairy tale; Henry James did so in *The Portrait of a Lady* and other novels. But Fitzgerald is alone in the twenties in drawing from the resources of the fairy tale to create his age, to touch the depths of its irrationality, and at the same time to create one of the most memorable characters in the American fiction of the 1920s.

Since World War II there have been novels published in America that have some claims to seriousness, and yet after one has read them one can hardly remember their characters. Compare with these the power of dramatic projection in *The Great Gatsby*, the way in which Jay Gatsby lives in one's imagination, refusing to be dislodged. Such enduring life is the mark of exceptional achievement, can only be the result of a creative conception of astonishing depth and power, which *The Great Gatsby* continues to give the impression of being.

Appendix
The Manuscript Versions of
The Great Gatsby

The extant manuscripts of *The Great Gatsby*, housed at the Princeton University Library, Department of Special Collections, are now available in book form, in Matthew Bruccoli's edition of them, *"The Great Gatsby"; a facsmile of the manuscript* (1973), an extremely useful and revealing volume. What makes it revealing is that the facsimile of the manuscript is not a revised typescript as it appeared just before the novel was printed, but a compilation of handwritten manuscripts and revised galleys, belonging to different stages of the novel's composition, which together show the evolution of the work. To read through this volume is virtually to enter Fitzgerald's workshop, to see his methods of composition, the problems he faced and overcame.

As the facsimile edition shows, Fitzgerald wrote *The Great Gatsby* in longhand, writing in pencil on sheets of unlined white paper; as he finished a chapter, he turned it over to a typist and began work on the next chapter. This, however, was only the beginning of the process of composition, since he revised the manuscript again, and again in a series of galley-proof sets (a method of composition that would be prohibitively expensive today), before a final galley-proof version of the novel was ready for publication. The earliest draft of the novel has been lost, but the later handwritten drafts and galley revisions give a substantial impression of how Fitzgerald refined his conception, his characters, and his prose, as he progressed, achieving a polished version only in a later stage of revision. In his introduction, Bruccoli has been interested chiefly in identifying the point in the composition at which each of the changes occurred; he provides some explanation for important changes, but by and large generalizes rather sparingly. I would like to generalize more than Bruccoli has done, without attempting to be definitive, and to suggest how Fitzgerald's changes reveal his craftsmanship, particularly in regard to some of my earlier observations on the novel's art.

Of the many changes Fitzgerald made in the novel perhaps the most startling occurs at the end of his first manuscript chapter, where Carraway first sees Gatsby at night. In the novel, he is shown with his arms outstretched toward the dark water "in a curious way," but in the early draft of the manuscript he reaches out toward the *sky*: "I saw him stretch out both hands toward the sky in a curious way. When I looked down again he was gone, and I was left to wonder whether it was really the sky he had come to measure with the compass of those aspiring arms" (MS, p. 37). In the later version, Gatsby regards not the sky but the watery darkness, which associates him more pointedly with illusion, and the green dock light, which gives definition more specifically to his quest. But it is not this difference that is so surprising. What is surprising is what follows, the coda that is later shifted to the end of the book and is expressed in the early manuscript draft in the following way:

> The sense of being a stranger in an unfamiliar place deepened on me and as the moon rose higher the inessential houses seemed to melt away until I was aware of the old island here that flowered once for Dutch sailors' eyes. . . .

And as I sat there brooding on the old unknown world, I could feel the motion of America as it turned through the dark hours—my own blue lawn and the tall incandescent city on the water and beyond that the dark fields of the republic rolling on under the night. (MS, pp. 137-38)

The passage indicates that Fitzgerald did not begin writing with a preconceived ending, but "discovered" his effective conclusion only later. In transferring the passage to the end, he also revised it, transferring Carraway's "blue lawn" to Gatsby's "blue lawn" and relocating Carraway's meditated vision from his own to Gatsby's lawn, placing it where it should be, in the closest proximity to Gatsby. In the final chapter of the manuscript version, Fitzgerald also makes other refinements of his conception. Earlier he had referred to "two" green lights at the end of Daisy's dock, which he changes, for a more concentrated effect, to a single green light, and at the end he concludes that Gatsby believed in "the green glimmer," which he alters, memorably, to "the green light." In the same passage, "a boat against the current" is changed to "boats against the current," giving a sense of a larger, more universal experience.

Another revealing feature of the manuscripts is that Fitzgerald had some difficulty in controlling his conception of Gatsby; he did not see him quite clearly and at one point was tempted to portray him as a melancholy romantic, a conception that would have devastated the novel. He is described early in the manuscript with rather too much emphasis upon his good looks and his startling blue eyes, which are reminiscent of Rudolph Miller's in "Absolution": "He was undoubtedly one of the handsomest men I had ever seen—the dark blue eyes opening into lashes of shining jet were arresting and unforgettable" (MS, p. 53). Somewhat later, Fitzgerald again calls attention to Gatsby's eyes: "He saw me looking at him, and suddenly he smiled—his eyes damp and shining like blue oil, opened up with such brilliance that it was an embarrassing brilliance" (MS, p. 66). Both passages have been deleted, undoubtedly because Fitzgerald realized he had tried to make Gatsbys' eyes do too much work in evoking his physical presence, that he was straining an effect. There is a similar temptation to overstatement in Fitzgerald's initial sketching of the uncertainty of Gatsby's social manners: "Yet he was somehow not like a young man at all," Fitzgerald writes, "there was a tremendous dignity about him, a reticence which you could fear or respect according to your temperament but on the other hand a formality that just missed being absurd, that always trembled on the verge of absurdity until you found yourself wondering why you didn't laugh" (MS, p. 53). This passage, which tends to make Gatsby seem a bit ridiculous, was shortened to the brief comment that his formality just missed being absurd.

Certain other minor changes in Fitzgerald's conception of Gatsby were prompted by Maxwell Perkins, after reading the first manuscript draft. He wrote, for example, that he had difficulty visualizing Gatsby physically and somehow imagined him as being older than he was; and he suggested that Fitzgerald add some small touches, certain expressions that Gatsby might use, for example, that would help to give a sharper sense of him. It was at this point that Fitzgerald had Gatsby adopt the expression "old sport," an improvement over his earlier use of "old man." In addition, Perkins thought that Gatsby's background, particularly his association with Wolfsheim and the means by which he acquired his money, had not been indicated fully enough. In line with these suggestions, Fitzgerald added new touches, such as the telephone call from Slagle in Detroit and Tom Buchanan's accusation that Gatsby had been involved in the illegal sale of bonds over the counters of drug stores. In adding these details, Fitzgerald at first implied that Gatsby and Wolfsheim were involved in some way with drugs and extortion, squeezing cab drivers and down-and-outers for money, an explanation that would have withdrawn the reader's sympathy for Gatsby. The details he finally used, implicating Gatsby in bonds and bootlegging (illegal but not necessarily vicious) are not really damaging. In any case, the additions were kept to a minimum and suggest that Fitzgerald had decided to take the risk of underspecifying Gatsby, rather than of overdrawing him.

He had, however, overdrawn Gatsby at one point in the manuscript, before removing the section entirely as a false start. There are traces of a rejected conception of Gatsby in an early draft of his first party, where he is shown alone by his house, the confusion of the cars on his drive in the background. In this draft, Fitzgerald writes: "An aching emptiness seemed to flow now from the windows and great doors, endowing with sudden loneliness the figure of Gatsby" (MS, p. 63). The words "aching" emptiness and "loneliness," which tend to evoke Gatsby as a figure of pathos, are removed in revision, so that the passage reads: "A sudden emptiness seemed to flow now from the windows and the great doors, endowing with complete isolation the figure of the host." Earlier in the same scene, Fitzgerald also evokes a morose Gatsby, when Jordan Baker recalls seeing him with Daisy in Louisville. "The officer looked at Daisy while she was speaking," she remarks, "his mouth drawn down into the corners—the most unhappy looking man I had ever seen" (MS, p. 86). How different from this desolate figure is Fitzgerald's redrawing of Gatsby at this same point: "The officer looked at Daisy while she was speaking, in a way that every young girl wants to be looked at at some time, and because it seemed romantic to me I have remembered the incident ever since." A similar change can be noticed in Jordan's account at the end of her conversation with Carraway in the original, and then in the revised, version. The original version reads: "That's why Gatsby bought that house and moved down on Long Island. He told me that that was the only reason he was alive at all" (MS, p. 91). Her statement is reduced in revision to: "Gatsby bought the house so that Daisy could be just across the bay."

These early draft depictions of a morose Gatsby lead up to the passage, after the party Daisy attends with Tom, in which Gatsby reveals his unhappiness and even sings a strange little ballad he has written about "lonesome night birds" singing, a "Southern moon," and crickets droning a "single tune." Even worse, Gatsby engages in a self-pitying conversation with Carraway. " 'I haven't got anything,' he said simply, 'I thought for a while I had a lot of things, my house'—He looked at it for an instant—'and things like that. But the truth is I'm empty and I guess people feel it!' " (MS, p. 162). Daisy, in this passage, has even offered to pack her suitcase that night and go off with him, but Gatsby rejects the idea, protesting that they would be running off like theives in the night. Moreover, it is apparent that Daisy cannot fulfill his romantic longing and that his love for her has opened a kind of wound that will not heal. This section is the single really serious mistake of the manuscript, but Fitzgerald did manage to resist the temptation of using it, striking it out entirely in revision as a false start. The section illustrates, however, that at a certain point Fitzgerald was wavering in his conception of Gatsby, was, in fact, working with a double conception of him, a romantically despairing Gatsby, and an exuberant Gatsby. With the excision of this section Fitzgerald redefined his conception of Gatsby as a still unfallen innocent, a votary of the green light, obviously recognizing that the self-indulgent Gatsby he presents midway in the work was unqualified for the dominant and heroic figure he had forecast in the opening pages. Once Fitzgerald resolved this problem, he shows no further conflict in his conception of Gatsby, a conception of him as a heroic figure of illusion that is continually deepened and sharpened.

With the character of Daisy Fay, Fitzgerald had fewer problems, although by the end there were one or two that he felt he had never fully resolved. Daisy's earliest name had been Ada, then Daisy Machen (Machen was the maiden name of Zelda Fitzgerald's mother), before she became Daisy Fay, a transformation that shows how Fitzgerald's naming conception grows increasingly symbolic. Curiously, on her first appearance in chapter 1, she is not golden haired, but "the dark lovely girl" (MS, p. 14) seated beside Jordan. It is even possible that Tom's reluctance to include Daisy among their group of Nordics, in the opening scene, may have been related to Daisy's being "dark." At any rate, the comedy of that moment is no less effective after Daisy has become a blonde; for whatever reason he hesitates, the incident brings out Tom's slow-thinking obtuseness and strict exclusions.

In the original manuscript of chapter 1, Daisy is made to seem somewhat more of a flirt than she is in the final version. When she goes out on the front porch with Carraway and is alone with him, she kisses him on the mouth, and then explains: "I just wanted to kiss you because I knew you when I was young" (MS, p. 28). The scene on the porch dramatizes a shade more fully than the final version the insincerity of Daisy's avowed sadness over the sophistication she has acquired. The Buchanan house has a double nature, since its shoreward side is banked by Italian rose gardens and is bathed by a flood of golden sunlight (a rich evocation of love, romantic possibility, and, indeed, of Gatsby himself); but at the front of the house the porch is darker, and it is in this "deep gloom" that Daisy kisses Carraway and tells him of her disillusionment, which is, in effect, her giving up Gatsby for Tom. Yet by the end of her remarks, as Carraway is about to believe her, she smiles smirkingly, and the illusion of her sadness is suddenly dispelled. The scene is thus an enactment in small of her whole relationship with Gatsby and suggests her lack of depth and essential affinity with Tom's world. The scene is reproduced in the book, but its effect is toned down. Daisy does not kiss Carraway, a touch of flirtatious enticement that suggests her earlier "playing" with Gatsby a little more pointedly than in the understated revision.

In a later scene, Daisy attends Gatsby's party with Tom, and in the manuscript she is obviously ill at ease among Gatsby's guests, responding to them with an "uneasy resentment," a reaction that is softened later to her admiring only the actress under the white plum tree. She is also depicted as being more romantically involved with Gatsby at this point than she is in the final version. They dance a foxtrot "as if it had some quality of a rite—perhaps they were thinking of another summer night when they had danced together in the old sad poignant days of the war." Later that evening, she is depicted as having drifted still further away from Tom. In the book, Fitzgerald speaks of Daisy's leaving as she hears the waltz "Three O'Clock in the Morning" being played inside Gatsby's house, and wondering if he might later that night meet some radiant young guest who would with a single glance blot out his five years of devotion. But in the manuscript this stray thought upon leaving was much more definitely part of her regret in leaving Gatsby: "As the car moved off she stretched out her hand with a quick flush of jealousy, seeking his once more." Daisy's involvement is subdued significantly in the final version; romantic involvement is seen almost wholly in Gatsby, not in Daisy. At no stage of the novel's evolution is Daisy's personality explored very fully; such personality as she has been given is, indeed, pared down in revision, so that she becomes almost an idea. Fitzgerald, of course, took great risks in not allowing Daisy to expand as a character; as a consequence, she does not become quite as fully living as the more minor figure Myrtle Wilson. Fitzgerald's instincts were right, however, or so it seems to me, in not permitting Daisy to develop, since her development would diminish Gatsby. Her existence largely as an idea in Gatsby's mind continually focuses Gatsby's overdreaming or reality and plays off his imaginative largeness against Daisy's incapacity for expansion.

Fitzgerald's adjustment in the conception of his characters as he continued to write and revise can be seen not only in his drawing of Gatsby and Daisy but also in his depiction of Myrtle Wilson, who is, in particular, closely related to the death motif in the novel, which was emphasized even more strongly in the manuscript. The death motif is introduced in the opening scene at the Buchanan house in one or two small allusions, which have been retained in the book. After the revelation that the Buchanans' marriage is not all that it should be, the Buchanans, Jordan, and Carraway go into the library "as if to a vigil beside a perfectly tangible body." Carraway also tells the Buchanans in the same scene that he stopped off in Chicago on his way east and that a number of people there told him they missed Tom and Daisy. He tells them, jokingly: "The whole town is desolate. All the cars have the left rear wheel painted black as a mourning wreath, and there's a persistent wail all night along the north shore." The images Carraway uses—the car wheel, mourning wreath, and wail—all prepare for later recurrences of cars (involving accidents), funeral wreaths, and mournful wailing in the work.

These inconspicuous allusions are retained by Fitzgerald, but in the early draft, there are additional references to death, later omitted. Carraway informs Buchanan in the opening scene that a mutual friend of theirs is dead, and Buchanan cries: "You don't mean to tell me he's *dead!*" (MS, p. 33), and thereafter they continue to discuss their dead friend. Moreover, when Carraway leaves he drives past the red gas pumps sitting out ("boldly" in the manuscript) under pools of light; and as he does, his thoughts turn to death: "I wanted something definite to happen to me—for I suppose that urge toward adventure is one and the same with the craving for a certain death" (MS, p. 36). These additional allusions have been deleted in a later stage of revision, almost certainly because Fitzgerald did not wish to accentuate his death motif too grossly.

A similar muting of effect is seen in connection with Gatsby and death. When Gatsby drives Carraway into New York, he says of his car: "It's the handsomest car in New York. . . . I wouldn't want to ride around in a big hearse like some of those fellas do" (MS, p. 68). It is in this section, as they enter New York in Gatsby's automobile that will later be described as "the death car," that they pass the motor-hearse and arrive at the Times Square café, where Wolfsheim mourns the dead. And at the burial of Gatsby, there is not only the motor-hearse, "horribly black and wet," but also a glimpse of "a 'mortician' in a black oilskin raincoat" (MS, p. 250), who, with his assistants, slides the casket out into the rain. Carraway adds here: "It was raining wildly now and growing darker minute by minute" (MS, p. 251). In revision, Fitzgerald has removed Gatsby's comparison of his car to a hearse, the mortician in the black oilskin coat, the rain beating harder while the sky darkens, muting his death motif further.

The death motif, as I have mentioned, also bears on Fitzgerald's conception of Myrtle Wilson and the valley of ashes. In the manuscript version, Fitzgerald describes the valley of ashes as "a desolate wasted mile of land . . . that could have passed for the back alleyway of Hell" (MS, p. 73). A line of gray cars, piled with cinders, enters the dumping ground, along an invisible track, and the cars creak "sepulchrally" (MS, p. 73) and come to rest; and the later-deleted word *sepulchrally* emphasizes further the association of the valley of ashes with a burial plot, with the gloomy and funereal. It is a place that, in a phrase later crossed out, "reeks of death" (MS, p. 94). This more pointed association of the valley of ashes with death than in the book may explain why it was that Fitzgerald originally chose the name for it he did. The valley of ashes does not lie in a valley after all, but on a featureless plain; yet the name becomes fitting if one remembers "the valley of the shadow of death" of the twenty-third Psalm: "Yea, though I walk through the valley of the shadow of death, I will fear no evil: for thou art with me; thy rod and thy staff they comfort me."

The early draft of the novel appears to substantiate that Fitzgerald began his conception of the valley of ashes, and of Myrtle, in the context of Christian allegory. In the manuscript, surprisingly, the valley-of-ashes section appears as chapter 3, follows rather than precedes the chapter devoted to Gatsby's

party; and it is Gatsby who drives Carraway through the wasteland on his way to New York, stopping for gas at the Wilson
garage; and it is Mrs. Wilson, rather than her husband, who is
shown at the gas tanks with "a panting vitality as she strained
at the handle of the pump" (MS, p. 75). In one version, she
is called "the hot woman," since the heat of the region, as they
pass through, is hellish, and makes her perspire; the first word
she addresses to them is "Hot!" Moreover, the heat with which
she is identified on her first appearance is lust, carnal desire,
implied in the way in which she stares directly into the eyes
of both Gatsby and Carraway and then wets her lips, a sexual
innuendo: "She was plump, hot, nearly middle-aged, carrying a
little fat sensuously as some women can, and she looked us both
in turn flush in the eye and wet her lips" (MS, p. 75). In a later
draft, the valley-of-ashes section appears earlier, as chapter 2,
and it is Tom Buchanan who stops with Carraway at the Wilson
garage. When Myrtle appears in the earliest version, she looks
at *both* men directly in the face and then wets her lips, a detail
that is changed to her looking only at Buchanan, an alteration
that shows how Fitzgerald gradually modified his conception of
Myrtle as a lust figure.

That Myrtle was intended originally to represent lust is not
implied merely on her first appearance. It is stated specifically
in a draft of the Washington Heights apartment scene where
Fitzgerald speaks of "the intense vitality that had seemed in
the garage like a scarcely restrained lust" (MS, p. 108). Moreover, Myrtle is captured with a spotlighted effect in the Times
Square café, where she has joined Tom Buchanan, a passage
that reveals her moral implications:

> There was a window above us which opened into the glaring
> noon of Broadway and from it a square beam, smoky with
> motes of dust, fell through upon the table where Tom had
> just been sitting. It brought out the plump faded bird that
> slept upon his companion's hat and the cheap rings that

glittered nervously upon her bulbous fingers. As I instinctly began to move toward the door she glanced around with a conscious, defiant movement of her shoulder and her face met the smoky beam. It seemed to be a face without skin, so close lust mounted to its surface until she and the beam were one and she partook of the same vital heat. (MS, p. 85)

In this passage, later canceled, Fitzgerald's heat motif appears to originate in a Christian morality conception of Myrtle, who embodies the deadly sin of lust. The brilliance of Fitzgerald's revision is that he was able to transcend this first conception, to envision Myrtle in terms of comedy and yet at the same time to suggest, very subtly, that she springs from some horrifying order of death and damnation.

In the Washington Heights apartment scene, as elsewhere in his picturing of Myrtle, Fitzgerald works continually toward subtlety, toward refining away whatever is too obvious. The walls and woodwork of the apartment were originally stained "a pale green" (MS, p. 105), a reminder perhaps, in a faded way, of the green light and Gatsby's different and greater vision; but the detail was removed. Similarly, the overenlarged photograph of Myrtle's mother, a deceased figure in black, becomes at a distance merely "a gray mass" (MS, p. 104), a detail that was changed, with attention called to the valley of ashes more effectively by the rising haze of cigarette smoke, through which people stumble in confusion. There is an interesting change, too, in the list of items Myrtle has "got to get." Fitzgerald has evoked the barrenness of Myrtle's inner nature comically by her meaningless pretensions, multiplied in effect by the emptiness of the pretensions of the subordinate characters, Catherine and the McKees. The effect is multiplied in other ways as well—in the furniture that is too large for the room and the photograph that is overenlarged into unrecognizability, which comment on Myrtle's pretensions. Her list of items to buy also undercuts her pretensions to largeness, since the items characterize her and reduce her existence to a few paltry commodities that can be enclosed within brackets—an ash tray, a dog collar, a cemetery wreath. That Fitzgerald intended these items to characterize her is confirmed by the manuscript, in which two additional items were included, "and a negligee, something in blue, and a box of writing paper with a monogram" (MS, p. 117).

There are also other small but effective changes in Fitzgerald's depiction of Myrtle, as can be seen in the detail of Myrtle's first appearing in a blue dress at the garage, revised as the blue polka dot dress of crepe de chine, which comments on her devastatingly. More frequently, Fitzgerald tends to compress his effects, to understate, to sharpen his irony. At one point, he describes her as revolving on a pivot "like a dummy" (MS, p. 38), a phrase he removes, letting the image speak for itself. At another point, Fitzgerald writes of Myrtle that the "intense vitality" that had been so remarkable in the garage was "converted into an absurd hauteur" (MS, p. 108), altered, with terse, surgical irony, to "an impressive hauteur." Similarly, when Myrtle is asked to strike a pose for the photographer McKee, she removes a strand of hair from her eyes and looks at the others "with a fatuous smile" (MS, p. 109), revised as "a brilliant smile." Myrtle offers a most unusual glimpse of a character as she is in the process of being created.

Of the other characters, Carraway and Tom Buchanan are changed very little, and Jordan Baker only somewhat (becoming a shade less approachable, less self-revealing, and somewhat more locked away in her "secret" world). More important are the changes in scene and in Fitzgerald's reordering of his chapters. The most striking of the chapter changes is the movement of chapter 2, devoted to Gatsby's party, to its later position as chapter 3. Book chapter 2, devoted to the valley of ashes and the apartment scene, had originally appeared as a later-stage insert to chapter 3. In the original scheme, Fitzgerald moved directly from the opening scene at the Buchanans' to Gatsby's first party, at which Jordan Baker is present and is a connecting link between the chapters. This plan provided an immediate contrast between the Buchanans' world and Gatsby's but it sacrificed suspense leading up to the appearance of Gatsby. At this early stage, Fitzgerald had not yet thought out his conception of Myrtle, who first appears at the Wilson gas pump, and then at the Times Square café with Buchanan, a version that was scrapped, and a new chapter dealing with the valley of ashes written. In this new chapter, Fitzgerald achieves many results at once, not only increased suspense leading up to Gatsby's appearance, but also a third socially contrasting sphere, and a memorable scene of spiritual inertia to heighten the impression of Gatsby on his first appearance.

Two other changes involved scenes Fitzgerald wrote but decided not to use. The first of these occurred at Gatsby's party that Daisy attends with Tom, a chapter Fitzgerald revised extensively. In the discarded version, the party was a costume affair, with many of the guests wearing rustic apparel. Coming as it does immediately after the reunion of Gatsby and Daisy, the "harvest dance," as it is called, was apparently intended to suggest the idea of a rich fulfillment; its harvesttime decorations include sunflowers and sheaves of wheat. But there may also be a suggestion of illusion in the decor, in Fitzgerald's reference to the bar, located in a (Quixotic?) windmill "whose revolving blades were studded with colored lights." There is irony, too, that Daisy, a rich girl attempting to enter Gatsby's world, should come dressed in a Provençal peasant costume. The harvest dance seems a reminder of Gatsby's farm origins and underlines the difference between Daisy (playing at being a "peasant," like Marie Antoinette) and himself. For it is in this chapter that Fitzgerald is attempting to bring out the sense of social differences that divide Gatsby and Daisy and Daisy's recognition at this point that Gatsby's world isn't hers. In revision, Fitzgerald began again, striking out the "harvest dance" scene, and making the party an extension, in kind, of the earlier party, except with more emphasis now on how the same gathering is seen through the eyes of Daisy. He has moved forward the figure of the actress from the first party, where she does not function to any particular advantage, to the later party, where she comments on Daisy's reactions to the party, since her artificiality is the only thing with which Daisy can identify.

The other discarded scene occurs on the day when Gatsby appears with Carraway at the Buchanan house, and they, with the Buchanans and Jordan Baker, drive into New York, a sequence that Fitzgerald had some difficulty conceptualizing. In his first attempt, he had them attend a baseball game, between New York and Chicago teams, at the Polo Grounds, and afterward stop at a café in Central Park, where an argument over Daisy develops between Gatsby and Tom. The heat motif was to have emerged at the Polo Grounds, where the ballgame forms a background of contention and competition, setting off the contention between Gatsby and Tom. In cutting out this scene and recasting it at the Plaza Hotel, Fitzgerald restricts his setting to an enclosed, indoor world, the suite of a fashionable hotel, which is more in keeping with the Buchanans' exclusivity. (The Plaza Hotel is also the setting in which Jordan Baker had first related to Carraway her witnessing of Gatsby's courtship of Daisy, a prelude to its ending in the same setting.) He is also able to introduce his motif of heat (and confusion) by the sweltering heat of that day and to insinuate the wedding motif by the bridal party taking place in the suite below. But in editing out the Polo Grounds–Central Park sequence, Fitzgerald manages to make use of all that is best in it—the quarrel between Tom and Gatsby, dialogue that he continues to polish and perfect.

Another important revision occurs in Fitzgerald's reordering of chapter 6, early in which the information about Gatsby's youthful meeting with Cody is added from its original position in manuscript chapter 8; and the scene in which Gatsby tells Nick of his love for Daisy is added, from its original position in manuscript chapter 7. Fitzgerald gave Maxwell Parkins credit for purposing this fragmentation of time, but in fact

Perkins had suggested only that Fitzgerald let more bits of information about Gatsby's background come out in the course of the novel. He had not proposed these flashbacks at all, and Fitzgerald's use of them was actually an extension of a technique he had already employed effectively in the work. In any case, some of the elements of the work in which parallels can be noted with Conrad's fiction—the creation of Dan Cody and Gatsby's youthful initiation aboard his yacht, the El Greco–like vision of New York, and the ironies of the "dying fall" did not come about until a later stage of revision, when Fitzgerald had resolved the problems of his characters' relationships, and was intent upon achieving a final, highly polished form for his narrative.

The manuscripts reveal, generally, a relentless process of polishing, seen even in the smallest details, as in his characters' names. Leo Epstein was originally to have been the composer of the "Jazz History of the World," but the change to Vladimir Tostoff does more "work" in suggesting the unanchored nature of the jazz idiom and the nature of the party. Wolfsheim's underling Mark becomes Katspaugh, and his friend Jack Rose becomes Rosy Rosenthal. Guest list figures had included the Wombats (another animal name), the De Coursey Abrahams (a crossbreeding of the Anglo-Saxon and the Jewish), the De Gongs (who become the De Jongs), and Miss Dewings (who becomes Claudia Hip). Moreover, there are many revealing alterations in small details of physical appearance and speech. Klipspringer was described as a "man with enormous thick glasses" (MS, p. 138), making him reminiscent of Owl Eyes, but in a contrasting way, as a figure antithetical to wonder, a means of pinpointing a likeness and difference Fitzgerald decided to omit. In his note to Carraway, begging off from attending Gatsby's funeral, Wolfsheim is "completely prostrated" (MS, p. 240), which Fitzgerald changed to the more vivid vernacular "am completely knocked down and out."

Carraway's saying good-bye to Gatsby after their long talk

in the late night and early morning at Gatsby's "ghostly" house is altered slightly and yet significantly. The manuscript version reads: " 'Good-bye,' I called, 'I enjoyed breakfast, Gatsby, Good-bye.' " In the revision the last good-bye is omitted, making it less conspicuous that Carraway, seeing Gatsby alive for the last time, is bidding him a formal farewell. Similarly, Fitzgerald has also refined upon Gatsby's two departures from Buchanan's presence. At the Times Square café, Carraway tells Tom that he has been having lunch with Mr. Gatsby and then turns to Gatsby to introduce him. "Then I realized that Gatsby had disappeared. He simply wasn't there. At the time it seemed quite casual— only a little odd" (MS, p. 84). In revision, however, the passage reads: "I turned to Gatsby, but he was no longer there." The change makes Gatsby's disappearance more dramatic than in the first version where Carraway comments on it. At the end of the Hotel Plaza scene, in the original draft, Gatsby leaves with Daisy: "They were gone, with scarcely a word" (MS, p. 200). In revision, Gatsby and Daisy not only leave but actually vanish: "They were gone, without a word, snapped out, made accidental; isolated, like ghosts." The revision increases tremendously the sense of their leaving as an extinguishing of their affair; and in having Gatsby "vanish," Fitzgerald makes his vanishing earlier at the Times Square café a foreshadowing of what is to come. (In fact, Gatsby vanishes three times in the work, the first when he is first seen on his lawn; but the revisions show that Fitzgerald did not *begin* with a conception of Gatsby's vanishing in a series of incidents, like a phantom.)

But there are a great many other small, revealing changes that might be noted. In the manuscript, for example, there are many more references to East and West than in the final version. Carraway comes originally from a "Western," changed to a "Midwestern," town; and in New York he works for the Eastern Shore Trust, changed to the Probity Trust. There is somewhat more emphasis on the "vanishing stimulus of the war" and the restless, unsettling effect it has had on everyone's lives; and there is at least one additional historical allusion in the book, since Carraway has among his books on capital the volumes of "the Alexander Hamilton business course" (MS, p.5). There are a number of small touches that make the portrait of Tom Buchanan more vivid. After Carraway speaks to him briefly on his porch at the beginning of the first scene, Buchanan says "let's go inside" (MS, p. 13), which becomes more peremptory when it is revised as "We'll go inside." Inside, Buchanan conducts Carraway into another room "as though he were moving a chess pawn to another square" (MS, p. 19); the image is good, insofar as it conveys his sense of other people as "pawns" to be moved about, but "checker," which it is changed to, is less conspicuous and suggests a game more on Buchanan's intellectual level. In a last view of Buchanan, Carraway sees him pushing his way through a Fifth Avenue crowd "in his alert, dynamic way" (MS, p. 254), revised as "alert, aggressive way."

In other revisions, Fitzgerald frequently trims his description of Daisy. The "golden air" and "blessed twilight" in which she is depicted in the opening scene are removed, together with her "enchanted murmurs" (MS, p. 134) as she enters Gatsby's house. When Carraway first enters the Buchanan living room and sees Daisy and Jordan, he says that he "must have stood a few moments on the threshold, dazzled by the alabaster light" (MS, p. 14), a deleted phrase that certainly emphasizes Daisy's identification with a dazzling "white" vision, but perhaps needlessly, since the impression speaks for itself without the added stress of this detail. Tom's bruising of Daisy's finger was spelled out more fully at first, since it occurred "yesterday when I was getting into the car" (MS, p. 21), and was to have emphasized the violence–car accident motif associated with Tom.

The picture of Dan Cody is at first "a prescience of forgotten violence" (MS, p. 43), and then "a token of forgotten violence." Chester McKee is shown asleep with his fists clenched "like the force of character in photographs of kings of finance" (MS, p. 118), changed to "like a man of action." In his opening introduction of himself, Carraway is contemptuous of the "creative temperament," comparing artists with garbage men as necessary evils, phrasing that is wisely removed. He calls the portrait of his great uncle "stern, pig-headed" (MS, p. 3), changed to "rather hard-boiled." He describes himself as the victim of "not a few colossal bores" (MS, p. 2), softened to "veteran bores." He remarks that the foul dust that floated in the wake of Gatsby's dream had "permanently" (MS, p. 3), changed to "temporarily," closed out his interest in other men. He comments that he had found in Gatsby a heightened sensitivity to life "that you might expect in some race yet unborn" (MS, p. 3), changed to "such as I have found in no other person."

Some of the most memorable phrases in *The Great Gatsby* come about only in the course of revision. Carraway's final recall of the old island had read: "The very trees that made way for Gatsby's house had once pandered with whispering leaves to the last and greatest of all human dreams" (MS, p. 38), which is later changed to "had once pandered in whispers." In the first draft, Gatsby weds his unutterable visions to Daisy's "sweet" (MS, p. 161), changed to "perishable," breath. On the last day of his life, Gatsby sees what a "bleak" (MS, p. 235), changed with stronger effect to "grotesque," thing a rose it. At the end, Carraway looks at that "huge horror of a house once more" (MS, p. 259), changed to "huge incoherent failure" of a house. Summing up Gatsby's quality at the beginning, Carraway says that "it was an extraordinary aliveness to life, an alert vitality" (MS, p. 3), corrected to "an extraordinary gift for hope, a romantic readiness."

Describing Gatsby as a host, Carraway comments that "he dealt out the raw material or romance" (MS, p. 91), changed to "he dispensed starlight and wine to half the world" (MS, p. 91), changed finally to "he dispensed starlight to casual moths." He says of Gatsby at one point that he was the son of God and must be about his Father's business, "which was the service of a vast, vulgar, meretricious beauty of America" (MS, p. 216), with "of America" removed in revision, a deletion that indicates how specifically Fitzgerald had identified Gatsby's largness with the largeness of America and its dream. And with these, are scores of other changes, each of which adds to the final effect of the work.

The manuscripts show the patterns of Fitzgerald's revision— his steady clarifying of his conception of his characters and their psychological relationships with one another; his rejection of several scenes that were false starts; his changing conception of Myrtle Wilson and the valley of ashes, which follows his refinement upon his vision; his tendency to think in symmetrical patterns and image clusters; and his concern with making language do a maximum amount of work. In a later introduction to *The Great Gatsby*, Fitzgerald remarked that he could have made another novel from the material he discarded; and while he did not literally discard a large amount of material, he did refuse to allow material to expand that would have jeopardized the novel's unity and direction. It is this kind of self-discipline, which Fitzgerald did not impose upon himself in the apprenticeship novels, that distinguishes the writing and revision of the novel.

Fitzgerald's self-discipline in writing *The Great Gatsby* can be seen on every page of the manuscripts in respect to his care for language. His concern with prose style is seen in two different ways—in his instinct for conserving what was valuable and in his determination to cut away whatever was weak or inessential in what he had written. Fitzgerald hoarded his phrases, and in rewriting a scene salvaged what had been best in it— the evocative phrase, the expressive gesture, the convincing line of dialague. Even in his worst scene, dealing with Gatsby's regrets at the second party, Fitzgerald saved lines that are among the most remembered in the work. At the same time, he continually pruned what he had written. Three words were rejected if his meaning could be compressed and sharpened in two. The effect of such revision is an intense compression that compels the reader to live deeply in Fitzgerald's vision, while conveying an impression of mysterious dimensions in the foreshortened world Fitzgerald has imagined, of much implied rather than stated.

But while *The Great Gatsby* achieves its final authority in revision, it might be noted that the initial manuscript version of the work was not unimpressive. It gives the impression that Fitzgerald has already taken possession of a richly evocative world; its richness of phrase and atmosphere and characterization is sustained throughout. After reading the manuscript, Maxwell Perkins wrote to Fitzgerald of the "brilliant quality" of the book: "The amount of meaning you get into a sentence, the dimensions and intensity of the impression you make a paragraph carry, are most extraordinary . . . it carries the mind through a series of experiences that one would think would require a book of three times its length. The presentation of Tom, his place, Daisy and Jordan, and the unfolding of their characters is unequalled so far as I know. The description of the valley of ashes. . . , the conversation and the action in Myrtle's apartment, the marvelous catalogue of those who came to Gatsby's house—these are such things as make a man famous." Fitzgerald's own letters to Perkins at this time indicate clearly that he himself felt that he was working on a level he had never before attained. Confirming the impression that the manuscripts provide, he described *The Great Gatsby* to Perkins as "a conscious artistic achievement."

Notes

Chapter 1   Toward *The Great Gatsby*: The Apprenticeship Period

1. Sergio Perosa, *The Art of F. Scott Fitzgerald* (Ann Arbor: University of Michigan Press, 1965), pp. 14–15.

2. Rupert Brooke, "Tiare Tahiti," in *The Collected Poems of Rupert Brooke* (New York: Dodd, Mead, 1915), p. 121.

3. F. Scott Fitzgerald, *This Side of Paradise* (1920; reprint ed., New York: Charles Scribner's Sons, 1948), p. 160. All quotations from this novel are from this edition. Subsequent references to this work appear in parentheses in the text.

4. Quoted in Henry Dan Piper, *F. Scott Fitzgerald: A Critical Portrait* (New York: Holt, Rinehart and Winston, 1965), pp. 44–45.

5. Arthur Mizener, *The Far Side of Paradise* (Boston: Houghton Mifflin. 1951), p. 59.

6. Cyril Connolly, *Enemies of Promise* (Boston: Little, Brown & Co., 1939). p. 39.

7. Compton Mackenzie, *Youth's Encounter* (New York: D. Appleton & Co., 1939), p. 39.

8. Edmund Wilson, "Fitzgerald before *The Great Gatsby*," in *F. Scott Fitzgerald: The Man and His Work,* ed. Alfred Kazin (New York: World, 1951), p. 79.

9. F. Scott Fitzgerald, "May Day," in *The Stories of F. Scott Fitzgerald* (New York: Charles Scribner's Sons, 1951), pp. 91–92. All quotations from this story are from this edition. Subsequent references to this work appear in parentheses in the text. Parenthetical page references to stories discussed later— "The Diamond as Big as the Ritz," "Winter Dreams," " 'The Sensible Thing,' " and "Absolution"—are from the same text.

10. Fitzgerald's first professional stories, "Babes in the Woods" and "The

Debutante" (both incorporated into *This Side of Paradise*), appeared in the September and November 1919 issues of *The Smart Set;* but Fitzgerald did not know of Mencken except as an editor when he submitted them. His mention of Mencken by name late in *This Side of Paradise* was added to the galley proofs in 1920 and reflects his first awareness of Mencken as an influential critic.

11. Carl R. Dolmetsch, ed., *The Smart Set: A History and Anthology* (New York: Dial Press, 1966), pp. 77–78.

12. Walter Lippmann, *Men of Destiny* (New York: Macmillan Co., 1928), p. 61.

13. F. Scott Fitzgerald, Introduction to *The Great Gatsby* (Modern Library Edition), reprinted in *The Great Gatsby: A Study*, ed. Frederick J. Hoffman (New York: Charles Scribner's Sons, 1962), p. 166.

14. Mark Schorer, *Sinclair Lewis: An American Life* (New York: McGraw-Hill, 1961), p. 290.

15. F. Scott Fitzgerald, *The Beautiful and Damned* (1922; reprint ed., New York: Charles Scribner's Sons, 1950), pp. 41–42. All quotations from this novel are from this edition. Subsequent references to this work appear in parentheses in the text.

16. Long out of print, the novel has recently been reprinted as part of the Lost American Fiction series, edited by Matthew J. Bruccoli. Stephen French Whitman, *Predestined: A Novel of New York Life* (New York: Charles Scribner's Sons, 1910; reprint ed., Carbondale: Southern Illinois University Press, 1974).

17. H. L. Mencken, "The National Letters," in *Prejudices: Second Series* (New York: Alfred A. Knopf, 1920), pp. 39–41.

18. Fitzgerald to Maxwell Perkins, December 20, 1924, in F. Scott Fitzgerald, *The Letters of F. Scott Fitzgerald*, ed. Andrew Turnbull (New York: Charles Scribner's Sons, 1963), p. 173.

19. H. L. Mencken, "The Niagara of Novels," *The Smart Set* (April 1922), p. 141. Review of *The Beautiful and Damned*.

20. Perosa, *Art of Fitzgerald*, pp. 48–49.

21. There is a certain typal resemblance between Bloeckman and Rosedale—in their role as newly monied Jewish men who rise socially in counterpoint to the decline socially and economically of a hero or heroine. At the beginning of *The House of Mirth*, Rosedale seems almost beneath Lily Bart's consideration. "Half obsequious, half obtrusive," he is pictured at this point "with smart London clothes fitting him like upholstery, and small sidelong eyes which gave him the air of appraising people as if they were bric-a-brac." Shrewd, ambitious, unruffled by rebuffs, Rosedale rises to a position of financial power and begins to be "received" by established society. Lily Bart, at the same time, becomes a kind of outcast, and at the end their roles are reversed, a situation somewhat similar to the later relation of Anthony to Bloeckman. *The House of Mirth* and *The Beautiful and Damned* are both set in New York City and are concerned, to an unusual degree, with social mobility.

22. Fitzgerald to Charles Scribner, April 19, 1922, in Fitzgerald, *Letters,* pp. 155-57.

23. Fitzgerald's less well known stories before *The Great Gatsby* have been treated most fully by John A. Higgins in *F. Scott Fitzgerald: A Study of the Stories* (Jamaica, N.Y.: St. John's University Press, 1971). One of the early stories he points to as anticipating *The Great Gatsby* is "The Offshore Pirate," in which Toby's rags-to-riches tale and his lavishing money on an elaborate scale to win the girl he desires prepares for Gatsby's career. Arthur Mizener has also found a preparation for Gatsby in Fitzgerald's theme in the story that "an imaginative conception of the possibilities of life is the only thing worth living for."

A number of other relevant stories were published in 1924, shortly before Fitzgerald began to devote his time exclusively to *The Great Gatsby;* and they are all concerned with an intensely experienced early love and with a character's attempt at a later time to recapture it. In "Diamond Dick and the First Law of Woman" (*Hearst's International* [April 1924]), a woman tries to recover the lover she has lost and waits five years for the opportunity to speak to him again alone, forgetting that time has passed and that people have changed. Higgins notes that certain passages in the story are strikingly similar to passages in Fitzgerald's novel. At one point, for example, the heroine is shown on the shore of Long Island Sound in the moonlight where, in her imagination, she "stretched out her arms as far as they could reach into the night . . . her eyes fixed upon the points of light on the other shore." This passage reads like a rough sketch of Gatsby, on his first appearance, as he stretches out his arms toward the green dock light that marks Daisy's house on the opposite shore. Further still, another passage in the story has been used by Fitzgerald in *The Great Gatsby* virtually word for word: "All night the saxophones wailed the hopeless comment of the Beale Street Blues, while five hundred pairs of gold and silver slippers shuffled the shining dust. At the gray tea hour there were always rooms that throbbed incessantly with this low sweet fever, while fresh faces drifted here and there like rose petals blown by the sad horns around the floor." The corresponding passage appears in *The Great Gatsby* on page 115 (of edition subsequently cited), in Gatsby's reverie of Daisy at the height of their early romance.

In a slight story that Higgins describes as "perhaps an unconscious parody of *Gatsby,*" "Rags Martin-Jones and the Pr-nce of W-les" (*McCall's* [July 1924]), Fitzgerald's plot concerns a hero's preoccupation for five years with his love for a rich girl who spurned him because he was not rich enough and his use of his money to create an elaborate show to impress her. More relevant still is "John Jackson's Arcady" (*Saturday Evening Post* [July 1924]), in which the hero is a wealthy and successful middle-aged man whose life is actually empty without the lost love of his youth. They meet again, however, and for a moment reexperience their first love. In his apparent recapturing of his romantic past, Jackson "felt that he had established dominance over time itself, so that it rolled away for him, yielding up one vanished springtime after another to the mastery of his overwhelming emotion." The passage is strongly suggestive of Gatsby, in his reunion with Daisy. Similar, too, is the reversal dealt to his hopes when Alice decides, after all, to stay with her husband. "It's so hot and I'm so confused," she tells him, very much like Daisy to Gatsby. And like Gatsby in the Hotel Plaza scene, Jackson, stunned, "fought blindly . . . as he felt his own mood of ecstasy slipping away." Since these stories of 1924 were written after his earliest draft of *The Great Gatsby* and before he began work on the manuscript again, it seems likely that Fitzgerald was exploring in popular fiction the theme of an attempted recovery of an early love that he had begun to deal with in the novel. They all comment, in any case, on the Gatsby-Daisy aspect of the novel.

Chapter 2   *The Great Gatsby* and Conrad

1. For details, see Piper, *Fitzgerald: A Critical Portrait*, pp. 112–20.

2. Robert Sklar, *F. Scott Fitzgerald: The Last Laocoön* (New York: Oxford University Press, 1967), p. 163.

3. Mizener, *Far Side of Paradise*, pp. 171–72.

4. Andrew Turnbull, *Scott Fitzgerald* (New York: Charles Scribner's Sons, 1962), p. 136.

5. Donald Elder, *Ring Lardner* (Garden City, N.Y.: Doubleday, 1956), p. 181. Fitzgerald's friendship with Lardner during the period when they were neighbors in Great Neck has been treated more recently by Ring Lardner, Jr., in *The Lardners: My Family Remembered* (New York: Harper & Row, 1976), and by Jonathan Yardley in *Ring: A Biography of Ring Lardner* (New York: Random House, 1977).

6. Elder, *Ring Lardner*, p. 191.

7. Quoted in Turnbull, *Scott Fitzgerald*, p. 147.

8. Perosa, *Art of Fitzgerald*, p. 54.

9. H. L. Mencken, *A Book of Prefaces* (New York: Alfred A. Knopf, 1917), p. 54.

10. H. L. Mencken, "The Monthly Feuilleton," *The Smart Set* 69 (December 1922): 141–44. Reprinted in Mencken, *Prejudices: Fifth Series* (New York: Alfred A. Knopf, 1926), pp. 34–42.

11. Joseph Conrad to George T. Keating, December 14, 1922, quoted in William H. Nolte, *H. L. Mencken: Literary Critic* (Middletown, Conn.: Wesleyan University Press, 1964), p. 206.

12. H. L. Mencken, "Joseph Conrad," *The Nation* 119 (August 20, 1924): 179.

13. Fitzgerald to President John Hibben of Princeton, June 3, 1920, in Fitzgerald, *Letters*, p. 462.

14. Noted by Sklar, *F. Scott Fitzgerald*, p. 72 and p. 351 n. 20; I noted the same independently. Mencken was himself using a phrase from Hugh Walpole's book on Conrad.

15. Fitzgerald, "The Baltimore Anti-Christ," in *The Bookman* 53 (March 1921): 79–81. Reprinted in *F. Scott Fitzgerald in His Own Time: A Miscellany*, ed. Matthew Bruccoli and Jackson Bryer (Kent State University Press, 1971), pp. 119–21.

16. Fitzgerald, Introduction to *The Great Gatsby,* reprinted in *The Great Gatsby: A Study,* ed. Hoffman, pp. 166–67.

17. Fitzgerald to H. L. Mencken, May 4, 1925, in Fitzgerald, *Letters,* p. 482.

18. Fitzgerald to H. L. Mencken, May or June 1925, in ibid.

19. Richard Foster points out that Miller's account of Fitzgerald's increasingly classical "form" ignores the development at the same time of an increasingly romantic imagination. Richard Foster, "Fitzgerald's Imagination: A Parable for Criticism," *Minnesota Review* 7, no. 2 (1967): 144–56.

20. Robert Wooster Stallman, "Conrad and *The Great Gatsby,*" *Twentieth Century Fiction* 1 (April 1955): 5–12. Reprinted in R. W. Stallman, *The Houses That James Built* (Ann Arbor: University of Michigan Press, 1961), pp. 150–57.

21. Joseph Conrad, *Almayer's Folly,* in *The Complete Works of Joseph Conrad,* Canterbury Edition (Garden City, N.Y.: Doubleday, 1924), p. 3. All quotations from this novel are from this edition. Subsequent references to this work appear in parentheses in the text.

22. F. Scott Fitzgerald, *The Great Gatsby,* in *Three Novels of F. Scott Fitzgerald* (New York: Charles Scribner's Sons, 1953), p. 4. All quotations from this novel are from this edition. Subsequent references to this work appear in parentheses in the text.

23. The roles of Nina and Daisy as simultaneously objectifying and denying the heroes' dreams are highlighted by the detail of the white dresses they both conspicuously wear. Nina's white dress is alluded to so often that it becomes closely associated with her and with the role she plays. Dreaming of her, Dain closes his eyes "trying to evoke the gracious and charming image of the white figure . . . that vision of supreme delight" (p. 166). In the climactic scene in which Nina goes away with Dain, Almayer has a final view of his daughter: "He followed their figures moving in the crude blaze of a vertical sun, in that light violent and vibrating, like a triumphal flourish of brazen trumpets. He looked at . . . the tall, slender, dazzling white figure" (p. 194). White in *Almayer's Folly,* as well as in other of Conrad's novels, is associated with illusion. The idea of illusion is implied in the scene in which the young lovers drift in their canoe under the white mist of the river, oblivious of the world and dreaming of an ideal life that will be unattainable. It is present when Almayer's imagination soars beyond the treetops "into the great white clouds away to the westward . . . to the paradise of Europe" (p. 63). Remembered always by her white dress, Nina stands for an enchanting but illusory vision. So, of course, does Daisy in *The Great Gatsby.*

24. Joseph Conrad, "Youth," in *"Youth" and Two Other Stories,* in *The Complete Works of Joseph Conrad,* Canterbury Edition (Garden City, N.Y.: Doubleday, 1924), p. 42. All quotations from this story are from this edition. Subsequent references to this work appear in parentheses in the text.

25. F. Scott Fitzgerald, "Under Fire," *New York Evening Post,* May 26, 1923, p. 715. Reprinted in *Fitzgerald in His Own Time,* ed. Bruccoli and Bryer, p. 143. Review of Thomas Boyd's *Through the Wheat.*

26. Joseph Conrad, *Lord Jim,* in *The Complete Works of Joseph Conrad,*

Canterbury Edition (Garden City, N.Y.: Doubleday, 1924), p. 339. All quotations from this novel are from this edition. Subsequent references to this work appear in parentheses in the text.

27. The use of a central symbolic scene, as Frederick Karl points out, is a convention of the Conradian novel. It appears not only in *Lord Jim*, but also in many of Conrad's other works. See Frederick Karl, *A Reader's Guide to Joseph Conrad* (New York, Farrar, Straus and Cudahy, 1960), pp. 16–17 passim.

28. Dorothy Van Ghent's well-known essay on *Lord Jim* examines the relationship between "the conscious will and the fatality of our acts." She cites Marlow's comment that one's destiny is predetermined (the quotation this note refers to) to support her contention that Conrad's world view is a closed and static system "incapable of origination though intensely dramatic in its revelations." She compares Conrad, in this regard, with Henry James, whose system is open and fluid and whose characters are self-creating. Fitzgerald's "system" in *The Great Gatsby* is like Conrad's—closed and predetermined. Dorothy Van Ghent, *The English Novel* (New York: Harper & Row, 1953), pp. 229–44.

29. The heroes' preoccupation with time is underscored in the novels, in part, through the use of clock imagery. In his confinement as he first reaches Patusan, Jim is given an old clock to repair, and later with an irony of which he is unconscious, his thoughts keep returning to the idea of "mending the clock." *The Great Gatsby* is filled with reminders of time, including clocks. When Gatsby was a boy in North Dakota, "a universe of ineffable gaudiness spun itself out in his brain while the clock ticked on the washstand." When he meets Daisy again at West Egg, he seems, in his reaction, to be "running down like an overwound clock." In the same scene, Gatsby brushes against a mantlepiece clock, and for a moment it seems almost as if the clock had fallen and smashed; as if in being reunited with Daisy, the clock had stopped, as for Gatsby it had when he lost Daisy.

30. Carraway's habit of reserving judgment is the result of his father's advice not to judge men too hastily. Jim's father also advises his son not to "judge men harshly or hastily" (p. 341).

31. Morton Zabel refers to Conrad's romanticism as endowing appearances with an "internal glow"; its effect, he feels, is a heightened sense of moral implication involved in occurrences. The "realism" of Conrad and of certain other modern writers, including Fitzgerald, he continues, was "always conditioned by an abstracting tendency and mythopoeic habit." Morton Dauwen Zabel, Introduction to *"Youth": A Narrative and Two Other Stories*, by Joseph Conrad, in *The Complete Works of Joseph Conrad* (1924; reprint ed., New York: Doubleday, 1959), pp. 9–10.

32. Joseph Conrad, *Heart of Darkness*, in *The Complete Works of Joseph Conrad*, Canterbury Edition (Garden City, N.Y.: Doubleday, 1924), p. 61. All quotations from this novel are from this edition. Subsequent references to this work appear in parentheses in the text.

33. The correspondence between the apartment scene in *The Great Gatsby* and Eliot's "Sweeney Agonistes" has been noted by various critics. "Sweeney Agonistes" was written first, but was not completed in its final form until after

the publication of *The Great Gatsby*. Eliot himself called attention to the correspondence.

34. The use of a great modern city as a culture symbol places both *Heart of Darkness* and *The Great Gatsby* in a tradition of social criticism developing from the nineteenth century. The city of Paris in Baudelaire's *Les Fleurs du mal* had already been one of the great culture symbols of the nineteenth century, and its influence on *Heart of Darkness* is very likely. Baudelaire was among Conrad's favorite poets, and he used a passage from one of Baudelaire's poems, "Le Voyage" (which contains the phrase "the horror!") as an epigraph to one of his own works. Baudelaire had written that evil, although destructive, is more human than passive nonentity, and this vision of evil forms a criticism of the spiritual inertia of modern life. The same criticism applies in *Heart of Darkness*, where the unexplored potentialities of the soul are evoked by Kurtz, contrasted to the complacency of the "monstrous town." The theme of the dehumanization of contemporary society appears later in the century in T. S. Eliot's *The Waste Land* (1922), which is also focused by a great modern city, in this case London. As in Conrad's "city of the dead," the inhabitants of Eliot's London lead an existence that is a form of death-in-life ("So many, I had not thought death had undone so many"). Eliot was conscious of *Heart of Darkness* when he wrote *The Waste Land,* and he had intended to use a passage from it as the poem's epigraph. Fitzgerald admired *The Waste Land* particularly, and its influence may be seen, in part, in the valley of ashes. His use of a large city as a culture symbol, however, is more closely related, in a structural sense, to Conrad than to Eliot.

Chapter 3   *The Great Gatsby*—the Intricate Art

1. Quoted in Mizener, *Far Side of Paradise*, p. 170.

2. The strongly visual nature of the novel has a quality, too, that is at times cinematic. Fitzgerald's observation of his characters, and the scenes in which they function, becomes a kind of camera, which moves in close, fades back, pans over a crowd, records moments at odd, foreshortened angles, makes use of flashbacks, and employs abrupt transitions that are like ingenious camera cuts.

Fitzgerald's experience in Hollywood and the cinematic aspect of his fiction have been treated by Aaron Latham in *Crazy Sundays: F. Scott Fitzgerald in Hollywood* (New York: Viking, 1970). More recently, Fitzgerald's experience as a scenarist has been considered by Tom Dardis in *Some Time in the Sun* (New York: Charles Scribner's Sons, 1976), an account of the Hollywood years of Fitzgerald, Faulkner, West, Huxley, and Agee.

3. Perosa has commented on the pattern of three separate parties: "Fitzgerald presents them at three different parties, given at distinct places at distinct times, in order to show immediately their various psychological natures, their diverse aspirations and ambitions, and the different social environments from which they spring and which they somehow embody." Perosa, *Art of Fitzgerald*, p. 62.

4. "Clay's *Economics*" refers to the text dealing with basic economic theory by the British scholar Henry Clay. (*Economics* [New York: Macmillan Co., 1918]).

It is curious that of all the textbooks on economics Fitzgerald should have chosen one by an author named Henry Clay, a name that is historically relevant to the theme of *The Great Gatsby*, since the American Henry Clay was strongly involved with the history of the frontier. Daisy Fay is from Louisville, Midwestern insofar as it touches the southern border of Indiana; but it is located, of course, in Kentucky, Henry Clay's own state and the site of the original frontier. Clay was always associated with the frontier dream, was an ardent expansionist, with an extremely optimistic vision of the West. One of his biographers, Bernard Mayo, remarks that "he described the unsatisfied needs of the great West in stirring terms, and then opened once more that glorious perspective of the great ocean-bound republic which his ardent mind was so fond of contemplating." Politically, Clay was a prominent figure in the National Republican or Whig party, which was dominated by the mercantile and industrial classes. His "American system" called for protective tariffs, favoring the expansion of industry, and government support for internal improvements (such as roads and canals), which would help to open up the West. Arthur Schlesinger, in *The Age of Jackson,* discusses the alliance Clay forged between the West and the big financial-industrial interests of the Northeast as a form of neo-federalism. Clay clashed with Jackson most dramatically, in fact, over the issue of the Second Bank of the United States, the big financial corporation Clay defended passionately and as an attorney represented. So strong was Clay's identification with the upper economic classes that after his defeat for the presidency in 1844, the merchants of New York proposed to raise a statue to him, to be placed "in the rotunda of the Merchants' Exchange or some other suitable place."

Clay thus stood for both the optimistic dream of the West and the interests of great corporate wealth that stood to gain by this Western dream; and he becomes a historical footnote of a kind to Dan Cody. Gatsby's glancing absently at a book on economics by Henry Clay, just before the appearance of Daisy Fay, would reinforce an impression that Gatsby will see the "vision" but not the realities that underlie it.

5. A useful work for the study of color and other imagery in the novel is the *Concordance to F. Scott Fitzgerald's "The Great Gatsby"*, ed. by Andrew Crosland (Detroit, Mich.: Gale, 1974).

6. An account of Fitzgerald's handling of chronology is given in Kenneth Eble, *F. Scott Fitzgerald* (New York: Twayne, 1963):

The construction of *The Great Gatsby* is the more remarkable because the crucial ordering of the material did not come until the book was in galley proof. In its simplest form, the change was that of taking the true story of James Gatz's past out of Chapter Eight, and bringing it forward to the beginning of Chapter Six. Thus, as I have noted, the static center of the novel—that moment when Gatsby's alone with Daisy and can hold past and present together—extends itself on into Chapter Seven. The story of the Gatsby who sprang from his Platonic conception of himself is placed precisely where it will make its greatest impact: between the moment of suspended time at the end of Chapter Five and Gatsby's beginning to be aware of the vanity of his own dreams in the party scene of Chapter Six. (P. 92)

7. Fitzgerald's comic guest list has few modern precedents, but one with which Fitzgerald must have been familiar, since he had read the novel many times, can be found in Thackeray's *Vanity Fair*. Thackeray's guest list, a satirical sketching of a motley social group, may be illustrated by a few lines from the *Morning Post* account in the novel: "Yesterday, Colonel and Mrs. Crawley entertained a select party at dinner, at their house in Mayfair. . . . H. E. Papoosh Pasha, the Turkish Ambassador. . . . Mr. Wagg . . . Comte de Brie, Baron Schapzuger, Chevalier Tosti, Countess of Slingstone . . . Major-General and Lady (Grizzel) Macbeth, and (2) Miss Macbeths . . . Sir Horace Fogey . . . Bobbachy Bahawder."

In recent times, Fitzgerald's guest list appears to have influenced other writers, including William Styron, in *Lie Down in Darkness* (1951). Included in his description of Southern country club life is a "guest list" that with its coupling of grotesque names and fates, seems inspired by Fitzgerald's guest list in *The Great Gatsby*:

There were the Appletons and the La Farges and the Fauntleroy Mayos, who were F.F.V.s, and the Martin Braunsteins, who were Jews, but who had been around long enough to be accepted as Virginians. Then there was a contingent of doctors and their wives—J. E. B. Stuart and Lonergan and Bulwinkle (they all smelled faintly of ether)—and there was Dr. Pruitt Delaplane, making his first hesitant public appearance after his trial and acquittal for criminal abortion. There was poor Medwick Ames and his wife—who threw fits. . . . Among the young people were the Walker Stuarts and the P. Moncure Yourtees and George and Gerda Rhoades, who were, everyone knew, on the verge of divorce, and a man's clothing dealer named "Cherry" Pye. The Blevinses had come, and the Cappses and John J. Maloneys. Also the Davises and the Younghusbands and the Hill Massies, who had once won ten thousand dollars in a slogan contest; and a dentist named Monroe Hobbie, who limped. . . .

8. Carraway is effective in many ways as a contrast to Gatsby, but he also creates a blurred edge in the novel. At the end, for example, he returns to the Midwest, where he can keep his moral distinctions clear; but his return involves a contradiction in terms, since the concluding image of the novel indicates a darkness spreading across the entire continent, including the Midwest, which Carraway imagines as a sanctuary. Even further, his return seems like a retreat from adult experience into a childhood or adolescent world. Fitzgerald apparently intends the reader to feel that there is a degree of illusion in Carraway's return, an experience that is the counterpart of the normal man's to Gatsby's. Gatsby's gardens strung with colored lights like a "Christmas tree" (p. 31) is a leitmotiv of Carraway's return to adolescent memories at the end, the Christmas vacations in the Midwest, where he experienced his own youthful illusion, as

Gatsby had in North Dakota. But if Carraway is *actually* returning to a land of adolescent illusion, rather than, as he claims, to an adult world where distinctions can be perceived clearly, he does not serve as a standard of reality against which Gatsby can be measured. Carraway attempts, apparently, to go back to the past, even after he learns from Gatsby's experience that one cannot.

Hugh Kenner, in *A Homemade World* (1975) has argued, also, that there is a fundamental flaw in Carraway's role as narrator, since he has become fused with Fitzgerald himself, the narrator-behind-the-narrator. Kenner is, of course, right that there is a double-image effect in Carraway's conception as narrator, one that makes him a less perfect, "homemade" version of Conrad's Marlow. Despite this flaw, however, and the flaw of Carraway's ambiguous return to the Midwest, Fitzgerald's art in the novel shows an impressive degree of sophistication and cannot in fairness be characterized as awkwardly "homemade."

9. Florenz Ziegfeld lived in Great Neck at the same time as Fitzgerald, and Fitzgerald was conscious of him partly through his friend Ring Lardner, who contributed lyrics for the 1922 *Follies*. Moreover, Gene Buck, chief assistant and general manager for Ziegfeld, was a personal friend of Lardner's. Buck's huge house in Great Neck was the scene of many parties that were in the Ziegfeld style, and Fitzgerald and Lardner have been described by Lardner's biographer, Donald Elder, as being "vastly amused by the scale of grandeur on which the Bucks' lived." Ziegfeld is relevant to Gatsby's parties in many ways—certainly in his love of theatrical and opulent display, and in his fascination with "dream girls." It was the famous and often quoted remark of Ziegfeld that he had "glorified the American girl." Sought after and ardently desired, Ziegfeld girls were practically an American cult. With his garish opulence and uncritical worship of Daisy Fay, Gatsby assumes something of the public role of Ziegfeld in his own personal life.

The allusion to Gilda Gray, who starred in the 1922 *Follies,* also helps to fix Gatsby's parties in the context of their time. Gilda Gray's obituary in the New York *Times* (December 23, 1959) describes her as having "epitomized the era of the Roaring Twenties." The New York *Herald Tribune* obituary is more informative still. It comments: "There is no doubt that Gilda Gray . . . was one of the symbols of that era that is now called the time of the speak-easy, bath tub gin, the flapper who danced to the 'shimmy,' the 'Charleston' and the 'Black Bottom,' jazz and other phenomena considered gay and wild. . . . Ziegfeld called her 'My Golden Girl,' but whether he was referring to the color of her hair or to the money people paid in order to see her was never made certain." In fact, Gilda Gray was the name assumed by Marianne Michalski, a poor Polish immigrant who sang in Milwaukee and Chicago saloons before Ziegfeld discovered her. The originator of a dance called the "shimmy," she was for a time the highest-paid performer in the world. In his use of the contemporary cult of the "golden girl," as in the worship of success, Fitzgerald comments on the values of his period.

10. The circle that Gatsby's blood makes on the water appears to refer back to

the three circlings by water of the continent, aboard Cody's yacht, in which Gatsby was initiated into wonder. Gatsby's body borne on the air mattress now closes the circle, and wonder ends in death. The idea of the circle now closed reinforces the sense of finality at the end of the work, the contrast between the openness of Gatsby's vision and the definiteness of his failure.

11. Lionel Trilling, "F. Scott Fitzgerald," in *F. Scott Fitzgerald: A Collection of Critical Essays,* ed. Arthur Mizener (Englewood Cliffs, N.J.: Prentice-Hall, 1963), p. 17.

12. F. Scott Fitzgerald, "My Lost City," in *The Crack-Up* (New York: New Directions, 1945), pp. 23–33.

13. Gertrude Stein to Fitzgerald, May 22, 1925, in Fitzgerald, *The Crack-Up,* p. 308.

Chapter 4   Conclusion: *The Great Gatsby* and the Twenties

1. As Kenneth Lynn points out in *The Dream of Success,* the veneration of success and riches had a very central place in the American culture of the 1890s and its imaginative literature. Its survival in the era of the twenties is seen in the immense popularity of the Horatio Alger books for boys. Alger published approximately 135 volumes, with titles like *Strive and Succeed* and *Bound to Rise,* in which the setting for fortune making was transferred from the West to New York City, the modern mecca of success.

2. It is clear from his letters that early in the twenties Fitzgerald read both the three-volume biography of Mark Twain by Albert Bigelow Paine, and Brooks's *The Ordeal of Mark Twain.* Fitzgerald to Maxwell Perkins, December 12, 1921, in Fitzgerald, *Letters,* p. 150.

Fitzgerald's having read *The Ordeal of Mark Twain* is noted in Sklar's *F. Scott Fitzgerald,* pp. 137–48, as part of a discussion of money and its effect upon the careers of Twain and Fitzgerald. Sklar does not, however, discuss Brooks's treatment of the frontier as it applies to *The Great Gatsby.*

3. Van Wyck Brooks, *The Ordeal of Mark Twain,* rev. ed. (New York: E. P. Dutton, 1933), pp. 45–46.

4. Ibid., p. 83.

5. Ibid., p. 246.

6. Ibid.

7. Van Wyck Brooks, "The Literary Life," in *Civilization in the United States,* ed. Harold E. Stearns (New York: Harcourt, Brace & Co., 1922), p. 179.

8. Randolph Bourne, "Trans-National America," in *History of a Literary Radical* (New York: B. W. Huebsch, 1920), p. 281.

9. Edmund Wilson, "The Delegate from Great Neck," in *F. Scott Fitzgerald,* ed. Kazin, pp. 54–66.

10. John Berryman, "Dreiser's Imagination," in *The Stature of Theodore Dreiser,* ed. Alfred Kazin and Charles Shapiro (Bloomington: Indiana University Press, 1955), pp. 149–53.

Bibliography

Publications of F. Scott Fitzgerald

This Side of Paradise. New York: Charles Scribner's Sons, 1920.

Flappers and Philosophers. New York: Charles Scribner's Sons, 1920.

The Beautiful and Damned. New York: Charles Scribner's Sons, 1922.

Tales of the Jazz Age. New York: Charles Scribner's Sons, 1922.

The Vegetable. New York: Charles Scribner's Sons, 1923.

The Great Gatsby. New York: Charles Scribner's Sons, 1925.

All the Sad Young Men. New York: Charles Scribner's Sons, 1926.

Tender Is the Night. New York: Charles Scribner's Sons, 1934. Reprinted with the author's final revisions. Edited by Malcolm Cowley. New York: Charles Scribner's Sons, 1948.

Taps at Reveille. New York: Charles Scribner's Sons, 1935.

The Last Tycoon. Edited with an introduction by Edmund Wilson. New York: Charles Scribner's Sons, 1941.

The Crack-Up. Edited with an introduction by Edmund Wilson. New York: New Directions, 1945.

The Stories of F. Scott Fitzgerald. Edited with an introduction by Malcolm Cowley. New York: Charles Scribner's Sons, 1951.

Afternoon of an Author. With an introduction by Arthur Mizener. New York: Charles Scribner's Sons, 1957.

The Pat Hobby Stories. With an introduction by Arnold Gingrich. New York: Charles Scribner's Sons, 1957.

The Letters of F. Scott Fitzgerald. Edited with an introduction by

217

Andrew Turnbull. New York: Charles Scribner's Sons, 1963.

The Apprenticeship Fiction of F. Scott Fitzgerald, 1909–1917. Edited with an introduction by John Kuehl. New Brunswick, N.J.: Rutgers University Press, 1965.

Dear Scott/Dear Max: The Fitzgerald–Perkins Correspondence. Edited by John Kuehl and Jackson Bryer. New York: Charles Scribner's Sons, 1973.

As Ever, Scott Fitz———; Letters Between F. Scott Fitzgerald and His Literary Agent Harold Ober 1919–1940. Edited by Matthew J. Bruccoli. New York: J. B. Lippincott, 1972.

The Basil and Josephine Stories. Edited with an introduction by John Kuehl and Jackson Bryer. New York: Charles Scribner's Sons, 1973.

"The Great Gatsby"; a facsimile of the manuscript. Edited with an introduction by Matthew J. Bruccoli. Washington, D.C.: Microcard Editions Books, 1973.

F. Scott Fitzgerald's Ledger. Edited by Matthew J. Bruccoli. Washington, D.C.: Microcard Editions Books, 1973.

Bits of Paradise; 21 uncollected stories [of F. Scott and Zelda Fitzgerald]. Edited by Scottie Fitzgerald Smith and Matthew J. Bruccoli. London: Bodley Head, 1973.

Fitzgerald Scholarship: A Selective Bibliography

Bruccoli, Matthew J. *F. Scott Fitzgerald: A Descriptive Bibliography.* Pittsburgh: University of Pittsburgh Press, 1972.

Bruccoli, Matthew J., and Bryer, Jackson R., eds. *F. Scott Fitzgerald in His Own Time: A Miscellany.* Kent, Ohio: Kent State University Press, 1971.

Bruccoli, Matthew J.; Smith, Scottie Fitzgerald; and Kerr, Joan P., eds. *The Romantic Egotists: A Pictorial Autobiography from the Scrapbooks and Albums of Scott and Zelda Fitzgerald.* New York: Charles Scribner's Sons, 1974.

Bruccoli, Matthew J. *"The Last of the Novelists": F. Scott Fitzgerald and "The Last Tycoon."* Carbondale: Southern Illinois University Press, 1977.

———. *Scott and Ernest: The Fitzgerald–Hemingway Friendship.* New York: Random House, 1978.

Bryer, Jackson. *The Critical Reputation of F. Scott Fitzgerald.* Hamden, Conn.: Shoe String Press, 1967.

Callahan, John F. *The Illusions of a Nation: Myth and History in the Novels of F. Scott Fitzgerald.* Urbana: University of Illinois Press, 1972.

Crosland, Andrew, ed. *Concordance to F. Scott Fitzgerald's "The Great Gatsby."* Detroit, Mich.: Gale, 1974.

Eble, Kenneth. *F. Scott Fitzgerald.* New York: Twayne, 1963.

———, ed. *F. Scott Fitzgerald: A Collection of Criticism.* New York: McGraw-Hill, 1973.

Gallo, Rose Adrienne. *F. Scott Fitzgerald.* New York: Frederick Ungar, 1978.

Greenfeld, Howard. *F. Scott Fitzgerald.* New York: Crown, 1974.

Higgins, John A. *F. Scott Fitzgerald: A Study of the Stories.* Jamaica, N.Y.: St. John's University Press, 1971.

Hoffman, Frederick J., ed. *"The Great Gatsby": A Study.* New York: Charles Scribner's Sons, 1962.

Kazin, Alfred, ed. *F. Scott Fitzgerald: The Man and His Work.* New York: World, 1951.

Latham, Aaron. *Crazy Sundays: F. Scott Fitzgerald in Hollywood.* New York: Viking, 1971.

Lehan, Richard D. *F. Scott Fitzgerald and the Craft of Fiction.* Carbondale: Southern Illinois University Press, 1966.

Lockridge, Ernest, ed. *Twentieth Century Interpretations of "The Great Gatsby."* Englewood Cliffs, N.J.: Prentice-Hall, 1969.

Mayfield, Sara. *Exiles from Paradise: Zelda and Scott Fitzgerald.* New York: Delacorte, 1971.

Miller, James E. *The Fictional Technique of Scott Fitzgerald.* The Hague: Martinus Nijhoff, 1957. Revised as *F. Scott Fitzgerald—His Art and His Technique.* New York: New York University Press, 1964.

Mizener, Arthur. *The Far Side of Paradise.* Boston: Houghton Mifflin, 1951.

———. *Scott Fitzgerald and his World.* New York: Putnam's Sons, 1972.

———, ed. *F. Scott Fitzgerald: A Collection of Critical Essays.* Englewood Cliffs, N.J.: Prentice-Hall, 1963.

Perosa, Sergio. *The Art of F. Scott Fitzgerald.* Ann Arbor: University of Michigan Press, 1965.

Piper, Henry Dan. *F. Scott Fitzgerald: A Critical Portrait.* New York: Holt, Rinehart and Winston, 1965.

Sklar, Robert. *F. Scott Fitzgerald, the Last Laocoön.* New York: Oxford University Press, 1967.

Stern, Milton. *The Golden Moment: The Novels of F. Scott Fitzgerald.* Urbana: University of Illinois Press, 1970.

Turnbull, Andrew. *Scott Fitzgerald.* New York: Charles Scribner's Sons, 1962.

Index

221